Installing Red Hat® Linux® 7

Bill von Hagen

Copyright ©2001 by Sams Publishing

All rights reserved. No part of this book shall be reproduced, stored in a retrieval system, or transmitted by any means, electronic, mechanical, photocopying, recording, or otherwise, without written permission from the publisher. No patent liability is assumed with respect to the use of the information contained herein. Although every precaution has been taken in the preparation of this book, the publisher and author assume no responsibility for errors or omissions. Nor is any liability assumed for damages resulting from the use of the information contained herein.

International Standard Book Number: 0-672-32084-3

Library of Congress Catalog Card Number: 99-66104

Printed in the United States of America

First Printing: November, 2000

03 02 01 00 4 3 2 1

Trademarks

All terms mentioned in this book that are known to be trademarks or service marks have been appropriately capitalized. Sams cannot attest to the accuracy of this information. Use of a term in this book should not be regarded as affecting the validity of any trademark or service mark.

Warning and Disclaimer

Every effort has been made to make this book as complete and as accurate as possible, but no warranty or fitness is implied. The information provided is on an "as is" basis. The author and the publisher shall have neither liability nor responsibility to any person or entity with respect to any loss or damages arising from the information contained in this book or from the use of the CDs or programs accompanying them.

Associate Publisher
Michael Stephens

Acquisitions Editors
Carol Ackerman
William E. Brown
Neil Rowe

Development Editor
Tony Amico
Mark Renfrow

Managing Editor
Matt Purcell

Project Editor
Natalie Harris

Copy Editors
Kim Cofer
Krista Hansing

Indexer
Sheila Schroeder

Proofreaders
Kathy Bidwell
Candice Hightower

Technical Editors
Bill Bruns
Ray Cotten

Team Coordinator
Pamalee Nelson

Media Developer
Dan Scherf

Interior Designer
Karen Ruggles

Cover Designer
Aren Howell

Production
Darin Crone

Overview

Contents

About the Author

William von Hagen is the president of Move2Linux.com, a firm specializing in migrating legacy COBOL applications, associated data, and computing environments (midrange, mainframe, Novell, and Windows) to Linux systems. Prior to founding Move2Linux.com, he had been a UNIX systems programmer, systems administrator, and writer since 1982. He is also a well-known computer collector (see `http://www.vonhagen.org/collection.html` for more information).

Contact Bill at `vonhagen@vonhagen.org` or `wvh@move2linux.com`.

Dedication

To my wife, Dorothy Fisher, for all her love, patience, and support over the years and today. This book is also dedicated to my brother-in-law and business partner, Edward R. Fisher, whose death was a tragedy for all who had the pleasure to know him and to be part of his life.

Acknowledgments

Thanks to the folks at Sams for the opportunity to write this book, for putting up with my "late-i-tude" and for making this a better book than it could otherwise have been: All errors are mine, but many improvements are theirs. Thanks to Neil Rowe, William Brown, Carol Ackerman, Christina Smith, Tony Amico, Elizabeth Roberts, Krista Hansing, and Natalie Harris, as well as Ray and Bill for technical comments. I promise to learn how to use a calendar in the future!

I'd also like to thank Ruth Leicht and Mrs. Stevick for inspiring and putting up with me when I fell in love with books as a child and incurred late fees that could still haunt me today if not for their kindness.

One final word of thanks: to Jeff Kaminski, who supported and inspired me when others questioned my abilities, and is still a great friend today. Jeff, it's midnight on Saturday, so you might want to think about leaving work soon! Imagine this message being mumbled over the PA system…

Tell Us What You Think!

As the reader of this book, *you* are our most important critic and commentator. We value your opinion and want to know what we're doing right, what we could do better, what areas you'd like to see us publish in, and any other words of wisdom you're willing to pass our way.

As an Associate Publisher for Sams Publishing, I welcome your comments. You can fax, email, or write me directly to let me know what you did or didn't like about this book—as well as what we can do to make our books stronger.

Please note that I cannot help you with technical problems related to the topic of this book, and that due to the high volume of mail I receive, I might not be able to reply to every message.

When you write, please be sure to include this book's title and author as well as your name and phone or fax number. I will carefully review your comments and share them with the author and editors who worked on the book.

Fax: 317-581-4770

Email: `linux_sams@macmillanusa.com`

Mail: Michael Stephens
Associate Publisher
Sams Publishing
201 West 103rd Street
Indianapolis, IN 46290 USA

CHAPTER 1

Introduction to Red Hat Linux

Linux is a multiuser, multitasking operating system that is taking the personal and professional computing worlds by storm. A modern implementation of UNIX, Linux is most commonly associated with systems using 80386, 80486, Pentium, and compatible processors from Cyrix and AMD; however, it actually runs on a much wider variety of computer systems. Versions of Linux run on Power PC (PPC) systems such as newer Macintosh and IBM RS6000 systems, systems using Sun Microsystems' SPARC processor family, systems using Alpha processors from Compaq or DEC, and several others.

The subject of this book, Red Hat Linux, is the most popular Linux distribution ever—it's the darling of the stock exchange and trade press, and the best-supported Linux distribution available. Red Hat Linux is the leader of the Linux pack because the folks at Red Hat are dedicated to packaging, testing, delivering, and supporting the most robust, usable Linux distribution possible. You'll see this from the moment you see Red Hat's easy installation process, thorough hardware detection, usable configuration utilities, and stability. Primarily for systems using Intel x86 and compatible processors, Red Hat is also kind enough to distribute a version of Red Hat for Linux users on the SPARC platform and for the few people who have systems using DEC (now Compaq) Alpha processors.

Red Hat is the best-supported, most popular Linux distribution for good reason. Along with access to thousands of powerful, free applications, Red Hat Linux provides the following:

- Fully graphical installation and configuration.
- Automatic hardware detection, identification, and configuration through Red Hat's Kudzu hardware monitor. The one socially redeeming feature of Windows is now available for Linux.

- Built-in support for more network interface cards, sound cards, video cards, PCMCIA cards, and other hardware than any other Linux distribution.
- Sophisticated application installation and management through the Red Hat Package Manager (RPM). The Red Hat Package Manager automatically identifies any additional software that you need so that you can install and use desired applications.
- Easy system administration and configuration through linuxconf, a centralized administrative tool that eliminates the need to manually edit configuration files.
- Automatic system updating over the Internet, giving you immediate access to system and security updates to provide the most secure, stable system possible.
- Lightweight Directory Access Protocol (LDAP) support. LDAP lets all your systems and applications share access to a centralized hierarchy of authentication and configuration information.
- Up-to-date versions of the GNOME and KDE graphical desktops, as well as most other window managers available for the X Window system. Unlike other Linux distributions, Red Hat does not limit you to a single desktop environment or window manager.

Today, more than 30% of the Web pages on the Internet are hosted and delivered by Linux systems. A recent industry survey from the International Data Corporation (IDC) stated that companies are increasing their use of Linux while delaying deployment of Microsoft's latest offerings. Thirteen percent of the respondents said they now use Linux, compared to essentially zero in 1997. Major hardware companies, including IBM, Dell, and Silicon Graphics, now provide Linux as one of the operating systems options for many of their systems. This level of commitment from IBM and SGI is especially interesting in light of the fact that both IBM and SGI have their own versions of UNIX: AIX and IRIX, respectively. Getting companies such as IBM and SGI to admit that there might be value in a not-invented-here (NIH) operating system makes a pretty strong statement that there's something exciting going on in computing—and that something is Linux!

Table 1.1 lists the most common versions of UNIX and UNIX-like operating systems in use on the World Wide Web today, the vendor they are available from, and the version of UNIX they are primarily descended from.

Table 1.1 The Most Common UNIX and UNIX-like Operating Systems

Version of UNIX	Vendor	UNIX Parent
AIX	IBM	SYSV
BSDI	BSDI	BSD
Digital UNIX	Compaq	BSD
FreeBSD	(free)	BSD
HP-UX	Hewlett-Packard	SYSV
IRIX	Silicon Graphics	SYSV
Linux	(Many—see later in this chapter)	SYSV
NetBSD	(Free)	BSD

Table 1.1 continued

Version of UNIX	Vendor	UNIX Parent
SCO Unix	Santa Cruz Operation	SYSV
Solaris	Sun Microsystems	SYSV
SunOS	Sun Microsystems	BSD

Why Red Hat?

Linux is an Open Source operating system, which means that the complete source code for the operating system is freely available. Because the source code is freely available, it doesn't serve the interests of any one software or hardware company. Instead, Linux serves the interests of the growing community of Linux users everywhere, providing a free, stable, and powerful operating system that doesn't cost an arm and a leg to purchase and that easily can be enhanced and extended to support new hardware and software.

Unfortunately, the fact that Linux is free and that thousands of developers are working on improving it at this very moment is small consolation if your system is down and deadlines are approaching. A major key to using Linux as a viable alternative to other operating systems is whether you can get product support when you absolutely, positively must have it. Businesses have a responsibility to their customers and shareholders to deliver on their promises in a timely and efficient fashion.

Red Hat's easy installation and thorough testing of the set of packages it delivers with each release already have won the hearts of system administrators who must install and configure systems. However, even more valuable than these is that Red Hat provides customer support for its Linux distribution. If your system has fallen off the network and can't get up, you can actually call Red Hat, talk to a human, and get assistance with your problem. Red Hat offers 30 days of free technical support when you register a version of Red Hat Linux. After you've passed this period, you can buy additional support on a per-problem basis for a certain number of machines, for an entire network, or even for the 24×7 support required by many businesses.

In addition to technical support for system and hardware problems, Red Hat also offers per-incident support for software developers. Red Hat provides special support programs for general application development, GUI development (including GNOME development), device driver development, and even RPM construction if you want to distribute applications.

People often find it confusing that although Linux is free and can't be charged for, firms such as Red Hat charge for their distributions and also charge for support. The ability to sell Linux-related services is spelled out in the points of the GNU Public License (GPL), under which Linus Torvalds released Linux to the world. Among its provisions, the GPL requires that no company can change for the source for any GPL'd application, but a fee can be charged for "the physical act of transferring a copy" and for warranty protection, software support, and so on.

Linux and Other Free UNIX-Like Systems

Many free UNIX-like systems are available today. The more modern of these easily separate themselves into two camps that reflect the two general paths of the evolution of UNIX since its birth at Bell Labs in 1969. The two basic flavors of UNIX are SYSV, the lineal descendant of the original UNIX invented at Bell labs (later AT&T), and BSD UNIX, a descendant of a set of enhancements made to Bell Labs UNIX by people (among them Bill Joy, one of the founders of Sun Microsystems) at the University of California at Berkeley, known as the Berkeley Standard Distribution.

Table 1.2 shows some of the primary differences between the BSD and SYSV flavors of UNIX—depending on how deep you want to go, there are many more, but these are the ones that spring to mind for most UNIX fans:

Table 1.2 The Primary Differences Between BSD and SYSV

Concept	BSD	SYSV
System startup scripts	`/etc/rc, /etc/rc.single, /etc/rc.local` (Run Command files)	`/etc/rc.*` (directories of scripts for different run levels)
Networking model	sockets	STREAMS API
Printing system	lpr, lpc, lpq, lprm	lp, lpstat, cancel
Process status command options	ps alxww	ps ef
Shell	csh	Sh, ksh
Terminal control	termcap	termio, terminfo
Terminal initialization	`/etc/inittab`	`/etc/ttys`

Where Does Linux Fit In?

Linux tends to err on the side of making everyone happy, often supporting both the BSD and the SYSV models but promoting SYSV-ims wherever possible. For example, the Linux `ps` (process status) command supports both the BSD and SYSV families of command-line options so that you can figure out what's running regardless of your UNIX orientation and preferences. Similarly, Linux provides an odd mixture of scripts to run during the system startup process, focusing on the `/etc/inittab` and `/etc/rc.d` models of per-run-level directories containing per-process or per-subsystem scripts, but also providing scripts such as `/etc/rc.d/rc.local`. These can be used by hopeless Berkeley-ites to start processes and subsystems with some semblance of familiarity. In general, Linux follows the SYSV model much more closely than the BSD model, but is happy to accept enhancements and generally good ideas from anywhere.

Free Versions of BSD UNIX Available Today

Several free versions of UNIX based on BSD UNIX are available today. A BSD codebase called 4.4BSD-Lite, which is free of any Bell Labs or AT&T code, serves as the reference system for all the free versions of BSD UNIX. These include FreeBSD, which grew from 386BSD, a free research implementation of BSD UNIX developed in 1992 by William Jolitz. With the eventual merger of code from 4.4BSD-Lite, FreeBSD became the premier BSD UNIX for Intel 386 and better Intel systems. The other major players in today's free BSD UNIX market are NetBSD, which focuses on supporting as many different platforms as possible, and OpenBSD, son of NetBSD, which focuses on security and is legendary for its thorough and repeated system security audits.

The Berkeley variants that are still out there are elegant and powerful systems that you can use at home and in business to do real work. They work well, are stable, and are actively supported and enhanced. Many companies, such as Yahoo!, run their Internet business on FreeBSD servers—OpenBSD is quite popular. Similarly, if you want to run a version of UNIX on some random old workstation or PC, NetBSD is for you, period—it runs on everything from extinct workstations to 386 and better Intel systems, and ports are underway for anything it doesn't currently run on. However, if you ask me whether a better career choice would be learning BSD-like UNIX or Linux, I'd answer by handing you a copy of this book.

Free Versions of Commercial UNIX Systems

Trying to grab themselves a seat on the free software express, some existing UNIX vendors have adopted the policy of giving away free copies of their versions of UNIX for personal use. Companies in this camp include Sun Microsystems and the Santa Cruz Operation (SCO), both long-term UNIX vendors. Sun provides personal use copies of Solaris for its SPARC systems, as well as for Intel X86 systems. SCO, which long ago partnered with Microsoft but is much better now, offers personal copies of its SCO UNIX.

Unless you're already running one of these version of UNIX at work and need to be compatible, or unless you are genetically unable to learn more than one version of UNIX, there's really no reason to use these. These are the worst of both worlds: proprietary systems without customer support (unless you pay for it) that cut you off from most of the free software that's out there (unless you compile it yourself). Having a whole free bucket of zeroes isn't any more valuable than having a single one.

Comparing Different Linux Distributions

The "versions" of Linux that are important to most people are actually Linux distributions consisting of some version of the Linux kernel, a set of device drivers, a set of libraries that provide support for various applications, and a set of applications. If you're lucky (as with Red Hat Linux), a distribution also includes powerful but usable installation and configuration utilities that make it easy for you to get the power of Linux without also having to get your Ph.D. in Computer Science. (Though it's not a problem if you already have one.)

This chapter discusses the most popular Linux distributions other than Red Hat, organized alphabetically, including their hardware requirement, how they are installed, and the system administration and software installation tools they provide. Although you've already made a decision by purchasing this book, it's useful to compare and contrast the installation and configuration tools used by other versions of Linux. The final section of this chapter discusses issues in running applications that have been compiled for these other Linux distributions under another Linux distribution, such as Red Hat.

Caldera OpenLinux

URL: `http://www.calderasystems.com`

Caldera's OpenLinux is an easy-to-use, easy-to-administer Linux distribution that is available only for Intel x86 and clone systems. Caldera has put a lot of thought and effort into bringing Linux as close as possible to the idyllic, trouble-free installation that most people expect and someday hope to see in a computer operating system. Part of the ease of installation and use can be attributed to Caldera's own installer and configuration tools, and part to the company's thoughtful bundling of special versions of commercial applications such as PartitionMagic and BootMagic, which aid in the installation and configuration process. PartitionMagic provides an easy-to-use graphical interface that enables you to optimize your disk by packing all your existing data together, and then makes it easy for you to create new partitions in the unused space, even formatting them for you and assigning the appropriate partition types for Linux. BootMagic provides an easy way for you to select which OS you want to boot each time you restart your machine.

OpenLinux is the only popular Linux distribution that you can begin installing from Windows—no need to reboot, create a boot floppy, light a candle, or perform other bootstrapping tasks. When you start the installer, you can use PartitionMagic to repartition an existing disk without reformatting, which comes in handy if you have data that you want to preserve. After creating the partitions necessary for OpenLinux, the rest of OpenLinux installation is fast and almost automatic. This is due to Caldera's OpenLinux Linux Installation Wizard (LIZARD), which is easy to use and does an impressive job of automatically detecting video cards, sound cards, PCMCIA cards, network adapters, special disk controllers, and just about anything else that you can stuff into a slot on your PC.

On the GUI front, Caldera's OpenLinux is committed to the KDE desktop environment to the exclusion of other popular ones such as GNOME. This won't be troubling to the new user, however, because KDE provides an easy-to-use, drag-and-drop veneer over the standard X Window system. However, administrators and those who want to more fully customize their systems might find this a serious limitation because many interesting developments (office suites, standalone word processors, new browsers, and so on) are GNOME-based.

As with all Linux distributions, the space requirements for OpenLinux depend on the type of installation that you are performing. Your options are as follows:

- 160MB for a minimal system.
- 500MB for recommended Linux end-user packages, without any of the bundled commercial Linux applications.
- 800MB for recommended Linux end-user packages and all the bundled commercial Linux applications.
- 1.4GB for every application on the Caldera CDs. Targeted toward software developers and power users, this includes every Linux binary package, all commercial applications, and all software development tools.

These space requirements do not include any swap space you've allocated on your disk.

After you have installed OpenLinux, Caldera provides you with a variety of administrative tools, the nicest of which is Caldera's Open Administration System (COAS), which provides both graphical and command-line interfaces. The graphical interface provided by COAS is intuitive and usable, while the command-line interface lets you assemble COAS commands into shell-scripts for easy, automated administrative purposes. To prevent other Linux distributions from having to reinvent the administrative wheel, Caldera has made COAS itself Open Source software, releasing it under the GPL, and has set up a Web site for coordinating COAS development (`http://www.coas.org`).

COAS is a modular administrative environment, written in C++ and Python, that makes it easy to write COAS modules for various administrative tasks. Although COAS itself is Open Source, modules that work within the COAS framework need not be—this fine line has served as a trip wire to prevent the adoption of COAS in other Linux distributions. If Linux distributors can learn to focus more on usability and standardized administration than on philosophical or theological issues, COAS should see more widespread use in the future, hopefully in other Linux distributions as well as Caldera's.

Corel Linux

URL: `http://linux.corel.com`

Corel is the newest member of the Linux distribution club, but it is getting a significant amount of attention. Corel Linux is the product of an established software firm with years of experience in things that have only recently come to Linux, including usability, sensitivity to customer needs, and so on. The fact that Corel's other Linux offering is WordPerfect, far and away the best and most powerful word processing and document production software for Linux, doesn't hurt either. WordPerfect stumbled badly when porting to Windows (some would say over a foot stuck out by someone at Microsoft), and Corel's early commitment to the Linux market shows that the company isn't eager to make that mistake again.

Corel's Linux is based on the Debian Linux distribution and comes in three different packages: a somewhat minimal downloadable version that's still quite usable, a standard version with email customer support and extra bundled applications, and a deluxe version with email and telephone support and even more applications.

One cute application that is unique to Corel's Linux basic distribution is Corel's File Manager, which provides the standard file/folder/drag/drop model for accessing your files, albeit with a sexy set of nicely done icons that let you know that Corel has done this user interface stuff before.

As for GUIs, Corel has committed to the KDE desktop environment to the exclusion of other popular ones such as GNOME. Again, this won't be troubling to the new user because KDE provides an easy-to-use, drag-and-drop veneer over the standard X Window system. However, administrators and those who want to more fully customize their systems might find this a serious limitation because many interesting developments (office suites, standalone word processors, new browsers, and so on) are GNOME-based.

The installation process for Corel Linux uses the Install Express application, a friendly graphical installation based on the X Window system that does a good job of probing and identifying hardware and that also hides much of the complexity associated with things such as disk partitioning. As with most other Linux distributions, Corel's offers several different installation classes: minimal, workstation, server, and custom, each with specific disk space requirements. Corel's Linux is designed for a Pentium or Pentium-class machine with a minimum of 24MB of RAM, 500MB of disk space, a CD-ROM drive, and a PCI video card with 2MB or better of memory running in at least VGA mode.

One nice installation option is the capability to install Corel's Linux into a directory named `\CDL` in an existing Windows file system. To run Linux, you then reboot your machine, press F8 to get the boot menu, and select Safe Mode Command Prompt Only. When you have a prompt, you change to the `\CDL` directory and execute a batch file to start Linux. This is a great way to experiment with Linux without making a real commitment, although it's impossible to get an accurate feel for the performance of Corel's Linux when run in this mode. Because Linux runs out of the FAT file system and uses a file for swapping, its performance in this mode is a fraction of what it would be if installed in its own partitions.

As with Red Hat Linux, Corel's Linux distribution includes a software package, corelupdate, that lets you locate software updates on the Internet and install new packages from a local source or over the Internet. There are usually two keys to success for updaters such as these: how usable they are and how well Corel keeps up its central database of patches, updates, and enhancements. Having a nice silver doorknob isn't all that useful if the door itself is full of termites. Time will tell.

Debian Linux

URL: `http://www.debian.org`

Debian is pronounced Deb'-ian, with a soft e, and is a contraction of the names of the founders of the Debian Project, Debra and Ian Murdock. Debian is an interesting departure from other Linux distributions in that it is designed to be kernel-independent. This means that someday the Linux kernel that is currently used with Debian could be replaced by other free, Open Source kernels that are under development. For now, Debian distributions ship with the Linux kernel, so it's fair to call this a Linux distribution.

The Debian Linux distribution is currently available for DEC/Compaq Alpha systems, Intel x86 (and clone) systems, Motorola 680x0 systems (Commodore Amiga, Atari St family, and older Apple Macintosh computers), and SPARC systems. Work on porting Debian to systems using ARM microprocessors is in progress. The number of supported platforms makes Debian the most widely ported Linux distribution, and thus the savior of more new and old hardware than any other Linux.

Disk space requirements for a Debian Linux installation span a similar spectrum. At the low end they consist of 40MB for the base system, 16MB of swap space, and no X Window system. At the high end, a full-blown system requires 850MB for a system supporting several users and including the X Window system and a few other similarly large applications. Debian systems can be booted from disks or bootable CD-ROMs and can be installed from disks, CD-ROM, local disk partitions, or over the network.

Debian installation and initial system configuration is handled by a fairly crude, text-based application called dbootstrap. For more information about installing and configuring Debian, see *Installing Debian GNU/Linux*, by Thomas Down, another book from Sams Publishing.

The Debian package manager dpkg provides some useful enhancements to the package managers used to install software in other Linux distributions. With dpkg, it is possible to use additional information that developers provide when creating Debian software packages. As with packages used by the Red Hat package manager, packages used by the Debian package manager identify any other packages that are required by a package you are using. Debian packages also can identify recommended and suggested packages. Recommending one package for use with another declares a strong but not absolute dependency between them. Suggesting one page for use with another declares that one package can enhance the usefulness of another but that installing the latter without the former is fine.

Mandrake

URL: `http://www.mandrake.org`

Mandrake is a popular Linux distribution that in many ways resembles Corel's: Like Corel's, the Mandrake Linux is based on another popular Linux distribution—in this case, Red Hat's.

Administratively, Mandrake provides some additional administrative applications such as initscripts and a very powerful, customized installer, but otherwise it is largely identical to Red Hat Linux. As an enhancement to the installation process, Mandrake provides Lothar, a useful application for identifying hardware and subsequently detecting hardware changes. This is typically the bane of any operating system that runs on ISA and PCI hardware, where anyone with a tent and a wave solder machine can make boards and sell them over the Net for pennies. In spirit and functionality, Lothar is much like the Kudzu application used by Red Hat Linux to do the same sort of things, but it's great to see the Mandrake folks at least trying to add some value to the Red Hat code base.

Mandrake is readily available by FTP, can be purchased for the cost of the CD from places such as Linux mall (`http://www.linuxmall.com`), or can be purchased off-the-shelf for $100 or so. With the $100 comes 100 days of email customer support. Some prepackaged versions of Mandrake include PartitionMagic and BootMagic (described in the section "Caldera OpenLinux," earlier in this chapter).

Slackware

URL: `http://www.slackware.com`

Alas, poor Slackware was the Linux distribution that truly got the Linux ball rolling and was the subject of most early Linux books. First released in 1992, the Slackware Linux Project intended to produce the most UNIX-like Linux distribution available. The emergence of well-supported, commercially backed Linux distributions has almost totally eclipsed Slackware, but it is still well known and hence discussed here.

In general, Slackware has the lowest hardware ante of any Linux distribution. Its official, minimum requirements are the following:

- 386SX processor
- 4MB of RAM
- 20MB of hard disk space
- 5.25-inch floppy drive

Anything better than these entry-level requirements is, well, better. For example, you will need more memory to provide any network services such as the X Window system at a usable speed.

The Slackware Linux installation program is called setup and is a text-based, menu-driven program that's relatively easy to use after you accept that it has the graphical sophistication of the vi editor.

Subsequent configuration is done by invoking specific, standard Linux utilities for various aspects of Linux—there is no single, unified configuration and administration utility as there is with most other Linux distributions. For example, to configure your network cards, addresses, and associated information, you use the netconfig utility. You use the XF86Setup application to configure your X Window system server, and you use the xwmconfig application to select the window manager or desktop environment that you want to use when the X Window system starts.

As with Corel's Linux, one especially nice feature of the Slackware Linux distribution is that it enables you to install Slackware into a directory on your existing Windows disks and run Linux from there (although not at the same time as Windows). Slackware outdoes Corel in running out of the Windows file system mode by providing two different subsets of the Slackware distribution that are specifically designed to run from within the FAT file system. These are called ZipSlack and BigSlack.

- ZipSlack is a special version of Slackware Linux that can be installed onto any FAT file system and that requires slightly less than 100MB of free space. (Therefore, it fits on an Iomega Zip disk, hence the name).
- BigSlack is similar to ZipSlack, but it actually includes most of a complete Slackware installation, including the X Window system and KDE. BigSlack requires about 800MB of disk space but will give you an accurate picture of an installed Slackware Linux distribution without requiring that you actually repartition your disk.

For installing software, Slackware provides an interactive program called pkgtool for managing your packages. The pkgtool application uses a terminal-mode interface that helps you add and remove packages. If you would prefer to avoid quasigraphical tools in classic UNIX style, you can even use separate command-line packaging commands such as `installpkg`, `removepkg`, `upgradepkg`, `makepkg`, and `explodepkg`. Two especially nice commands are `rpm2tgz` and `rpm2targz`, which enable you to convert Red Hat RPM packages to Slackware's gzipped tar file package format; this is often desirable because it's much easier to find packages for Red Hat than for Slackware.

SuSE Linux

URL: `http://www.suse.com`

SuSE, a German Linux distribution, is the most popular Linux distribution in Europe. SuSE (pronounced "Soose") stands for Gesellschaft für Software und Systementwicklung mbH, which roughly translates into Company for Software and System Development. The SuSE distribution has its roots in Slackware but has added significant value by providing excellent installation and configuration utilities, as well as an incredible amount of software.

SuSE is a complete Linux distribution that comes with easily more than a thousand applications and utilities, packaged on six CD-ROMs when you buy the commercial, supported version. SuSE users who purchase a commercially packaged SuSE distribution kit can get customer support via email, telephone, or fax for 60 days following the purchase date. Additional support is available for a fee. For researching and (hopefully) solving problems more quickly or without purchasing additional support, the SuSE Web site provides an extensive knowledge base of common questions, answers, and suggestions.

The SuSE Linux distribution runs on 386SX or better Intel systems or compatible processors, and also on DEC/Compaq Alpha systems. It requires a minimum of 8MB, with a minimum of 16MB required (32MB recommended) if you use the X Window system. SuSE also requires a minimum of 300MB of disk space and can use up to 4GB if you install the contents of all six CDs.

The SuSE Linux distribution includes an excellent installation and administration tool called Yet Another Setup Tool (YaST). YaST is a terminal-mode graphical application that simplifies all the tasks you need to perform to install SuSE Linux, partition and format disks, and configure SuSE Linux. Although the type of graphical interface provided by YaST pales beside similar tools that use an X Window system interface (such as those used by Corel, Red Hat, and Mandrake), the fact that you can run it from any terminal or terminal emulator is probably more important. This means that you can use YaST to configure systems on systems where you do not plan to install the X Window system. YaST is well designed and walks you through the mandatory set of installation and configuration options necessary to successfully install SuSE Linux.

SuSE Linux uses the Red Hat Package Manager (RPM) for distributing and installing software packages. Using a common package format such as RPM simplifies the process of installing compatible packages from other Linux distributions.

As with Red Hat, the SuSE Linux distribution does not restrict you to a specific X Window system desktop environment; SuSE provides both KDE and GNOME, so you can select the desktop environment you are most comfortable with and that supports the applications you want to use.

TurboLinux

URL: `http://www.turbolinux.com`

TurboLinux is the most popular Linux Distribution in Japan and the Far East, and is available for systems with Intel Pentium and compatible processors. A version of TurboLinux for systems with Alpha processors is under development.

As with most other Linux distributions, both workstation and server versions of TurboLinux are commercially available and come with high-quality, thorough, and readable documentation. TurboLinux also provides a TurboCluster Server package, which is a version of TurboLinux designed for use within a group of servers that work together, dynamically distributing user requests and processes across the systems in the cluster (known as load-balancing).

A TurboLinux workstation installation requires approximately 750MB of disk space, and a server requires at least 1GB. TurboLinux can be installed directly from a bootable CD-ROM or can be booted from a disk and loaded from CD-ROM or over a network if your CD-ROM drive isn't bootable or if your TurboLinux distribution is located on a remote system. The commercial version of TurboLinux comes with preconfigured disks for local or network installations.

The TurboLinux Linux distribution provides a well-designed general installation process that invokes specialized, custom TurboLinux tools (such as TurboProbe, for identifying the cards in your system) as needed during installation. The TurboLinux installation and configuration tools are terminal-mode graphical applications. As with the terminal-mode tools used by other Linux distributions such as SuSE, the type of graphical interface provided by the TurboLinux tools pales beside similar tools that use an X Window system interface (such as those used by Corel, Red Hat, and Mandrake). However, the fact that you can run them from any terminal or terminal emulator means that you can use the TurboLinux tools to configure systems on systems where you do not plan to install the X Window system.

After you have partitioned your disk(s) and installed the basic TurboLinux package, you use the TurboPkg application to select and install specific software packages; you use the TurboCfg application to configure your system. After your system is up and running, you can use these same tools to install other packages or modify your system's configuration.

In the GUI department, TurboLinux provides a customized X Window system desktop known as TurboDesk, which is based on the AfterStep window manager. AfterStep is modeled after the window manager used on NeXT workstations and in the OpenStep operating system. TurboDesk is a nicely designed desktop environment that provides familiar features such as a row of icons from which you can start specific applications, icons for running applications so that you can switch between them more easily, and a trash can for deleting files. If you already are accustomed to another window manager or desktop environment, TurboDesk provides menu options that let you switch to window managers such as fvwm, fvwm95, and Window Maker.

Mixing and Matching Software from Linux Distributions

The bewildering assortment of Linux distributions available can make it frustrating if you're looking for a specific software package but can't find a version compiled for the Linux distribution that you are using. One great fringe benefit of Linux as an Open Source project is that you should be able to locate the source for any Linux application that has been released under the GPL. However, if you don't have the time or ability to compile your own applications, the Open Source nature of Linux also means that programs compiled for one Linux distribution often can be executed on another as long as two key factors match. These factors are the version of any shared libraries that the application requires, and the kernel versions on your system and the one where the software was compiled.

Shared Libraries and Versioning

In most cases, shared libraries are a great step forward in the evolution of how applications access system functions. Computer libraries are precompiled sets of functions that applications call to perform a specific task. Grouping related functions into libraries that any application can call is more efficient than requiring that each application provide its own version of each function. For example, any graphical application that needs to draw a line can call a central library function to draw that line rather than having to implement and maintain its own line-drawing function.

In the old days, compiling an application that used library functions actually linked that version of the library into the application. This is known as static linking. The advantage of static linking is that the compiled applications can be moved more easily from one computer system to another because they are self-contained. The disadvantage of static linking is that applications that have been compiled and linked against a specific version of a library can't take advantage of any subsequent enhancements to that library without recompiling and relinking to the application. For example, if someone found a bug in a library function, fixed it, and released a new version of the library, applications compiled against the earlier, buggy library still would use the buggy version of the function because it had been built in when they were compiled.

Shared libraries are libraries to which an application links when it is executed, often referred to as "at run time." Because the libraries are loaded whenever an application that uses them is executed, this is referred to as dynamic linking. Because every application needs access to functions in that library at run time, the libraries must be capable of being loaded by multiple applications at the same time, hence the term shared libraries. Applications compiled against shared libraries contain an internal reference to the library in which required functions are found and to the version of the library against which they were compiled. Shared libraries typically have names such as libc.so.2.6—any application compiled against this library "knows" that it must be capable of find version 2.6 or better of this library when it is executed. The phrase *or better* is critical because applications linked against a shared library can use other, newer versions of that shared library as long as they differ only by minor number. For example, applications linked against libc.so.2.6 could dynamically link to libc.so.2.7, but not to libc.so.3.0.

Linux applications built for one Linux distribution usually can run on another if the same shared libraries exist in both distributions or if the shared libraries in the new distribution differ only by having a higher minor number than the ones used when the application was compiled.

Kernel Version Numbers

As you would hope, the Linux kernel has improved over time. Older versions of the Linux kernel used a different object file format (`a.out`, now ELF) for applications. Older kernels also did not use things such as the `/proc` file system for centrally storing process information. As with shared library versions, applications from one Linux distribution usually will run on another as long as both have the same kernel version or if the two kernel versions differ only by the smallest number (2.1.3 versus 2.1.7).

In reality, most user-level applications use few kernel-level functions that are prone to radical change, so you might be able to run user-level applications on other kernels with more radical differences in version numbers. Applications for system administration, or those that directly access system devices or data structures, are a different story. Because they use more low-level functions to provide access to internal system features, kernel versions should be as close as possible if you want to try running such applications on Linux distributions other than the one on which they were compiled. As a general rule, you should avoid trying to run administrative or system-level applications on Linux distributions other than the one for which they were compiled.

CHAPTER 2

Preparing Your System for Red Hat 7.0

This chapter provides planning discussing information, the various Red Hat installation classes and the content and organization of each. In addition, it explains different ways of collecting information about system hardware that you might need during installation. The chapter concludes by discussing how to configure systems on which you want to be able to run Red Hat Linux and one or more other operating systems.

Red Hat Linux can be installed in three general configurations, known as installation classes. These classes (workstation, server, and custom) represent different uses for the Red Hat Linux system that you are installing and configuring, and they determine the software packages that are installed by the Red Hat Installer. You can subsequently add other packages at any time, but each requires a different amount of disk space and has different memory requirements. Some of these installation classes also use different disk partitioning schemes for content and performance reasons.

Selecting Your Red Hat Installation Class

Red Hat Linux systems are grouped into three basic classes that you can select during installation. Two of these, the workstation and server classes, are designed to be used in certain ways and therefore include automatic installation of the software packages associated with those kinds of tasks. The third basic installation class, a custom class, is designed for more advanced Linux users and developers who need a mixture of the services and applications included in the workstation and server installs. Selecting the custom class forces you to specify how you want the installer to partition your disk and requires that you manually select the specific packages that you want to install on the system.

Any Red Hat installation requires a bootable CD-ROM drive or 3.5-inch floppy drive to begin the installation process, and at least 16MB of RAM in which to run the installer. The class of Red Hat system that you choose to install serves as the starting point for your new machine. Using the Red Hat Package Manager (RPM), you can subsequently install other packages on your system, configuring it to exactly suit your personal requirements or the special needs of users within your organization. Regardless of the installation class you select, the packages associated with that class are always installed in the correct order so that any libraries or auxiliary software required by one package are installed before the libraries or software for a package that depends on them.

When installing a Red Hat Linux system, selecting the correct installation class is an important starting point. Different installation classes have very different contents and disk partitioning schemes. In terms of software, it can be time consuming to subsequently locate and install the packages containing the right combination of libraries and applications, for example, to convert an existing server installation into a workstation installation. With hardware, it is impractical to convert a workstation installation into a server installation due to the differences in the disk partitioning schemes used by the two. In general, to change installation classes on a system, it is easiest to back up any data that you want to preserve onto some removable media or over the Net to another system, and then reinstall your machine with the new class.

The next few sections examine the different Red Hat installation classes and provide overviews of their content and target audiences.

The Workstation Installation Class

A Red Hat workstation is intended to be the desktop machine for one or more users. Workstations provide a graphical user environment (GUI), compilers, tools for formatting documents and printing them, and many other tools. When installing Linux, Red Hat offers two different workstation installation classes that primarily differ in the default desktop environment they install on your workstation. These are the GNOME (GNU Network Object Model Environment [GNU stands for "GNU's Not UNIX"]) and KDE (K Desktop Environment) workstations.

NOTE

> Unlike previous versions of Red Hat Linux, Red Hat 7.0 does not offer separate GNOME and KDE workstation classes on its installation class dialog. You must specify the type of workstation you are installing on a subsequent Package Group Selection dialog.

The GNOME and KDE workstation installation classes each require approximately the same amount of disk space (exclusive of swap space, which is the same for both). The basic Red Hat workstation installation class requires approximately 570MB of disk space. The GNOME and/or KDE installations add the following amount of disk space to that requirement:

- A GNOME installation adds approximately 115MB to your basic Red Hat Linux workstation installation.
- A KDE workstation installation adds approximately 120MB to your basic Red Hat Linux workstation installation.

The next sections provide additional detail about GNOME and KDE workstation installations and examine the disk-partitioning scheme shared by both these workstation installation classes. Which one you choose is up to you. GNOME is the darling of the Linux set right now, and has been selected by vendors such as Sun Microsystems as their desktop environment for future versions of operating systems such as Solaris. GNOME is probably where the most interesting GUI and application development will take place on Linux in the near future. On the other hand, if you come from a UNIX background and want a familiar environment, KDE's similarity to CDE will help you be productive quickly. I prefer GNOME, but generally install both on systems where I have sufficient disk space. This makes it easy to experiment with and compare the features of the different desktop environments. Red Hat's support for both of these desktop environments is a significant difference from many other Linux distributions, which only support one or the other.

GNOME Workstations

GNOME is an Open Source desktop environment on free steroids, a bell and whistle farm for the most adventurous X Window system advocates. GNOME is not a window manager, but it requires that one is present on your system. By default, the Sawmill window manager is included, but you can use any other GNOME-compliant window manager, including Enlightenment, Window Maker, and IceWM (in addition to FVWM, SCWM, AfterStep, and QVWM, in the near future). As with all X Window system environments, GNOME can be configured and personalized in an infinite and occasionally bewildering number of ways. By default, GNOME provides a large desktop with a panel at the bottom of the screen. This control panel (pardon the expression, Windows haters) provides access to menus containing GNOME and X Window system applications, four different virtual workspaces (handy for hiding games when your boss comes around), and icons representing any X Window system or GNOME tasks that you are currently running. This panel is just a GNOME application that is started by default—other control panels, such as xfce, are available for GNOME if you don't like this one.

GNOME is the desktop environment of choice for many Linux users because it provides an incredible number of features, with many more under active development. For example, all GNOME applications are session-aware, meaning that applications retain knowledge of the previous times they were used. For example, each time you restart a GNOME tool, it reopens the last file that you were working with and even positions the cursor at the last location you edited. This is not only technically interesting, but also useful.

In general, the GNOME folks can claim adherence to more buzzwords and acronyms than any other desktop environment. For example, GNOME uses CORBA (the Object Management Group's Common Object Request Broker Architecture) for interoperability and network transparency. GNOME is also working on an OLE (Microsoft's Object Linking and Embedding) clone called Bonobo, uses the DocBook SGML (Standard Generalized Markup Language) DTD (Document Type Definition) for all its documentation, and supports Mesa, which is a free software implementation of the OpenGL (Open Graphics Library) standard. You probably get the idea.

For more information about GNOME, visit the GNOME Web site at `http://www.gnome.org`.

KDE Workstations

KDE is a desktop environment that is designed to provide users with a standard, easy-to-use graphical desktop environment. KDE was initially inspired by the Common Desktop Environment (CDE), which was cooperatively designed by major UNIX vendors such as IBM and Sun Microsystems. CDE was designed and built using the Open Group's Motif X Window system libraries, which meant that vendors wishing to deploy CDE had to license Motif. This obviously was unsuitable in the free, Open Source environment of Linux, so KDE was written to provide a free, Open Source alternative. The KDE project originally was sponsored by a number of Linux vendors, including Caldera, Delix, O'Reilly Associates, and SuSE. For more detailed information about KDE, see the K Desktop Environment Web site at `http://www.kde.org`.

The major features of KDE are standardized drag-and-drop operations, a graphical system for easy desktop configuration, integrated national language support (NLS), a unified help system that works the same way for all KDE applications, and network transparency at the application level. Most of these features are provided as a result of the common application development framework used by KDE, called KOM/OpenParts (K Object Model/OpenParts), which is built using open industry standards such as the CORBA object request broker 2.0. KDE applications display a wonderful similarity to each other that you never could find in older X Window system applications written using different developers' favorite portions of various X toolkits and widget collections.

KDE is not a window manager in the classic X Window system "window decorations and menu support" sense. KDE includes its own KWM window manager and provides a complete desktop work environment, not just the window manipulation and X Window system controls that a window manager provides.

As with all X Window system environments, KDE can be configured and personalized in an infinite and occasionally bewildering number of ways. By default, KDE provides a large desktop with a panel at the bottom of the screen. This control panel is similar to the one used by GNOME, providing access to menus containing KDE and X Window system applications, four different virtual workspaces, and icons representing any X Window system or KDE tasks that you are currently running.

Planning Disk Partitioning for Red Hat Workstations

By default, Red Hat's workstation installation class creates a swap partition for use by Linux's virtual memory support and two disk partitions for storing files. The Linux partitions created by a workstation class install are the following:

`/`—The root of the standard Linux file system, this contains all the files that Linux actually uses when it runs, as well as all user directories.
`/boot`—This contains files used during boot time. The most important of these is the kernel, usually named `vmlinuz-`*`<kernel-version>`*.

By default, workstation partitions have the following sizes:

Swap partition—Approximately the same size as the amount of memory in your system, rounded up based on the parameters of your disk drive
`/`—Assigned the remainder of your boot drive
`/boot`—Approximately 20MB in size

The only potential problem in the default partitioning scheme used by Red Hat's workstation class install is that it does not create separate partitions for system and user files. You typically want to locate any directories where users can create files (such as their home directories, usually located in the directories `/home` or `/usr` on older UNIX systems) on a partition other than the one on which system files are located. Locating user and system directories on the same partition gives users the opportunity to accidentally fill up the partition where the system needs to write such files as temporary and log files. Whenever a system partition fills up, you will always begin to get severe error messages on the console, and the system might actually crash.

As mentioned earlier, Red Hat's default installation classes are a good starting point for any Red Hat installation because they ensure that you will install all the packages necessary for what you want to do—and in the correct order to avoid your seeing "missing dependency" messages. If you're concerned about the temporary file issue, you can always add another disk to your system after completing a workstation install and create a partition on that disk to mount as `/tmp`. See Chapter 9, "Using Local and Network Storage," for more information about adding new disks and partitions to your system.

The Server Installation Class

A Red Hat server provides centralized services for FTP, the World Wide Web, and so on. Red Hat servers are not intended to be desktop machines, so they do not include software such as the X Window system, window managers, and so on. A default Red Hat server installation requires approximately 1.6GB of free disk space, exclusive of the amount of disk space allocated for swap space. More swap space is typically allocated for server systems than for workstations because centralized servers are expected to be servicing multiple network requests simultaneously. By default, the Red Hat Installer allocates swap space equal to 2.5 times the amount of memory in your system when installing a Red Hat server. This number is rounded up slightly, based on the parameters of the disk drive on which you are installing the server.

Server Disk Partitioning

By default, Red Hat's server installation class creates a swap partition for use by Linux's virtual memory support and several disk partitions for storing files. The Linux partitions created by a server class install are listed here:

- `/`—This is the root of the standard Linux file system, which contains all the files that Linux actually requires to run and provides mount points (directories) for any other disk partitions.
- **`/boot`**—This contains files used during boot time. The most important of these is the kernel, usually named `vmlinuz-`*`<kernel-version>`*.
- **`/home`**—This contains the login (home) directories for all users.
- **`/usr`**—This contains executables and associated files used by the system or users that are not mandatory for the system to boot. Red Hat uses `/usr` as the location into which to install applications and related files that are not expected to be changed by the average user. The only exceptions to this rule are subdirectories such as `/usr/local`, where systems administrators install "sanctioned" applications, and `/usr/tmp`, historically a location for programs to store temporary files but now usually a symbolic link to `/var/tmp`.
- **`/var`**—This contains the directory where system log files are stored, as well as directories that store temporary files and contain executables and support files associated with third-party applications.

When dividing up the disk onto which you are installing Red Hat, the swap partition is allocated approximately 2.5 times the amount of memory in your system; the partition mounted at `/boot` is approximately 18MB in size. The remainder of the space on your boot drive is divided among the other partitions, with approximately 50% allocated to `/home`, 35% to `/usr`, and the remaining 15% to `/var`.

The Custom Installation Class

The Red Hat custom installation class is designed for special-purpose machines that don't easily fit the model of a desktop user machine or a dedicated, user-free server. When installing a system using the custom installation class, you must specify how your disk will be partitioned and the directories where different partitions will be mounted.

There are almost as many different ideas of optimal partitioning schemes for Linux and UNIX systems as there are Linux and UNIX system administrators. Most Linux and UNIX system administrators agree on several points, namely:

- `/` must have its own partition to serve as the root of the Linux or UNIX file system.
- **`/boot`** should have its own partition to isolate files required for booting the system and to simplify experimenting with different kernel versions. (This also is because Linux is designed to look for the kernel on `/boot` by default.)
- **`/usr`** should be a mount point for a separate partition whenever possible, to isolate noncritical software from that required to boot the system and to help minimize

the amount of disk space required for the `/` partition. Note that if `/usr` is its own partition and you configure your system to automatically start the X Window system at boot time, you will receive various severe error messages when you reboot your system if the partition associated with `/usr` cannot be mounted. Some people also advocate a separate partition for `/usr/local`, which is where software developed or compiled at your site usually is installed by a system administrator.

`/tmp` should be a mount point for a separate partition whenever possible, to prevent temporary files allocated by the system or user processes from accidentally filling up a system partition.

`/home` should be a mount point for a separate partition whenever possible. In networked environments, `/home` is typically located on a centralized file server, to isolate users' home directories from being located on a single workstation. This simplifies backups and enables home directories to be accessed from any workstation.

`/opt` and **`/var`** should be mount points for separate partitions whenever possible to isolate external packages from those required to boot the system. Note that if you create a separate partition for `/var`, the `/var` directory on your system's boot drive must contain a subdirectory named log to enable the system to boot correctly if the partition associated with `/var` cannot be mounted.

In general, separate partitions are associated with different directories for one or more of the following reasons:

- To isolate the contents of those directories from the system itself.
- To simplify increasing the amount of space associated with those directories.
- To reduce the overall sizes of the partitions and associated file systems on your system. The system fsck utility (file system consistency check) can verify and repair smaller file systems more quickly than large ones at boot time, especially now, when fsck can check multiple partitions in parallel.
- To reduce the impact of the failure of any single disk or disk partition. You can restore one or more smaller file systems from backup media more quickly than you can a single huge partition. Smaller partitions also can be backed up more quickly during standard daily maintenance.

New partitions easily can be retrofitted to existing systems by adding and partitioning new disks, copying the files from an existing directory hierarchy into the new partitions, deleting the files in the old directory hierarchies, and then mounting the new partitions on the directories whose contents they now contain. The fact that Linux and UNIX use standard directories as mount points for partitions makes this easy. Adding new disks to an existing Linux system, partitioning them, and integrating them into your system is explained in Chapter 9.

On systems with reasonable amounts of disk space that are designed to be used as both workstations and server systems, you might want to consider assigning separate partitions to the directories associated with those servers. Typical examples of directories associated with specific servers are `/home/ftp` (associated with the FTP server) and `/home/httpd` (associated with a Web server).

The following is a sample custom layout that I typically use for systems with 64MB of main memory and two disks that are designed to be used both as workstations and servers.

```
Filesystem    1k-blocks      Used  Available    Use%     Mounted on
/dev/hda10       101485     32841      63404     34%     /
/dev/hda1         19487      2647      15834     14%     /boot
/dev/hdc1       5039560      3112    4780444      0%     /home
/dev/hdc6       3005656      6372    2846600      0%     /home/httpd
/dev/hdc5       5039560        20    4783536      0%     /opt
/dev/hda8        101485        37      96208      0%     /tmp
/dev/hda6       1511936   1255592     179540     87%     /usr
/dev/hda7       1007960     32852     923904      3%     /var
/dev/hda9        206899        99     196117      0%     /var/log
```

This table shows two hard drives, `/dev/hda` and `/dev/hdc`, that have been partitioned to help minimize the chance that any partition will ever fill up. `/dev/hda` is the boot drive, the first drive on the primary IDE interface on this system. `/dev/hdc` is the first device on the secondary IDE interface on this system. `/dev/hdb` is not listed because it is the CD-ROM drive, the slave device on the primary IDE interface, and no disk is currently present. If there were another IDE drive in the system, it would be `/dev/hdd`. Different disk interfaces (IDE, SCSI, and so on) have different naming conventions. Hard drive and removable media naming conventions are discussed in more detail in Chapter 9.

Note that `/var/log` is assigned its own partition. This is because system logs can fill up quickly for server systems, especially if problems are occurring. Disk space is cheap. On Linux and UNIX systems, `/usr/tmp` is the other temporary directory used by system dn user processes and is usually a symbolic link to `/var/tmp` (to increase the default chance that it will not be located on the same partition as `/tmp`). If you have sufficient disk space, isolating the partition where `/var/tmp` is located from the partition where `/var/log` is located will help reduce the chance that overly full log files will prevent user processes from being capable of storing temporary files in `/var/tmp`. The cost of wasting disk space is typically much less than the cost of dealing with irate users.

On file servers, you might want to allocate multiple partitions for user directories and mount them under `/home` to improve performance. If you have large numbers of users, the system cost of listing hundreds or thousands of directories under `/home` can be substantial, especially when done by the system when looking up a home directory each time a user logs in. Many large sites create directories such as `/home/a-l` and `/home/m-z` and use these to segregate the home directories of users whose logins begin with those letters. An alternative is to create group-specific subdirectories under `/home`, such as `/home/research`, `/home/sales`, or `/home/losers`, and put the home directories of users associated with those groups in those subdirectories. The latter approach makes it more difficult to guess the home directory of a specific user, but you can always look in the password file, `/etc/passwd`, for this information.

Installing Red Hat on Systems with Multiple Disks

The Red Hat workstation and server installation classes assume that your system has a single disk and allocate partitions based on percentages of the size of that disk. If you are installing Red Hat Linux onto a system with multiple disks, you should either use the custom installation class or allocate partitions on your other disks after finishing a default installation. As mentioned earlier, you can always retrofit new partitions to an existing system by copying the files from an existing directory hierarchy into the new partitions, deleting the files in the old directory hierarchies, and then mounting the new partitions on the directories whose contents they now contain. The fact that Linux and UNIX use standard directories as mount points for partitions makes this easy.

Adding new disks to an existing Linux system, partitioning them, and integrating them into your system is explained in Chapter 9.

Collecting Information About Your Hardware

Before starting your Red Hat installation, you should always prepare a list of the hardware in your system and its configuration. If you're using cards that set IO addresses and IRQs using jumpers, you will not be able to yank them out to verify their values while you're installing Linux. In general, I've found that documenting the contents of a system is tedious and rarely necessary, but one single case in which you need that information will make you want to do this forever. (I have had my one such experience—I'd suggest that you try not to get yours now.) A good rule of thumb for getting card names, chip type, and jumper information is that the one bit of information you need will always be unreadable or obscured by another card. Take the time to capture this information now.

In general, Red Hat Linux is much better than any other version of Linux in terms of detecting hardware and selecting appropriate drivers to get you up and running quickly. A good example of this is in one of my systems, where the default installer identified my video card as a Banshee, which was sufficient to get the X Window system working. When the system was up and running, I was able to run the Xconfigurator manually and more correctly identify the card as a Banshee with 3dfx support, enabling me to run the X Window system at higher resolutions and greater color depths. Beyond providing good detection support during installation, Red Hat also provides a software package called Kudzu to detect changes to hardware made after you install your system.

Before installing Red Hat Linux, collect the following information about your system:

- Amount of main memory.
- Device information, including manufacturer, model number, and size (where appropriate) of all hard drives, CD-ROM drives, and removable media drives in your system.
- Video card manufacturer and model and the amount of onboard memory

located on the card. If you have multiple video cards, make sure that you record this information for each.

- Monitor manufacturer and model, as well as any available specifications for the monitor itself, such as its horizontal refresh rate, vertical sync rate, and its supported (and maximum) resolutions.
- Sound card manufacturer and model, as well as the IO address and IRQ that it currently is using.
- Network card manufacturer and model, as well as the IO address and IRQ that it is currently using. If you have multiple network cards, make sure that you record this information for each.
- Any permanent network configuration information that you currently use on the machine. This would be the IP address (if fixed), the host and domain names, the netmask, and the default gateway and name servers used by the system.
- The IO address and IRQ used by your serial ports (COM1 and COM2) and your parallel port (LPT1).
- The type (PS/2 or serial), manufacturer, and model of your mouse.
- The IO address of any game or joystick port on your system.
- The manufacturer and model of any other cards in your system, such as cards providing additional serial/parallel ports, high-speed disk interfaces, and so on.

If you are lucky enough to still have the documentation for the boards and other components of your system, it should contain all the information you need. The next sections discuss how you can obtain this information from your system itself if you are already running Microsoft Windows or another version of Linux.

Collecting Hardware Information on a Windows System

Installing Red Hat Linux is one of those rare cases when it actually might be handy to already be running Windows 95, 98, or 2000. If your hardware is already working in your Windows box, you should be able to get accurate information about it by using the Windows System Control Panel, which you surely know how to find if you're using a Windows system. (Just in case: Start menu, Settings, Control Panel, System.) Selecting the Device Manager tab displays a nicely organized list of all the devices and interface cards in your system, organized into groups.

Collecting Hardware Information on a Linux System

If you're already running some other version of Linux but don't know or remember much about the hardware in your Linux box, Linux provides various ways of obtaining information about your system hardware:

- The file `/var/log/messages` provides a record of the console messages displayed when your system rebooted.
- If you currently are running the X Window system, the file `/etc/XF86Config` provides information about the horizontal synchronization and vertical refresh rates in the entries for the HorizSync and VertRefresh keywords.

- Systems utilities for the ISA bus (isapnp), general plug-and-play detection utilities (pnpdump), and PCI bus (lspci and pciutils) provide information about the devices on those buses.
- The `/proc` file system (available only if your system is running a Linux kernel later than v2.0) provides a hierarchical collection of device type and status information:
    - `/proc/ide/ide0` and `/proc/ide/ide1` contain information about the IDE devices on your system, organized by interface and device. For example, `/proc/ide/ide0/hda/settings` contains information about the master device on your system's first IDE interface.
    - `/proc/sys/dev/cdrom/info` provides information about the CD-ROM devices in your system.
    - `/proc/parport/hardware` contains information about the IO address and IRQ used by your system's parallel port(s).
    - `/proc/tty/driver/serial` contains information about the serial ports that are available on your system.
    - `/proc/scsi/scsi` contains a list of all SCSI devices in your system.

Preparing Dual-Boot or Multiboot Systems

In some circumstances it might be useful or necessary to create systems that can boot multiple operating systems. You select the operating system you want to boot each time you power-cycle the system. There are two main reasons for this: First, like it or not, you may not always have enough computer systems available to put a Linux system in every pot (so to speak). This is especially true of home computer systems, of which you may have only one, but it also can be true in companies that watch their hardware budgets carefully and will not purchase systems exclusively for use as Linux systems until there is a good business reason to do so. Secondly, and even less attractive, is the grudging admission that you might not be able to do all the work that you currently need to do from a Linux system. This is unfortunately true in companies that mandate the use of applications such as Lotus Notes (although work on a Linux Notes client for Linux is in progress) or require the use of specialized, standard packages for contact management, PC-only databases, and so on.

Creating a system that can boot and run different operating systems isn't that hard to do and requires only the following:

- Your hardware is good enough to satisfy the requirements of each of the operating systems you want to run.
- You have enough disk space to store the partitions required by all these different operating systems.
- You have a boot loader that lets you select which operating system you want to run each time you turn on a machine.

For practical purposes, it is generally best to aim for supporting only two different operating systems on a single system, with an upper limit of three (after all, you might want to add the BeOS). You certainly can run more than that on a single system, but this generally transcends the realm of usability and heads firmly into the realm of experimentation—perhaps even sadism.

Creating systems that boot both some flavor of Microsoft Windows and Linux is the most common case for systems that can run multiple operating systems. Windows is egocentric and therefore generally believes that it should be the only operating system on a computer. A standard step when installing any version of Windows is the one in which it formats your disk for you and then lets you create any partitions you want in the newly freed space. This is not a good thing to do if your disk contains partitions used by other operating systems that you'd like to preserve. I generally suggest, therefore, that if you must use Windows, you should install it first and then use smarter, less megalomaniacal applications to create free space or partitions to be used by other operating systems. You then can easily install whatever other operating system(s) you want in the free space.

The simplest way of making a multiboot system out of one that already runs Microsoft Windows is to add another disk to your Windows system and install Linux on that other disk. Unfortunately, this costs money, ruling it out in many cases. The low-cost key to installing multiple operating systems on a system that currently runs Microsoft Windows is to split existing Windows partitions into multiple partitions. Several utilities that run the gamut of software purchasing options let you split existing Windows partitions. FIPS (First nondestructive Interactive Partition Splitting program) is a freeware utility, the Ranish Partition Manager is shareware, and PartitionMagic from PowerQuest is a full-fledged commercial application.

The next section explains how to prepare a Windows file system for division before using any of these utilities. The remainder of the sections in this chapter discuss each utility, providing general information about its use. For more detailed and possibly more current information, see the documentation that accompanies these utilities.

Preparing Windows Partitions for Fission

First, back up any data on your Windows system that you can't afford to lose forever. I have never had a problem when splitting a Windows partition, but you might. The time you "waste" in backing up your system is worth a thousand times less than the pain you will feel if you lose your data. When backing up your system, you also might want to use RegEdit (or any similar utility that you prefer) to save a copy of the registry with your backups. Chances are that you will never need or use these backups—however, if you do, you will be eternally grateful to me for this paragraph.

After backing up your data (you did back it up, right?), you should reboot your system, enter the BIOS setup screens, and disable virus checking. Motherboard virus checking is usually done by scanning the MBR of your disk for byte sequences that match viruses, or simply by reporting that the MBR has changed. Disabling this option is a good idea, because your MBR will eventually change as a result of the partitioning described in this chapter.

Reboot your machine into Windows and run ScanDisk from Start, Programs, Accessories, System Tools, and do a thorough test of your disk surface. This is necessary to verify that the disk you'll be using for Linux is indeed usable. When the

ScanDisk dialog displays, select the disk that you want to check and select the options for Thorough (Performs Standard Test And Scans Disk Surface For Errors and Automatically Fix Errors). Click Start to proceed, and then go out for a latte, a cup of real coffee, or a cola. Caffeine can be handy, because this (and the next step) can take quite a while. But you should expect that—after all, it's still just a Windows system at this point.

After successfully checking the disk surface, you must next defragment the disk. Defragmenting the disk is necessary to guarantee that all the data used by Windows is packed at the front of your current disk partition. When you split the current disk partition, you must split it into a portion that contains all the files and other data used by Windows, as well as one or more other portions that consist entirely of space that is not used by Windows.

To defragment your disk under Windows, select the Disk Defragmenter command from Start, Programs, Accessories, System Tools. This displays a dialog box that asks you to select the disk you want to defragment and enables you to configure various defragmentation settings. Click the Settings button to display the Settings dialog box; make sure that the Check The Drive For Errors disk is selected. Next, perform the appropriate step:

- On Windows 95 systems, select the Advanced menu's Consolidate Free Space option.
- On Windows 98 systems, make sure that the Rearrange Program Files So My Programs Start Faster option is not selected. Then click OK to close the Settings dialog box.
- On Windows 2000 systems, you simply select the drive that you want to defragment and click the Defragment button.

After correctly configuring the defragmentation settings, click OK to begin the defragmentation process. Defragment your disk even if you see a dialog box saying something along the lines of Your Disk Is Barely Fragmented. Are You Sure?. Yes, you are sure. Completely defragmenting your disk is critical in terms of knowing exactly how much space your current Windows installation requires. This enables you to maximize the amount of space that you can devote to Linux.

Repartitioning Disks When Using a Disk Manager

Disk managers are special software packages that help older versions of Windows and motherboards with older BIOS versions deal with large disks (large by the standard of the time, that is, not by today's standards, in which disks larger than 10GB are standard).

Disk managers were used as a workaround for limitations in the BIOS used on older motherboards, which could use only hard drives with a maximum of 1024 cylinders, 16 heads, and 63 sectors. A little math shows a maximum size of approximately 528MB for drives used with these older BIOS versions. Because your disk is (probably) much larger than this, disk managers work by tricking the system into believing that drives have a different number of heads than they actually do—up to 256.

The most common disk manager is OnTrack, which usually is loaded from a special sector when booting from hard drives that require it. Some drives might display an OnTrack splash screen when booting your system. If you are installing Linux onto a new disk or are willing to completely reformat your disk, you can skip the rest of this section—you can completely ignore any OnTrack messages.

And now, the bad news: If your system uses OnTrack and you need to preserve existing data on a disk managed by OnTrack, the only way to do it is to totally back up the contents of your system and reformat the drive. You cannot split partitions managed by OnTrack. You then can create a DOS/Windows partition at the beginning of your disk that is less than the maximum size supported by your BIOS without OnTrack's help and restore your data into the new partition. Linux can use the remainder of the disk, and everyone will be happy.

Repartitioning Disks When Using Disk-Compression Software

Disks are so cheap nowadays that it's rare to find someone using disk-compression software, but you never know. Disk-compression packages such as Stacker, DoubleSpace, and DriveSpace (which is included with Windows) work by creating a huge file within an existing partition and compressing the files that were previously located on the partition into that file. Because all the files are compressed, you save space. When you boot your system, it loads a driver that enables it to read and write directly to the compressed file, remaps drive letters if necessary, and then loads the compressed software (Windows or whatever) from the compressed file. The compressed file often is referred to as a compressed volume or partition because it is read from and written to like any other disk partition. Remapping drive letters usually is necessary because you want the compressed file to be accessed through the same drive letter it formerly used, even though it is now a file located within that partition. It would truly be a pain to have to change every drive letter reference in the registry or in INI files after compressing a partition.

Partitions containing a compressed volume cannot be reduced in size below the sum of the size of the compressed volume and any other files that are actually located within the partition containing the compressed volume.

Nowadays, disk space is cheaper than dirt—if your time is worth anything, it's almost cheaper to add disks to a system than to delete files. (Well, not really, but I couldn't resist saying that.) At any rate, if you're currently using disk-compression software, the best suggestion I can make is to buy another disk and install Linux on that disk—don't mess with the compressed disk. However, if you absolutely can't afford another disk and must live with your existing disk-compression software, you can do the following:

1. Delete any files that you can from the partition containing the compressed volume and from the compressed volume itself. If you're still running Windows 3.X or Windows for WorkGroups on the compressed volume, make sure that you are using a temporary swap file, and delete any permanent swap files located in the real partition. You will have to leave sufficient space in the real

partition for it to be re-created, but you might be able to get away with using a smaller file than the one you were using.

2. Use the disk verification utilities provided with the disk-compression software to verify that the compressed volume is valid and consistent.
3. Use utilities provided with the disk-compression software to defragment the compressed volume.
4. Use the software provided with the disk-compression software to decrease the size of the compressed volume to the minimum size you can live with. This must be larger than the size of the files that the compressed volume currently contains, with a little extra space left over for any new files that you might want to create.
5. Use any of the partition-resizing software discussed in the next few sections to split the real partition into two partitions: one that contains the compression drivers, boot software, and the compressed volume, and one onto which you can install Linux.

Defragmentation Problems and Solutions

The following list details some situations that could prevent you from completely defragmenting your disks and offers ways of solving them:

- If you still are cruelly tied to a Windows 3.X system, are trying to split the partition on which Windows is located, and are using a permanent swap file (through the Control Panel's 386enhanced control), that permanent Windows swapfile for Windows 3.x will not be moved by defragmentation. You will have to use this control panel to switch your system back to using a temporary swap file and then reboot before using FIPS.
- If you are running older system snapshot software such as MIRROR, these programs store information in a hidden file that uses the last sector on your disk. You must delete this file before you can run FIPS (it will be re-created the next time you run MIRROR).
- Some applications create hidden files because they are necessary for correct operating and shouldn't accidentally be deleted, or because they contain authorization information and serial numbers. Do not try to move the ones created by DOS and Windows themselves (`MSDOS.SYS` and `IO.SYS` on MS-DOS and Windows systems, and `IBMBIO.SYS` and `IBMDOS.SYS` on IBM PC-DOS systems) because these are usually located at or near the beginning of your boot partition in the first place. For nonsystem hidden files, you should try making the files visible (for example, using the DOS `DIR /A` command to identify their names and using `attrib -r -s -h filename` to make them visible and movable). You can then try moving them, changing their attributes to the way they were before, and running the application to which they belong. If this works, fine—if not, you should just uninstall the software package associated with those files (which can be tricky to determine, but is usually a backup or system snapshot utility) and reinstall it after changing your partition sizes.

Using FIPS

FIPS (First nondestructive Interactive Partition Splitting program) is a freeware DOS program by Arno Schaefer, portions copyright by Gordon Chaffee. FIPS enables you to split primary FAT-16 and FAT-32 partitions so that you can use the newly created partitions with other operating systems, such as Linux. The FIPS home page is located at `http://www.igd.fhg.de/~aschaefe/fips` and always contains the latest version, as well as documentation and a FAQ.

To use FIPS, create a bootable disk and expand the `FIPS.EXE`, `ERRORS.TXT`, and `RESTORRB.EXE` files from the zip file onto that disk. After defragmenting the partition that you want to split (as explained earlier in this section), print and read the FIPS documentation (the file `FIPS.DOC` in the zip file—note that this is not a Microsoft Word file, as the name suggests, but is a standard text file). You then can reboot your machine from the disk, execute FIPS, and follow its instructions to split the partition. Figure 2.1 shows the FIPS startup screen.

Before using FIPS to split an existing partition, be sure of the following:

- Back up any data on your system that you are not prepared to lose forever. FIPS is an excellent utility, and I have never had a problem with it, but I wouldn't want your experience to be the first time.
- Make sure that the drive containing the partition you want to split is connected to the primary IDE interface in your system. It's not a bad idea to explicitly disconnect all other drives in your system, to guarantee that you are working with the right one.

When FIPS starts, it first examines the state of the partition table on your disks, reports any suspicious abnormalities it detects, and exits if it detects any problems that it can't deal with. (See the next section for information about resolving problems detected by FIPS.)

```
Info: Partition table inconsistency

FIPS has detected that the 'physical' start or end sector (head/cylinder/
sector) do not match with the 'logical' start/end sector. This is not
an error since the 'physical' values are redundant and not used anyway.
There are many configurations where the values differ. This message is
meant only to inform you that FIPS has adapted the 'physical' values
according to the current drive geometry. So don't be alarmed by an unex-
pected cylinder range.

Press any key

Partition table adapted to the current drive geometry:

     |        |     Start        |      |      End         | Start  |Number of|
Part.|bootable|Head Cyl. Sector|System|Head Cyl. Sector| Sector |Sectors  |  MB
-----+--------+----------------+------+----------------+--------+---------+----
1    |     yes|   1    0      1|   0Ch| 254  526     63|      63|  8466192|4133
2    |      no|   0    0      0|   00h|   0    0      0|       0|        0|   0
3    |      no|   0    0      0|   00h|   0    0      0|       0|        0|   0
4    |      no|   0    0      0|   00h|   0    0      0|       0|        0|   0
OK

Press any Key
```

Figure 2.1

FIPS in action.

Next, FIPS checks for free (unused) space on the partition and lets you choose a starting cylinder for the new partition based on where the free space begins. Make sure that the partition on which your Windows files are still located has enough unused space to store the temporary Windows swap file used by Windows. You also should make sure that you leave enough unused space in that partition to enable you to create any new files that you might need when running Windows.

After splitting the partition, but before actually writing the new partition table to your disk, FIPS offers you the chance to save a copy of your current partition table, which you always should do. If something goes wrong, you can use the `RESTORRB.EXE` utility to restore the saved partition table—this might be your only chance to recover from a potential disaster.

After you have split an existing partition, you might see an error message when you exit from FIPS. Do not panic. Remove the bootable FIPS disk and reboot your machine. If your machine does not reboot correctly, shut it down, reboot from the FIPS disk, and restore the old File Allocation Table using `RESTORRB.EXE`. You then should reread the FIPS documentation for clues to what the problem was.

Using the Ranish Partition Manager

The Ranish Partition Manager is a relatively new contender in the DOS split existing partitions software market. If you use this shareware, you should send the suggested contribution of $10, which is truly reasonable for such a nice and powerful package. The Ranish Partition Manager is written and maintained by Mikhail Ranish. Figure 2.2 shows the Ranish Partition Manager's startup screen.

As with FIPS, the Ranish Partition Manager enables you to split primary FAT-16 and FAT-32 partitions so that you can use the newly created partitions with other operating systems, such as Linux. Unlike FIPS, it provides a graphical DOS interface that many will find more comfortable than the FIPS simple text interface. The Ranish Partition Manager home page is located at `http://www.users.intercom.com/~ranish/part/` and always contains the latest version, thorough documentation, and a FAQ.

Aside from its graphical interface, another nice feature of the Ranish Partition Manager is that it is bootable—you can install it on a disk so that it boots `PART.EXE`, eliminating the need for a bootable DOS disk. See the documentation for more information about how to do this.

One unfortunate shortcoming of the current version of the Ranish Partition Manager is that it does not allow you to save a copy of your partition table before it makes changes (although it claims to). This shortcoming certainly will be addressed in the future.

To use the Ranish Partition Manager, first defragment the partition you want to split, as described in the "Preparing Windows Partitions for Fission" section earlier in this chapter. Next, print and read the documentation and FAQ from the Ranish Partition Manager Web site. You can then boot from the disk containing the Partition Manager, and execute the program PART.EXE. To split a partition, you must change the partition size in both the partition table at the top of the screen and in the boot sector at the bottom. You then can save your changes, remove the disk, and reboot your system. As with FIPS, you should immediately run ScanDisk on your Windows partition to verify that the Windows partition is still consistent and usable.

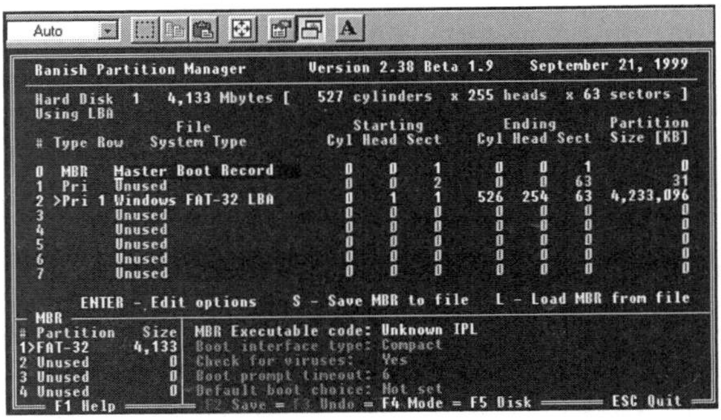

Figure 2.2

Ranish Partition Manager in action.

Using PartitionMagic

PartitionMagic is a commercial, nondestructive disk-partitioning package available from PowerQuest. At the time of this writing, the current version is 5.0. PartitionMagic is an excellent program that always gets rave reviews—for good reason. PartitionMagic provides a powerful, easy-to-use graphical interface that makes it easy to dynamically resize and move FAT, FAT32, and HPFS (older Windows NT) partitions on your hard disks. PartitionMagic also provides other features, such as enabling you to dynamically convert FAT partitions into HPFS partitions (although now that you'll be running Linux soon, that's hardly necessary).

As with the other repartitioning utilities discussed in this section, you should defragment your drive before running PartitionMagic. You can boot from the PartitionMagic disk and use its graphical interface to select the partition you want to resize and determine how you want to resize it. PartitionMagic's documentation walks you through the resizing process.

Limited-use and older versions of PartitionMagic are provided with certain Linux distributions, such as Macmillan's packaging of the Mandrake Linux distribution. However, if you will be creating multiple dual-boot systems, you should simply buy a full-featured copy. PartitionMagic is an excellent software package and a powerful addition to any tool chest of PC software, and it is well worth its $69.95 retail cost.

CHAPTER 3

Beginning Your Red Hat Installation

The previous chapters of this book provided background information about Linux, discussed the different Red Hat installation classes, and explained some preparations you should do to have information about your system handy and to prepare multi-OS systems for installing Linux.

In this chapter, the fun actually begins as you start the installation process by booting Red Hat from different types of media. This chapter also discusses Linux's virtual consoles, which can help identify any problems you encounter during installation and can collect problem reports for Red Hat support personnel. The virtual consoles used by Linux also can be very useful at many other times when running Linux, such as when installing and configuring the X Window system.

NOTE

Red Hat 7.0 is the first version of Red Hat Linux to require multiple CDs in order to install the executable software. The first and second disks contain the Red Hat software; the third disk contains documentation and source code. Throughout this chapter, any generic references to "insert the Red Hat CD" refer to the first CD in the Red Hat 7.0 CD set. Any references to the second or third CDs in the Red Hat 7.0 CD set explicitly identify those CDs by number.

Defining Your System's Boot Sequence

The BIOS (basic input/output system) chip is the heart of an IBM-compatible personal computer, enabling you to configure and save many of the basic characteristics of how your system interacts with its memory and peripherals. One important bit of information that you can configure in the BIOS is your computer's boot sequence—the devices that your system will search for bootable media and the order in which those devices are searched.

IBM-compatible systems typically use one of several different BIOS chips, each of which lets you configure the boot sequence in a slightly different way. Some BIOS chips let you individually select the first, second, and third devices that the system queries. Other BIOS chips let you select only from an assortment of predetermined boot sequences. The next few sections explain how to set the BIOS boot sequence option for different common BIOS chips.

Note that only ATAPI and SCSI CD-ROM drives are bootable. If you are installing Red Hat Linux onto an older system whose CD-ROM drive is not ATAPI-compatible, you will have to boot from a floppy disk. This is not a limitation of the Red Hat Installer, but is a hardware limitation of older CD-ROM drives.

American Megatrends AMIBIOS Boot Sequence Configuration

The AMIBIOS lets you specify the first, second, and third devices from which the system attempts to boot and provides a very complete list of bootable devices.

To access the BIOS configuration options on systems using American Megatrends AMIBIOS, reboot your machine and press the Delete key after any memory tests have completed but before the system lists the attached IDE devices. This displays the AMIBIOS Setup screen.

To specify the boot sequence, follow these steps:

1. Use the cursor control keys to select the Advanced CMOS Setup configuration option, and press Return.
2. To boot the Red Hat Installer from CD-ROM, use the cursor control keys to select the 1st Boot Device entry, and change it to CDROM by repeatedly pressing the Page Down key. To boot from a disk, change the value of the 1st Boot Device entry to Floppy.

   Do not select Network if you are planning to do a network install of Red Hat. Red Hat's network install must boot from local, physical media, but can subsequently install from a network device. You will be prompted for that information when doing a network install. Note that you also might want to change the entry for the second boot device to IDE-O, the first hard drive on IDE controller 0. This will enable you to automatically boot from the hard drive if there is no bootable CD in the CD-ROM drive and no disk in the floppy drive.
3. Press the Escape key to return to the main AMIBIOS screen, and use the cursor control keys to select the Save Settings & Exit option.
4. Enter **Y** and press Enter when the message "Save current settings and exit (Y/N)?" displays.

Put the first Red Hat CD in the CD-ROM drive, or put a Red Hat boot disk in the floppy drive. Your computer will reboot and will boot from whichever device you specified.

AWARD BIOS Boot Sequence Configuration

The AWARD BIOS lets you select from predetermined sets of boot sequences.

To access the BIOS configuration options on systems using the AWARD BIOS, reboot your system, and press the Delete key after any memory tests have completed but before the system lists attached IDE devices. This displays the AWARD BIOS Setup screen.

To specify the boot sequence, follow these steps:

1. Use the cursor control keys to select the BIOS Features Setup configuration option, and press Return.
2. To boot the Red Hat Installer from CD-ROM, use the cursor control keys to select the Boot Sequence entry, and change it to CDROM, C, A by repeatedly pressing the Page Down key.
   To boot from a floppy disk, change the value of the Boot Sequence entry to A, C, SCSI.
   To boot from a SCSI disk, change the value of the Boot Sequence entry to SCSI, A, C.
3. Press the Escape key to return to the main AWARD BIOS screen, and use the cursor control keys to select the SAVE & EXIT SETUP option.
4. Enter `Y` and press Enter when the message "SAVE TO CMOS & EXIT (Y/N)?" displays.

Put the first Red Hat CD in the CD-ROM drive, or put a Red Hat boot floppy in the floppy drive. Your computer will reboot and will boot from whichever device you specified.

IBM Aptiva Boot Sequence Configuration

To access the BIOS configuration options on an IBM Aptiva system, reboot your machine and press the F1 key when the IBM splash screen displays. This displays the IBM Configuration screen.

To specify the boot sequence, follow these steps:

1. Use the cursor control keys to select the Select Startup Options configuration option, and press Return.
   To boot the Red Hat Installer from CD-ROM, use the cursor control keys to select the Boot From CD-ROM entry, and change it to Enabled by pressing the right arrow key.
   To boot from a disk, change the value of the System entry to A then C.
2. Press the Escape key to return to the main AWARD BIOS screen, and press Escape again to exit.
3. Select Yes and press Enter when you see the message "Settings have changed. Do you want to save CMOS setting?"

Put the first Red Hat CD in the CD-ROM drive, or put a Red Hat boot disk in the floppy drive. Your computer will reboot and will first attempt to boot from the CD-ROM drive, then the disk, and finally the hard drive.

PhoenixBIOS Boot Sequence Configuration

Phoenix recently merged with AWARD, the manufacturers of the AWARD BIOS discussed earlier. Part of the agreement was that PhoenixBIOS chips no longer will be produced or sold. This BIOS is discussed here because it was very popular for years and might be found on many slightly older motherboards.

To access the BIOS configuration options on a system using a PhoenixBIOS, reboot the machine and press the F2 key after any memory tests have completed but before the system lists the attached IDE devices. This displays the PhoenixBIOS Setup screen.

To specify the boot sequence, follow these steps:

1. Use the cursor control keys to select the Boot Options configuration option, and press Return.
2. To boot the Red Hat Installer from disk, use the down arrow cursor control key to select the Boot Sequence entry, and change it to A then C by pressing the right arrow key.
3. Press the `F10` key to save the modified settings, and press Escape to exit.
4. Press the Spacebar when you see the message "Values have been saved to CMOS! Press `<space>` to continue."

Put a Red Hat boot disk in the floppy drive. Your computer will reboot and will boot from the floppy drive.

Installing from the Red Hat CD

After you have configured your system to boot from the first CD, as described in the previous sections, you should be able to boot from the Red Hat CD simply by inserting the CD in your CD-ROM drive and turning on the machine.

If you have problems booting from the CD, do the following:

- Inspect the nonprinted side of the CD for dirt or fingerprints, and clean it with a damp, lint-free cloth, Try booting from the CD again.
- If you already are running another operating system on your machine, verify that you can list and examine the contents of the CD from that operating system. If you cannot, either the CD or your CD-ROM drive could be bad.
- If you have access to another computer system, verify that you can list and examine the contents of the CD on some other machine. If you cannot, the CD probably is bad.

If you can list and examine files on the CD from another operating system but cannot boot from it, verify that you have correctly configured your BIOS to boot from the CD. If these settings are correct, you might not actually have a bootable ATAPI CD-ROM drive. Try creating a boot disk, as described in the next section, booting from that, and then loading Linux from the CD.

Creating and Using Boot Floppies

If the system on which you want to install Red Hat Linux can't boot from a CD-ROM drive, or if you want to install Red Hat Linux from your network, you will have to prepare a bootable 3.5-inch floppy disk. Red Hat Linux distributions that you purchase separately include a bootable disk, which this book does not. Luckily, creating a bootable disk is easy to do from any Windows, DOS, Linux, UNIX, or other UNIX-workalike system.

To create a boot floppy disk, you write a bootable disk image onto a floppy disk using special utilities that write directly to the disk rather than copying files as you normally would do. The system on which you're creating the bootable disk therefore must have a CD-ROM drive because the images of boot disks provided with Red Hat Linux are located on the CD.

NOTE

The bootable floppy images provided on the CD are for 3.5-inch disks only and are too large for high-density 5.25-inch disks. If you want to boot the Red Hat Installer from a floppy drive, it must be a 3.5-inch floppy drive.

The Red Hat distribution provides three different bootable floppy images:

- **`boot.img`**—A standard bootable image for installing Red Hat Linux from CD-ROM or another hard drive.
- **`bootnet.img`**—A bootable image for installing Red Hat Linux from a network device using the FTP, HTTP, or NFS protocols.
- **`paride.img`**—A bootable image for installing Red Hat Linux from an IDE device attached to the parallel port, much as the boot.net image installs Red Hat Linux from an IDE ATAPI CD-ROM or internal hard drive.
- **`pcmcia.img`**—A bootable image for installing Red Hat Linux from a PCMCIA device on your system, such as a PCMCIA CD-ROM drive or Ethernet card.

Internationalized versions of the `boot.img`, `bootnet.img`, and `pcmcia.img` boot disks are also provided in French, German, Italian, Japanese, and Spanish. These boot images are organized in subdirectories of the `\image` directory on the first disk of the Red Hat install set, where the directory name corresponds to the country code.

Creating Boot Disks on a DOS or Windows System

You can create bootable disks on a DOS or Windows system from any command prompt by using the `RAWRITE.EXE` application. This application is found in the `\dosutils` directory at the root of your Red Hat CD.

To create a bootable disk, follow these steps:

1. Open a command prompt window, and change directory to the CD.
2. Change directory to the `\dosutils` directory.
3. Execute the rawrite program (`rawrite.exe`).

4. Enter the disk image source filename, which is one of `\images\boot.img`, `\images\bootnet.img`, or `\images\pcmcia.img`.
5. Enter the name of the 3.5-inch floppy drive in which you will be creating the boot disk.
6. When prompted to do so, insert a formatted disk into that drive and press Enter.

The rawrite application displays status information as it copies the bootable image to the disk, and exits when the boot disk is complete. If you receive any write errors when writing the boot image to the disk, create another bootable disk using a different disk. After all, a bootable disk, not a copy of Microsoft Word where a flipped bit or two might not make a difference (or might accidentally fix a bug), must be an exact image.

Creating Boot Disks on a Linux or UNIX System

You create bootable disks on another Linux or other UNIX-like system from any command prompt, using the standard UNIX `dd` (dump data) command.

To create a bootable disk on a Linux or UNIX system, follow these steps:

1. From a shell window, mount the CD. Mount commands will differ based on the system you are using and the device that corresponds to the CD-ROM drive. A common command to mount the CD would be `mount /dev/hdb /cdrom`, assuming that the `/cdrom` directory exists and that the CD-ROM drive is the second (slave) device on the primary IDE interface on the machine that you are using.
2. Change directory to the `/cdrom/images` directory (or whatever directory name you actually used).
3. Execute this command:

   ```
   dd if=IMAGE_FILE of=/dev/fd0 bs=1440k
   ```

   Here, `IMAGE FILE` is one of `boot.img`, `bootnet.img`, or `pcmcia.img`.

You can remove the disk when the shell prompt returns. If you receive any write errors when writing the boot image to the disk, create another bootable disk using a different disk.

Installing Red Hat Over a Network

Installing Red Hat from a central location on your network offers several potential advantages over installing Red Hat from a local CD-ROM drive:

- It helps guarantee that Red Hat installations on multiple systems are identical by providing a single, centralized location from which to install.
- It frees you from having to carry a CD around with you when installing multiple systems.
- It lets you install Linux on multiple systems at the same time.
- It makes it easy for you to update a single installable image or to maintain a centralized set of updated packages that you want to apply after a generic system installation.

The procedures for installing Red Hat Linux over a network described in this section overlap somewhat with the standard installation instructions that begin in the next section. Rather than force you to jump around in this book, some information is duplicated in this chapter and the next. The goal of this book is to help you install Red Hat Linux and get up and running with the system as quickly and as easily as possible.

Installing Red Hat Linux Over a Network on a Desktop System

This section explains how to begin installing Linux on a desktop, desk-side, or laptop computer system with ISA or PCI Ethernet cards or with built-in Ethernet support. If you are installing Linux on a laptop that uses a PCMCIA Ethernet card, see the next section.

To install Red Hat Linux over a network, first create a bootable disk from the bootnet.img image, as explained in the section "Creating and Using Boot Floppies," earlier in this chapter:

1. Booting from this disk requires that you specify whether you are installing Red Hat Linux for the first time or are upgrading an existing system. The installer then lets you select other installation modes such as expert and Kickstart. Expert mode is beyond the scope of this book, but Kickstart installs are explained in a later section of this chapter. Press Enter to continue.

   The installer displays the standard screens that enable you to select the language used during the install process and the type of keyboard your machine has. These screens are explained in more detail in the next chapter.
2. You then are prompted to select whether you will be installing from an NFS image, FTP, or HTTP.
3. You then are prompted for basic network information, either questions of whether you are using DHCP, or the standard set of network questions:
   - Your IP address
   - Your netmask
   - Your default gateway address
   - Your primary nameserver address

   For more detailed information about these values, see Chapter 4, "Red Hat Installation: Basic System Configuration."
4. You then are prompted for the name or IP address of the appropriate server and the directory where the Red Hat installation can be found. This is the mount point of the Red Hat CD (or the root of a hierarchical copy of it). For example, if you export the Red Hat CD via NFS as `hostname:/mnt/cdrom`, you would enter **`/mnt/cdrom`**. If you mount the Red Hat CD as (or have created a hierarchical copy of it in) `/home/ftp/pub/redhat`, you would enter **`/pub/redhat`**. For HTTP servers, you would enter the directory where you mounted the Red Hat CD or installed a copy of it relative to the directory `/home/httpd/html`.
5. The local Red Hat Installer verifies that the location you specified was correct by trying to load the file `RedHat/base/stage2.img` from the directory you specified.

If this file is found, the installation proceeds normally; skip to the section "Specifying Your Red Hat Installation Class," in Chapter 4.

If this file was not found, see the section "Troubleshooting Network Installs," later in this chapter, for troubleshooting information.

Installing Red Hat Linux Using PCMCIA Ethernet Cards

Installing Red Hat Linux over a network using a PCMCIA Ethernet card is very similar to the standard network install. If you are installing Red Hat Linux over a network from a laptop with a PCMCIA Ethernet card, you will need to boot from a disk created from the pcmcia.img image, as explained in section "Creating and Using Boot Floppies," earlier in this chapter.

1. Booting from this disk requires that you specify whether you are installing Red Hat Linux for the first time or are upgrading an existing system. The installer then enables you to select other installation modes such as Expert and Kickstart. Expert mode is beyond the scope of this book, but Kickstart installs are explained in a later section of this chapter. Press Enter to continue.
2. After the kernel loads, you then see a separate screen with the message "Installing PC Card Devices…". Your system will beep once when installing the PCMCIA driver and then will beep once or twice, depending on the PCMCIA slots in which cards are detected.
3. You then see the standard screens that enable you to select the language used during the install process and the type of keyboard your machine has. These screens are explained in more detail in Chapter 4.
4. You then are prompted to select whether you will be installing from a local CD-ROM, NFS image, FTP, HTTP, or hard disk.
5. You then are prompted for basic network information, either questions of you are using DHCP, or the standard set of network questions:
   - Your IP address
   - Your netmask
   - Your default gateway address
   - Your primary nameserver address

   For more detailed information about these values, see Chapter 4.
6. You then are prompted for the name or IP address of the appropriate server and the directory where the Red Hat installation can be found. This is the mount point of the Red Hat CD (or the root of a hierarchical copy of it). For example, if you export the Red Hat CD via NFS as `hostname:/mnt/cdrom`, you would enter **`/mnt/cdrom`**. For FTP installs, if you mount the Red Hat CD as (or have created a hierarchical copy of it in) `/home/ftp/pub/redhat`, you would enter **`/pub/redhat`**. For HTTP servers, you would enter the directory where you mounted the Red Hat CD or installed a copy of it relative to the directory `/home/httpd/html`.

7. The local Red Hat Installer verifies that the location you specified was correct by trying to load the file `RedHat/base/stage2.img` from the directory you specified.

If this file is found, the installation proceeds normally; skip to the section "Specifying Your Red Hat Installation Class," in Chapter 4.

If this file was not found, see the previous section for troubleshooting information.

Using Red Hat's Kickstart Install

Red Hat's Kickstart installation process lets you create an installation script that automatically responds to prompts during the installation process. This can be especially useful when installing or updating Red Hat Linux on multiple, identical computer systems. Kickstart installations are typically done from disks that you can use to start the install process on individual systems, but they also can be done during other types of Red Hat Linux installs.

This section explains how to create a Kickstart configuration file and boot disk to use on a number of identical workstations on which you will be installing Red Hat Linux via NFS. For information on creating configuration files for other types of Kickstart installs, see the `Kickstart-HOWTO` file, located in the `doc/HOWTO` subdirectory of your first Red Hat CD.

1. After installing Red Hat Linux on the first machine of a given type, make sure that you have installed the package mkkickstart-1.3-1.noarch.rpm. This package installs a shell script called mkkickstart in `/usr/sbin`. This script creates a Kickstart configuration file that matches the configuration of the machine on which it is executed.
2. Assuming that you are installing via NFS, execute the mkkickstart script with the following command:

   ```
   mkkickstart --nfs 192.168.6.61:/mnt/cdrom > ks.cfg
   ```

   This creates the file `ks.cfg`, which contains instructions for a Kickstart install from the NFS file server 192.168.6.95, which exports the Red Hat CD-ROM as the directory `/mnt/cdrom`.
3. Edit the `ks.cfg` file, uncommenting the network line by removing the leading # symbol; also replace the default IP address of 10.0.0.1 and gateway of 10.0.0.254 with the ones that you want to use for the machines you are installing. I usually reserve a special IP address on my local subnet for Kickstart installs, using linuxconf to assign their actual IP address immediately after booting each installed system for the first time. If you have more than one person installing systems at the same time using the same `ks.cfg` file, you occasionally might see an IP address conflict if two of them come up at the same time with the default address, but this doesn't hurt anything.

   The `rootpw` line in the `ks.cfg` file sets the default root password. If you prefer to store this in encrypted form on your Kickstart boot disk, you can use the following Perl command to create an encrypted password:

   ```
   perl -e 'print crypt("foobar", "Xa") . "\n";'p
   ```

This returns Xa5xnxIELkl8Y, which is the encrypted version of the password foobar. You then would modify the rootpw line to begin with the following (the remainder of the line depends on the authentication options you enabled on the system you are cloning):

```
rootpw --iscrypted Xa5xnxIELkl8Y
```

At the end of the ks.cfg file (after the %post line), you can add any commands that you want to execute after completing the base installation. This is a good place to add rpm commands to add any other packages that you want to install. However, the install process must be capable of installing these from the same location as the other packages. If you are customizing your Red Hat install, you just might want to copy the Red Hat CD to the NFS install directory (probably not /mnt/cdrom, in this case) and copy the other packages to that directory so that they can be installed from the same NFS mount point.

4. Copy the modified ks.cfg file to the boot disk (made from either pcmcia.img or bootnet.img, depending on whether the Ethernet card in the systems you are installing is a PCMCIA card).
5. Modify the syslinux.cfg file at the root of the boot disk so that it contains the following:
   To boot over a network using pcmcia.img:

```
default ks
prompt 0
label ks
kernel vmlinuz
append ks=floppy initrd=initrd.img pcmcia
```

To boot over a network using bootnet.img:

```
default ks
prompt 0
label ks
kernel vmlinuz
append ks=floppy initrd=initrd.img network
```

You then can use this disk to install any number of machines. After verifying the Kickstart configuration file and changes to syslinux.cfg, you might want to create a floppy image from this disk and create several other copies. You can do this from a Linux system using this command:

```
dd if=/dev/fd0 of=kickstart.img bs=1440k
```

You can create additional boot disks from this disk on a Linux system using this command:

```
dd if=kickstart.img of=/dev/fd0 bs=1440k
```

The Kickstart installation process first was added to Red Hat Linux 6.0 and will continually be improved with each subsequent Red Hat Linux release. For complete information about Kickstart installs and configuration files, see the Kickstart-HOWTO file, located in the doc/HOWTO subdirectory of your Red Hat CD.

Troubleshooting Network Installs

The most common cause of problems doing a network install is an incorrect server IP address, server directory, or host IP information. If you encounter a problem, the first thing that you should do is to use the Back button to return to previous screens and verify that the information you entered is correct.

The second most common problem encountered is an authentication failure at the remote server—the CD or Red Hat installation directory is actually being exported by the server as the directory you specified, but you can't access its contents. Different problems can occur in remote installs, depending on the protocol being used. The following are the authentication and access requirements for the different types of Red Hat Net installs:

- When installing via FTP, anonymous FTP must be enabled on the remote FTP server. Make sure that the remote system has a user account called ftp in its password file and that anonymous FTP has not been disabled in the server through other means. Error messages from the FTP server usually are logged to the system log on the remote machine, which might provide you with useful information about the problem if you can access it. Otherwise, contact the administrator of the system on which the FTP server is running for help in resolving the problem.
- When installing via HTTP, the Red Hat CD or copied installation hierarchy must be installed somewhere under the doc root of the Web server, in a directory to which you have access. Error messages from Web servers such as Apache are logged into its access and error logs, and might provide an explanation of the source of the problem. By default, these files are located in the file `var/log` subdirectory of the directory where the server is installed and are named `access_log` and `error_log`, respectively. Contact the Webmaster of the machine on which the Web server is running if you do not know how to find these logs or do not have access to them.
- When installing via NFS from an NFS server, make sure that the CD-ROM device was exported in noauth mode, meaning that anyone can access it. In general, make sure that access to the CD does not require any special privileges.

Another problem can occur if you attempt to install Red Hat Linux over a network after booting from a disk that is not associated with the same Red Hat version. Be careful.

During installations done using PCMCIA Ethernet cards, you should check the activity lights on the card and your Ethernet hub to make sure that your card is correctly initialized. A correctly initialized PCMCIA Ethernet card will show a steady activity light on the card and hub. Incorrectly initialized cards, whether due to hardware, connectivity, or driver problems, may correctly initialize the PCMCIA interface, but will blink on and off once you have provided IP address, netmask, gateway, and nameserver information. Reseat your Ethernet card, check your cables and connections, reboot, and retry the installation process. If this does not resolve the problem, you will need to try using a different PCMCIA Ethernet card. If the PCMCIA installation process prompts you for the driver to try, your PCMCIA Ethernet card may not be supported by Linux. Try using a different PCMCIA Ethernet card.

If you are installing Red Hat on a laptop and the installation process requests a driver disk, your laptop may not have fully compliant PCMCIA hardware implementation. You may not be able to install Linux on this system. Explaining how to resolve problems with non-compliant PCMCIA hardware is outside the scope of this book. Call Red Hat for installation support if you encounter this problem.

Using Virtual Consoles During Installation

An interesting problem occurs when you try to log errors or status messages that occur during installation, especially before you have a file system in which to create and store log files. Linux solves this problem by creating virtual consoles, which are initially just devices to which the Red Hat Installer (anaconda) writes different types of messages. If, by some rare chance, you encounter a problem during installation, Red Hat's customer support personnel probably will ask you to provide a list of the messages displayed on one or more of these virtual consoles.

Red Hat Linux provides seven different virtual consoles during the installation process. To switch to any of these, hold down the Ctrl and Alt keys, and press the function key with the number of the virtual console to which you want to switch. For example, to switch to virtual console 1, you would hold down the Ctrl and Alt keys, and press F1.

The virtual consoles used during installation are as follows:

- **1**—Displays the installation dialog boxes and status messages. This is the default virtual console if the boot image from which you booted could not recognize your video card, and therefore could not start a low-resolution version of the X Window system.
- **2**—Provides a shell prompt for directly executing Linux commands to examine or modify parts of the system as it is being installed. The shell prompt is available only after you have specified the media from which you are installing.
- **3**—Displays log messages from the installation process.
- **4**—Displays log messages from the system, such as kernel messages. This virtual console is empty if no such messages have been received.
- **5**—Displays messages from applications executed by the install process. This virtual console is empty if no such messages have been received.
- **7**—Displays the X Window system-based install process. This is the default virtual console if you are running the low-resolution X Window system installer—in other words, if the boot image you booted from can recognize and use your system's video card.

The virtual consoles provided by Linux are not just useful during the installation problem, but they also provide an easy way for you to simultaneously log in as multiple users (yourself and the system administrator, for example) without using the `su` command or having to be running the X Window system. This is especially handy on Linux server systems on which the X Window system is not installed.

Virtual consoles also are extremely useful when experimenting with your X Window system configuration. For example, you can switch to a different virtual console to terminate X Window manager processes that have run amuck or are unresponsive. When using virtual consoles for X debugging, make sure that you start your X server or issue the `startx` or `xinit` command in the background so that you can use the command line to kill the errant X server.

CHAPTER 4

Red Hat Installation: Basic System Configuration

The exact steps of the Red Hat installation process and the installer itself differ based on the characteristics of your system, the type of install you are doing (PCMCIA, network, other floppy, CD-ROM), and the Red Hat installation class you select during the installation process. This chapter walks you through all the installation screens you might see during the first part of the Red Hat Linux installation process. The chapter also helps you provide or verify the basic information about your system that is required during installation.

Which Installer Will I See?

Red Hat provides two different installers: an X Window system-based installer that you interact with using the mouse and keyboard, and a text-mode installer that you interact with using the keyboard. The majority of the information you must supply these installers is the same and follows roughly the same order.

Red Hat's X Window system installer is simpler and easier to use than the text installer. The X Window system installer also is designed to help you get your Red Hat system up and running as quickly and easily as possible. The text-mode installer provides slightly greater control over specific aspects of your system's configuration, such as formatting partitions, installing the Linux boot loader, and running different types of authentication.

Red Hat 7.0 provides a substantially simpler installation process than that found in previous versions of Red Hat Linux. The steps in the X Window system installer and the text mode installer have been simplified and made more parallel than in previous versions of red Hat Linux.

Regardless of which installer you will be running, the first screen you see when you boot from a Red Hat boot disk or the first Red Hat Linux CD is the text-mode "Welcome to Red Hat!" screen. When you see this screen during a non-kickstart install, you can do any one of the following:

- Press Enter to start Red Hat's graphical installation program. This is usually the right choice to make; however, if you encounter any problems at this point, try using the text-mode Red Hat installer, as explained in the next bullet.

NOTE

Hardware such as older, low-resolution monitors and motherboards with integrated video hardware can cause problems when you use Red Hat's X Window system installer. If you encounter any problems using the X Window system installer, try rebooting your system and starting the text-mode Red Hat installer: Enter the word `text` and press Enter when you see the first "Welcome to Red Hat!" splash screen.

- Enter the word `text`, and press Enter to start the text-mode installer.
- Enter the word `expert`, and press Enter to the expert installer. This option prevents Red Hat from automatically attempting to detect the hardware in your system, enabling (or forcing) you to enter all the hardware information yourself. For that reason, discussing Red Hat's expert-mode installation process falls outside the scope of this book.
- Enter the words `linux rescue`, and press Enter to boot from Red Hat CD number 1 in rescue mode. Red Hat's rescue mode boot contains utilities and system tools to help you recover data from a corrupted system and restore it to proper functioning.
- Enter the words `linux dd`, and press Enter to cause the Red Hat text installer to prompt for a driver disk that supplies low-level drivers for many older, nonstandard boot devices.

You can get help about different aspects of installing Red Hat Linux by pressing the function keys at the bottom of the "Welcome to Red Hat!" screen. Pressing the function keys F1 through F5 displays different sorts of information that can be useful to you when using the different Linux boot options listed previously. These keys have the following meanings:

- Press F1 to return to the list of boot options originally displayed on the welcome screen.
- Press F2 for general information about the boot and installation process, including suggestions about when to use text mode installs versus the more common X Window system installer.
- Press F3 for more information about Red Hat's Expert installation mode.
- Press F4 for more information about other options that you might want to supply to the boot process, such as the amount of memory on your system and so on. If you have problems booting your system after installing Red Hat, the

information on this screen may help you correctly modify the lilo.conf file to resolve any problems you encounter.

- Press F5 for more information about Red Hat's linux rescue mode installer.

After pressing Enter to proceed with a standard Red Hat Linux installation, your system boots a generic Linux kernel from the boot media. This generic kernel is powerful enough to run either of Red Hat's installation programs.

If you do not press a key, the system automatically attempts to start the Red Hat X Window system installer after 60 seconds. To start the X Window system installer, the installation process probes your hardware as part of the boot process to identify your mouse type and video card. If the installer can correctly identify your video hardware and mouse, the X Window system installer begins; otherwise, the Red Hat installation process starts the text-mode installer.

The information you must supply during installation differs based on many variables, primarily these:

- The installer you are running
- The type of installation you are trying to do
- Whether Red Hat can identify your video card
- Whether that video card is powerful enough to run the X Window system
- Whether disk partitions already exist on the drive on which you are installing Linux

The screens that you see and the responses you need to provide are discussed throughout the remainder of this chapter. The next chapter completes the installation process by discussing X Window system configuration during installation and describing the actual installation process itself.

Configuring Your System

The sequence and content of some of the installer screens differ between Red Hat's text-mode and X Window system installers. Where sections of this chapter are specific to one or the other, the installer is clearly specified just after the section heading. This will make this chapter especially easy to follow.

In general, the installation screens in the remainder of this chapter are discussed in "installer-independent" terms—that is, these screens should make this book useful regardless of what installer you are using. In Red Hat's X Window system installer, you can use the mouse to select values, and you can use the mouse or the Tab key to move between different fields on each screen. In Red Hat's text installer, you use the cursor control keys (arrow keys) to select values in a field, and you use the Tab key to move from one field to the next. Pressing Shift+Tab takes you back to the previous field.

Selecting a Language, Keyboard, and Mouse

The first few bits of information you must supply about your system affect the remainder of the installation process. They also affect how you interact with your system after installing Red Hat Linux.

Specifying a Language

After you actually boot the generic Linux kernel and start the appropriate installer for your system, the installer displays a Language Selection screen. This screen enables you select the language that you want to use. This language is not only the language that will be used throughout the remainder of the installation process, but it also will be used to set variables for National Language Support (NLS) when your system is up and running. Your National Language support settings determine the language in which many applications will display error messages, prompts, and other interactions with the user.

Most modern computer systems and applications use external catalogs of messages when they need to display status information, a warning, or a dialog box. Because Linux is the Open Source product of thousands of developers from all over the world, you might expect it to feature integrated NLS support, and it does. To change the language in which system and NLS-aware application messages are expressed, you must use environment variables to identify the location of alternate message catalogs. Older applications used messages that were compiled into the application, making it difficult to easily translate the application. NLS-aware applications can do this quickly, just by changing the value of their LANG environment variable.

Red Hat's installers are still only partially NLS-compliant; you might see certain help panels, text entry field labels, or button labels in English. The number of these sorts of aberrations eventually will vanish over time.

Choosing the Keyboard Type and Configuration

If you are using Red Hat's X Window system-based installer, the Keyboard Configuration screen provides three selectable regions that enable you to specify the model of keyboard you are using, the layout of the keys on that keyboard, and a variant option for languages that require multiple keystrokes to compose characters. As with the Language Selection screen, this screen is intended to help you customize your Red Hat installation to a specific National Language and related hardware.

If you are using Red Hat's text-mode installer, the keyboard selection screen enables you to select the type of keyboard attached to your system. This is usually the type of keyboard most commonly used in your country, the name of which is often based on the name of your country—for example, "us" for keyboards used in the United States and featuring symbols for U.S. currency, "uk" for keyboards used in the United Kingdom featuring symbols for UK currency, and so on.

If you choose incorrectly, you can select Back to return to the previous screen to re-select the correct values, as you can on any of the text or X-Window system installer screens.

Designating the Mouse Type and Configuration

Red Hat's X Window system installer can't detect information about your mouse automatically because mouse devices are simple serial devices; however, providing the right information about your mouse can help Linux make the most of its buttons. This information is important even if you are not planning to run the X Window system because Linux provides mouse drivers for screens running in terminal mode. This enables you to cut and paste information just as though you were running in a graphical environment.

NOTE

If you are using Red Hat's X Window system-based installer, the Mouse Configuration screen lets you provide information about the mouse you are using on your system. The text-mode installer collects mouse information much later in the installation sequence. If you are using the text-mode installer, skip over this section for now.

Select the type of mouse you are using from the list at the top of this screen. If your mouse isn't listed, the most important bits of information about your mouse are whether it is connected to a serial or P/2 mouse port, and the number of buttons it has.

NOTE

The X Window system expects mouse devices to have three buttons, each of which displays different menus or performs different functions. If your mouse has only two buttons, you still can use it with the X Window system by checking the Emulate Three Buttons box. This lets you simulate pressing the middle mouse button by pressing both mouse buttons simultaneously. Clever, no?

If your mouse is connected to a serial port (or if you told the Red Hat Installer that it was), you must also specify the serial port to which the mouse is connected. You will not see this screen if you specified that your mouse is connected to a PS/2 port. If your mouse is a 9-pin serial mouse, it probably is connected to the serial port `/dev/ttyS1` (COM1), but you should verify this to eliminate potential problems down the road.

Specifying Your Red Hat Installation Class

Now that you've provided the basic information about your system that is required by the installer, the main Red Hat System Installer screen displays. Press Return to close this screen and proceed with installing Red Hat 7.0.

As discussed in Chapter 2, "Preparing Your System for Red Hat," Red Hat Linux provides several standard system templates, also known as *install types* or *installation classes*. After you specify language, keyboard, and mouse information, Red Hat displays a screen on which you must select the type of system you are installing. See the section "Selecting Your Red Hat Installation Class," in Chapter 2 for detailed information about the different Red Hat installation classes.

In addition to offering different installation classes, this screen in the Red Hat Installer also enables you to specify that you are upgrading an existing Red Hat Linux system. Selecting Upgrade preserves the current partitioning and user data on your system, installing only a new version of the Linux kernel and updating the system software on your system from the CD. During an upgrade, the installer does the following:

- Correctly mounts all the drives and partitions on your system
- Extracts a list of installed packages on your system from the RPM database on your existing system
- Installs a new kernel on the `/boot` partition of your existing system
- Installs any newer versions of packages that are currently on your existing system

After selecting Upgrade or the installation class that you want to install, select Next or OK to proceed.

Partitioning Disks for Linux

After you select any installation class other than Upgrade, the Red Hat Installer displays the Automatic Partitioning screen, which warns you that you are about to erase any existing Linux partitions on your system and gives you the option of manually partitioning your system.

- If you are installing a Workstation or Server system and want to use the default partitioning schemes implied by those installation classes, you can select Continue and OK to proceed. The default partitioning schemes associated with these installation classes are discussed in the section "Selecting Your Red Hat Installation Class," in Chapter 2. If you are using one of these default partitioning schemes, you can skip to the "Configuring Network Support" section after selecting OK or next.
- If you are installing a Workstation or Server system and want to customize how your system is partitioned, select Manually Partition. Red Hat's Disk Druid partitioning software displays.
- Installing a custom system implies that you will manually partition your disk, so the installer automatically displays a screen giving you the option of using Red Hat's Disk Druid tool or fdisk, an older, command-line oriented partitioning package. This chapter discusses using Disk Druid—for more information about using fdisk, see the manual pages for fdisk that can be found on the Web. For more information about suggested disk-partitioning schemes for the custom installation class, see the section "The Custom Installation Class," in Chapter 2. If you have access to the internet from another system, check `http://www.linuxdoc.org/HOWTO/mini/partition-5.html` for more information.

Red Hat's Disk Druid is a remarkably easy-to-use tool for disk partitioning. You can use Disk Druid only when you are installing Red Hat Linux; Red Hat does not provide a version of Disk Druid that you can execute when your system is up and running. The Disk Druid utility can be intimidating at first, but even on its worst day it is substantially friendlier than the standard run-time Linux disk-partitioning tool, fdisk.

It's important to realize exactly what Disk Druid does for you. Disk Druid makes it easy for you to specify a particular partitioning scheme for the disk(s) in your soon-to-be-Linux system, but it doesn't actually do the formatting or partitioning itself. While you're working in Disk Druid, the partitioning scheme you create is saved in the installer's memory. Partitioning occurs only after you accept the partitioning scheme that you've created on the main Disk Druid screen and move on to subsequent screen.

The Disk Druid display is divided into three main sections:

- The top portion of the screen shows a list of the disk partitions that are currently defined on your system.
- The middle portion of the screen can't be edited directly. This portion provides summary information about each of the drives that were detected in your system during the installation process. If you have more than one hard drive in your system, this portion of the screen lets you select the one on which you want to create specific partitions.

CAUTION

If your system contains any disk drives or partitions that are not listed on this screen, then those drives or partitions were not detected during the installation process. If you want to partition them now or are depending on the space that they provide for part of your installation, you should shut down your system; check your cabling, power connection, and the drives themselves; and restart the installation process.

- The bottom portion of the screen displays five buttons that enable you to add new partitions, edit a current partition or partitioning scheme, delete new partitions, select Next or OK to proceed with the installation process, or select Back to undo partitioning changes or return to a previous phase of the installation process.

Moving around in the Disk Druid screen is easy regardless of which installer you're using. Pressing the Tab key moves you from button to button and then to the Current Disk Partitions list at the top of the screen. In Red Hat's text mode installer, you can also use various function keys to activate these buttons directly. The function key shortcuts for these buttons are the following:

- **F1**—Displays generic help for using Disk Druid and provides detailed information about the various fields displayed in the Disk Druid.
- **F2**—Provides a shortcut for the Add button.
- **F3**—Provides a shortcut for the Edit button.
- **F4**—Provides a shortcut for the Delete button.
- **F5**—Resets the partition table to the values displayed the last time you executed the Disk Druid.
- **F12**—Provides a shortcut for the OK button, which verifies the changes you have made to the partition table, asks for confirmation of whether the Disk Druid should save your changes, and (if the answer is "OK"), saves your changes and proceeds to the next step in the Red Hat installer.

NOTE

If you manually partition your disk, you must specify the mount points and types of the various partitions you create. You will not be able to proceed in installing Red Hat without, at a minimum, identifying the partition to be mounted at the root of the Linux file system, "/" and creating a partition to be used for swap space.

If you manually partition your disk and your disk already contains existing partitions that use all of the space available on the drive where you want to install Red Hat Linux, you must delete some of the existing partitions before you can create new ones. If you want to retain all of your existing partitions on a specific disk and do not have another disk available on which to install Red Hat Linux, you must add another disk to your system and restart the installation process before continuing with the Red Hat Linux installation process.

Adding Partitions in Disk Druid

Linux assigns names to disk drives and other storage in your system in much the same way that Windows does, but uses different naming conventions. Storage devices on your system's primary disk interfaces, whether IDE or SCSI, are assigned names in the order that they are detected. For example, Linux assigns the name `/dev/hda` to the master device on IDE interface 0 in your system, which would be assigned the drive letter C: on Windows systems. The next storage device detected, whether a slave device on IDE interface 0 or a master or slave on IDE interface 1, is assigned the name `/dev/hdb` by Linux, which Windows would assign drive letter D: to. (In reality, `/dev/hdb` is usually your CD-ROM drive, which isn't listed in the Disk Druid window—regular CD drives aren't listed because they aren't writable, and CD/RW drives aren't writable at this point in a Linux install.)

Linux actually uses a slightly more understandable naming scheme for partitions on those devices than Windows does, because Linux doesn't have Windows' confusing notion of primary and extended partitions. Linux partitions created on `/dev/hda` are numbered from 1 to the maximum number of partitions you've created: `/dev/hda1`, `/dev/hda2`, and so on for each device in your system. Windows muddies the water here by assigning the drive letter C: to the first primary partition detected on the first drive in your system. It then doesn't assign subsequent drive letters to any logical partitions within extended partitions on your disk until all primary partitions on your storage devices have received drive letter assignments.

When adding partitions in Disk Druid, it's important to realize how this is done. Each time you add a new partition, space for that partition is allocated from the beginning of the disk, adjacent to any previous partitions you've defined. Therefore, you cannot modify any aspect of a partition (except its mount point) after you have created a partition that follows it on the disk. For example, if you already have defined partitions 1 and 2 on `/dev/hda`, you can't edit anything about `/dev/hda1` except its mount point. Unfortunately, you can't reduce its size, either, which should be valid. You can always delete `/dev/hda1` and re-create it with different parameters, but those parameters can't exceed its previous size unless there is free space on the disk that follows the partition you are modifying.

Of course, redefining partitions with smaller sizes is valid, but this tends to leave small portions of your disk unallocated. Disk space is cheap, but this type of wasted space is more than just wasted—your reasons for leaving unallocated portions of your disk would truly mystify any system administrator who worked on this system after you. If you are manually partitioning your disk(s), see the section "The Custom Installation Class," in Chapter 2, for suggestions and general information about manually partitioning your disks.

To create a new disk partition, use the mouse, the Tab key, or press F2 in the text-mode installer to select the Add button. The Edit New Partition screen displays, which lets you specify the following:

- The mount point for the partition you are creating. This is the name of the directory on which the partition you are creating will be mounted. UNIX uses standard directories as mount points; when a formatted partition is mounted on a directory, any files and directories copied or created in that directory actually are being stored on the mounted partition. You must specify a mount point for any non-swap partition that you create using Disk Druid.
- The size of the partition, in megabytes. This field lets you provide a suggested numeric value for the size of the partition you are creating. When you eventually close the Edit New Partition screen, the exact number you specified might be adjusted slightly to work better with the geometry (heads, sectors, cylinders, and so on) of your disk.
- Whether you simply want to grow this partition to use the remainder of your disk. You select this option with the mouse or by pressing the Spacebar when the cursor is in that field. This option provides an easy way to ensure that you don't waste any space on the hard drive you are partitioning because it forces the last partition that you create to use up all the remaining space on this disk.
- The drives on which this partition can be created, with the currently selected drive selected (indicated by a check mark in the X-Window system installer, or by an asterisk in the text-mode installer).
- The type of partition you are creating: Linux Swap, Linux Native, DOS 16-bit < 32M, or DOS 16-Bit >= 32M. If you select Linux Swap, the Mount Point field is deactivated because swap partitions aren't mounted as part of the file system. Instead, they are directly accessed as raw, unformatted partitions by Linux.

Selecting OK schedules the partition for creation and formatting; Selecting Back or Cancel returns you to the main Disk Druid screen.

It's important to remember that the Red Hat Installer doesn't actually create and format your partitions until the next phase of the installation process.

Example of Creating Partitions in Disk Druid

While Disk Druid is easy to use, disk partitioning is a complex subject that rarely comes up as a topic for casual conversation. This section provides an example of using Disk Druid to create a simple partitioning scheme.

NOTE

This example assumes that you are installing Linux on a disk that is solely for Linux and on which you are not preserving any existing partitions. This section is only provided as an example of how to use Disk Druid. See Chapter 2 for information about devising an optimal partitioning scheme for the type of system you are creating.

1. When the Disk Druid screen first displays, any existing partition on your disk is selected in the Current Disk Partitions portion of the Disk Druid screen. Select the Delete button in the X Window system-based installer, using the F4 key in the text-mode installer, or press Tab until the Delete button is highlighted and press Return to delete the existing partition.
2. Select the Add button in the X Window system-based installer, using the F2 key in the text-mode installer, or press Tab until the Add button is highlighted and press Return to display the Edit New partition screen.
3. To define a partition called `/boot` to hold the kernel and associated files for the boot process, enter **`/boot`** as the mount point, enter a size of 20MB, make sure that the Grow to Fill Disk check box is not selected, and specify "Linux Native" as the partition type. This example uses a system with a single disk, so "hda" is the only choice in the Allowable Drives list. Press Tab again to highlight the OK button and press Return to create the partition definition.
4. To define a swap partition, select the Add button again. On the Edit New Partition screen, skip the mount point field, enter a size of 96MB, make sure that the Grow to Fill Disk check box is not selected, and select "Linux Swap" as the partition type. Press Tab again to highlight the OK button and press Return to create the partition definition.
5. To define a single monolithic partition to hold your Linux files, select the Add button again. On the Edit New Partition screen, enter `/` as the mount point field, skip the size field, press space to activate the Grow to Fill Disk check box, and select "Linux Native" as the partition type. Press Tab again to highlight the OK button and press Return to create the partition definition.

You would then click next or select OK to proceed with the installation process.

Modifying Partitions in Disk Druid

Disk Druid is easy to use, which also makes it easy to occasionally create partition definitions that aren't exactly what you intended. This then makes it necessary to modify partition definitions after you have created them.

You can edit partitions only under certain circumstances—in many cases, it might be easier to delete a misdefined partition and then re-create it with the parameters you intended. The following list details the aspects of an existing partition definition that you can edit—and when:

- The mount point of any partition, at any time.
- The size of a partition, only if free space is available on the disk and if that free space is located after the partition you are editing. For example, if you already

have defined partitions 1 and 2 on `/dev/hda`, you can't edit anything about `/dev/hda1` except its mount point. Unfortunately, you can't reduce its size, either, which should be valid.

- The Grow to Fill Disk option, only if free space is available on the disk and if that free space is located after the partition you are editing (as in the previous point).
- The Partition Type option, only if free space is available on the disk and if that free space is located after the partition you are editing (as in the previous points). (You should actually be able to change this at any time, but that particular improvement is being left for a future version of Red Hat.)

If you want to modify a partition definition that is immediately followed by other partitions on your disk, you must delete the subsequent partition before you can modify the previous one.

To modify a partition after you have defined it but before leaving Disk Druid, simply select the partition that you want to modify in the list at the top of the Disk Druid window. Then use the mouse, the F3 function key in the text-mode installer, or the Tab key to select the Edit button. If you use the Tab key to select the Edit button, you must press Return in order to activate the Edit button and proceed with the installation. The Edit Partition screen displays, which lets you modify the following:

- The mount point of the partition (always).
- The size (in the cases described in the previous list).
- The Grow to Fill Disk flag (in the cases described in the previous list). When modifying partitions that are followed by previously defined partitions on your disk, the Grow to Fill Disk option actually means "grow to fill adjacent free space" because the space in a Linux partition must be contiguous on your disk.
- The partition type (in the cases described in the previous list).

After you have made any changes you want, select the OK button to save your changes, or select Cancel or Back to return to the previous Disk Druid screen without accepting any changes you have made.

It's important to remember that the Red Hat Installer doesn't actually delete, modify, create, or format your partitions until the next phase of the installation process.

Deleting Partitions in Disk Druid

To delete a partition that you have defined, simply select the partition that you want to delete in the list at the top of the Disk Druid window. Then use the mouse or the Tab key to select the Delete button. Disk Druid displays a confirmation screen that asks whether you really want to delete the selected partition. To delete the selected partition, select OK; to keep your current partition definitions, select Cancel.

It's important to remember that the Red Hat Installer doesn't actually delete, modify, create, or format your partitions until the next phase of the installation process.

NOTE

This screen appears only if you are using Red Hat's text installer. If you are using the X Window system installer, skip to the section "Configuring Network Support."

Formatting Linux Partitions

After accepting a manual partitioning scheme in the Disk Druid, the Formatter screen displays. This screen displays a list of all the partitions you selected in Disk Druid, enabling you to specify which partitions you want to format. Swap partitions are not listed because these are not formatted as file systems but are formatted by Linux using a special application that enables them to be written to and read from in raw mode.

NOTE

This screen appears only if you are doing a Custom install or have manually partitioned your disk using Disk Druid or fdisk.

You must format any new or resized partitions after defining them. Formatting them creates the basic Linux file system structure in each partition, enabling partitions to be mounted, to store files and directories, and so on.

When formatting partitions for the first time, it's a good idea to select the Check for Bad Blocks During Format option on this screen. Selecting this option causes the Red Hat installed to perform a read/write test while formatting each partition, marking any bad blocks as unusable.

By default, all Linux Native partitions for which you have specified a mount point are selected when this screen displays, as indicated by an asterisk in the text-mode installer or a check mark in the X Window system installer. If you are reinstalling Linux on a system whose partitions already have been formatted, you can deselect any partitions that you do not want to format by selecting the name(s) and pressing the Spacebar to toggle whether these will be formatted.

If you are installing Linux on a system that will also boot another operating system and that operating system is already installed on that partition, make absolutely sure that this partition is not selected for formatting. It should not be listed, but it's a good idea to double check—remember that formatting a partition destroys any existing data on it.

At this point, you can either schedule any selected partitions for formatting, return to the Disk Druid screen to modify your partition definitions, or click Next or Select OK to proceed.

Installing LILO, the Linux Loader

NOTE

If you are using Red Hat's X Window System or text mode installers and you are doing a Custom Installation Class install, the installer now collects information about where to install the Linux Loader. You will not see these screens if you are doing a Workstation or Server Class Installation because these installation classes use sets of default values for this information. If you are doing a Workstation or Server Class install, skip to the next section, "Configuring Network Support."

The Linux Loader is a small program that is used to determine which partition to boot from, and which operating system or Linux to boot from that partition. More complete information about the Linux Loader, its configuration file, and its participation in the boot process is given in Configuring the Linux Loader in Chapter 6, "Starting and Stopping Red Hat Linux." You can configure many aspects of LILO after it is installed by modifying its configuration file. If your system only boots Linux or Linux and DOS/Windows, you will probably never need to change anything about the way that LILO is installed and configured on your system.

In Red Hat's X Window System installer, one screen is used to collect all of the LILO information. In the text installer, several screens collect this information.

You can simply accept the default values unless:

- You do not want your system to be able to boot Red Hat Linux from your hard drive without a boot floppy. You may want to only boot Red Hat Linux using a floppy disk if you do not want anyone to run Red Hat Linux on your system without your knowledge or if you usually want to run a different operating system.
- You are installing Red Hat Linux on a system that will boot both Windows NT and Red Hat Linux. In this case, you will want to install LILO in the first sector of your Red Hat boot partition. See your Windows NT documentation for information about updating the NT boot loader to boot multiple operating systems.

See the online help for information about using and installing LILO in these and other rare cases.

Configuring Network Support

Red Hat's network configuration process consists of several screens that enable you to specify the basic network information necessary to configure TCP/IP support on your Red Hat system.

NOTE

You will see the second and third network setup screens only if your system contains a network card that is one of the default types supported by Red Hat. If yours does not and if you are using Red Hat's text installer, skip ahead to the section "Configuring the Mouse." If you are using Red Hat's X Window system installer, skip to the section of this chapter titled "Setting the Time Zone." If your system contains a network card that is not being recognized, you can configure that later, as explained in Chapter 6 in the section, "Resolving Module and Hardware Startup Problems."

The Hostname Configuration Screen

The Hostname Configuration screen enables you to set the hostname for your machine. This should be the unqualified, short name of your machine. For example, if your fully qualified hostname is rh70.vonhagen.org, you would enter `rh70` on this screen.

The Network Configuration Screen

The Network Configuration screen enables you to provide the basic information necessary for configuring TCP/IP (Transmission Control Protocol/Internet Protocol) support on your system.

When this screen displays, the Activate on Boot option is selected. This means that your network will be automatically enabled each time you boot your system, which is almost always correct. You may not want to automatically enable your network if your system is not attached to a network and is intended only for home or dialup use.

NOTE

If you are using Red Hat's text mode installer, references to DHCP also include references to Bootp, an older protocol for booting over a network using a centralized server. Bootp does not provide all of the features of DHCP but is included for compatibility with networks using older boot servers.

To automatically obtain IP address and host name information from your network, select the Configure Using DHCP option. This is a protocol that enables your system to obtain the basic network configuration information over a network by contacting the appropriate servers.

To use DHCP, one or more DHCP servers must be running on a machine that is already on your network. This could well be the case if you are installing a Linux system onto an existing corporate or academic network. Do not select this option unless you are sure that a DHCP server is available on your network. Contact your network administrator to determine whether a DHCP server is available on your network. You do not need to know the name or network address of the or DHCP server. When using DHCP, your system broadcasts a query for the location of a server each time your system boots, automatically connects to the first server that responds, and obtains the information that it requires from that server.

If you are not using DHCP, skip to the section "Assigning Fixed IP Information."

General Information About DHCP

The advantage of using DHCP is that you do not need to maintain permanent network information in specific files on your machine; your machine automatically gets the network information it needs each time it boots. From a system administrator's perspective, DHCP makes it easy to manage large networks—IP addresses aren't wasted on systems that are turned off, and DNS, gateway, and router information is maintained centrally and can be changed at any time. Client systems using BootP automatically obtain the updated information the next time they boot, and client systems using DHCP automatically obtain updated information at intervals that the administrator can specify (when their lease expires, for DHCP aficionados).

A DHCP server provides the following information:

- An IP address for your system
- The IP subnet mask (also known as netmask) appropriate for the network to which your system is connected
- The IP address of the default IP router (also known as gateway) appropriate for the network to which your system is connected
- The IP addresses of the primary and secondary Internet domain name servers (DNS) appropriate for the network to which your system is connected

A DHCP server can also provide additional information, but the items in the previous list are the minimum bits necessary to get your system up and running on a network.

A potential problem with using DHCP to obtain network information is that using DHCP to assign IP address and system name information each time your system reboots makes it difficult for other systems to locate your system. You can access other systems and services normally from your machine, but other systems will not know how to telnet to your system without your giving them its name and IP address information each time you boot.

Assigning Fixed IP Information

If you are installing your Linux system as a server, at home, or on a smaller network, chances are that you will have to provide your own network configuration information. In that case, deselect the Use bootp/dhcp option on this screen, and provide the following information:

- **IP address**—The IP address for your machine must be unique on the network where you are installing your system. If your Internet service provider (ISP) did not provide you with a permanent IP address, you still can assign one to your system from the blocks of freely available Internet addresses available for use on private networks that are not directly connected to the Internet. See the next section, "Assigning IP Addresses for Private Networks," for more information about these addresses.

- **Netmask**—The netmask is an IP bitmask that is used to quickly identify your machine and the subnet on which your machine is running. The most common netmask for home use is 255.255.255.0, which means that only the last portion of your IP address is required to locate your machine. On larger networks, a netmask such as 255.255.0.0 might be used, which means that systems that want to communicate with yours need to consider both the Class C address (the next-to-last portion of the IP address) as well as the last portion of your machine's IP address.
- **Default gateway (IP)**—This is the IP address of a computer system to which network requests that can't be resolved locally will be sent. This host is known as a gateway because it knows how to contact networks other than the one on which your host is located.
- **Primary nameserver**—This is the IP address of a computer system that can map hostnames to IP addresses. The Internet would be a mess if everyone had to remember the IP addresses of the hosts that they want to contact. DNS servers accept the name of a host that you want to contact and return the IP address of that host. This lets users remember somewhat meaningful hostnames and domain names (www.gethip.com, and so on), while the software gets the hardcore numeric IP information it requires. You must always specify the IP address of your primary nameserver rather than its name—after all, your system can't look up the IP address of the nameserver if it can't contact it in the first place. This presents an amusing electronic chicken-and-egg problem.

When you've specified these bits of information, select Next or OK to proceed to the next screen.

Assigning IP Addresses for Private Networks

The Internet RFC (Request for Comment, a proposal for feedback) 1918 sets aside blocks of IP addresses for use by computer systems that require IP connectivity but that do not need external connections to the global Internet. The following IP addresses are available for use on such private networks:

```
10.0.0.0 - 10.255.255.255          (10/8 prefix)
172.16.0.0 - 172.31.255.255        (172.16/12 prefix)
192.168.0.0 - 192.168.255.255      (192.168/16 prefix)
```

Anyone can use any addresses within these ranges of IP addresses without having to ask for permission or worrying about stepping on anyone's toes. These addresses are never forwarded through routers or injected in any other way into the Internet.

If you decide to use these private addresses on a network that you will eventually connect to the Internet, you will have to set up a gateway between the two that serves as a network address translator (NAT) between your local network and the Internet. NAT systems typically have at least two Ethernet cards: one for each private network to which they're connected, and one that is actually attached to the Internet and that therefore has a real, public IP address obtained from an ISP. The NAT system uses software such as ipchains (on Linux) to route requests from the private networks through its public IP address, keeping track of which private address is communicating with which

Internet hosts. Linux systems make excellent NAT boxes, but explaining how to configure NAT falls outside the scope of this book.

Configuring the Mouse

This screen appears only if you are using Red Hat's text installer. If you are using the X Window system installer, you provided this information earlier; skip to the next section, "Setting the Time Zone."

The next step in the text-mode Red Hat installation process is to provide information about your mouse. The Red Hat Installer can't detect this automatically because mouse devices are simple serial devices; however, providing the right information about your mouse can help Linux make the most of its buttons. This information is important even if you are not planning to run the X Window system: Linux provides mouse drivers for screens running in terminal mode, letting you cut and paste information just as though you were running in a graphical environment.

Select the type of mouse you are using from the list at the top of this screen. If your mouse isn't listed, the most important bits of information about your mouse are whether it is connected to a serial or P/2 mouse port, and the number of buttons it has.

The X Window system expects mouse devices to have three buttons, each of which displays different menus or performs different functions. If your mouse has only two buttons, you still can use it with the X Window system by checking the Emulate Three Buttons box. This will let you simulate pressing the middle mouse button by pressing both mouse buttons simultaneously. Clever, no?

After selecting the best fit for your mouse and the Emulate Three Buttons option (if necessary), select Next or OK to proceed to the next screen.

If your mouse is connected to a serial port (or if you told the Red Hat Installer that it was), another screen displays on which you must specify the serial port to which the mouse is connected. You will not see this screen if you specified that your mouse was connected to a PS/2 port.

If your mouse is a 9-pin serial mouse, it probably is connected to the first port, `/dev/ttyS1` (COM1). Select the serial port to which your mouse is connected, and then proceed to the next screen.

Setting the Time Zone

Information about the time zone in which your computer is located is used to make sure that your computer knows the right time, can handle daylight savings time correctly (where appropriate), and uses the correct time stamps when communicating with other systems using services such as email. If you have ever received email from someone whose system clock was set incorrectly, you know just how irritating that can be because many mailers sort messages by time. It can take a while to track down a new message that's dated in the 1990s, while messages from the latter part of the twenty-first century rarely will be sorted correctly.

If you are using Red Hat's text installer, select your computer's location from the list of available time zones. Activating the Hardware Clock Set to GMT option of your system's clock (on the motherboard) uses Greenwich Mean Time.

If you are using Red Hat's X Window system installer, select your computer's location from the list of available time zones. Activating the System Clock uses UCT option of your system's clock (on the motherboard) uses Universal Coordinated Time.

Configuring Initial Accounts, Passwords, and Authentication

The next few screens let you provide initial passwords for your system, create any user accounts that you want to begin using immediately, and select the type of security that your system uses.

Setting the Root Password

The root password is the single most powerful password on a Linux system (or any UNIX or UNIX-like system, for that matter). Logged in as root, you can delete or modify any files or partitions on the system. Choose your root password more carefully than any other password—it should be easy to remember but not obvious. When selecting the root password, the same "clever password" rules apply as with any password, but more so: Mix uppercase and lowercase letters, use numbers and nonalphabetic characters, and so on. If you set the root password of your system to something obvious and other people have access to your system, you might just as well put it in your car and drive it over to their house—or at least never make that person angry.

As with any password, the root password is not echoed to the screen when you enter it, and it must be entered twice to make sure that you didn't make any typographical errors when you entered it. (Or, at least, that you made the same ones twice.)

Creating an Initial User Account

It generally is good practice to always log in on your Linux box using a standard user account; use the su command to become root only when absolutely necessary. This is good practice for working in the real world, where walking away from a node or terminal and leaving yourself logged in as root could get you fired—or at least will earn you verbal abuse and disdain from your coworkers.

To create an initial user account, specify the following:

- User ID (the login for that account)
- Full name (your first and last names)
- Password (entered twice, as usual)

NOTE

When creating accounts, Linux automatically creates default groups of which the new users are the only member. These have the same name as the new user's name. This simplifies giving multiple users access to the files owned by any single user, but takes a bit of getting used to if you're used to more "classic" UNIX group assignments. On most other UNIX systems, groups are created before users, and users are assigned to groups when their accounts are created. The Linux model has the same eventual goal, but tends to produce `/etc/group` files with many more entries than are found on other UNIX systems.

After providing this information a subsequent screen displays on which you can create other user accounts by selecting the Add button; this displays the same screen you used to create your first user account. I rarely create multiple accounts when installing a Linux system because they aren't really necessary at this point. After you have installed your Linux system, you can easily create any other accounts that you need by using linuxconf, the Linux configuration tool.

In addition to the root account and any initial user accounts you create, the Red Hat Installer automatically creates a number of system accounts for you, such as adm, bin, daemon, ftp, games, gopher, halt, lp, mail, news, nobody, operator, shutdown, sync, and uucp. These accounts are used by various system services and are not (for the most part) accounts that you should use to log in. Depending on the software that you install, the Red Hat Installer also might create other accounts, such as postgres for one of the Linux database systems, and xfs for the X Window system font server.

Specifying Authentication

If you are doing a custom install, Red Hat also displays a screen that enables you to specify the type of authentication you want to use in your new system. The options are

- MD5 passwords: Enable you to use passwords longer than 8 characters.
- Shadow Passwords: Enable you to store passwords in the file /etc/shadow for security purposes, rather than in the standard password file.
- NIS: Enables you to use Sun's Network Information System (NIS) for authentication purposes.
- LDAP: Enables you to use the networked Light-weight Directory Access Protocol (LDAP) for authentication purposes. This is a networked authentication system that stores passwords on a central server.
- Kerberos: Enables you to use the Kerberos authentication system (developed by MIT and used with systems such as AFS and Microsoft's Windows 2000 for authentication purposes.

CHAPTER 5

Red Hat Installation: Basic Software Installation

After you've supplied the information about your system that is required by the Red Hat text and X Window system installers, and after you optionally have modified the default configurations, you're almost ready to begin the installation and launch your personal computer into the world of Red Hat Linux.

This chapter discusses the basics of selecting and installing software when installing Red Hat for the first time. The first two sections discuss the groups of software that you can select for installation when installing Red Hat, and they also explain how you can optionally add specific packages to the installation process. For information about installing, updating, or removing packages after you've installed your system, see the discussion of the Red Hat Package Manager (RPM) in Chapter 10, "Installing Other Software."

The third section of this chapter introduces the X Window system and its client/server model, and explains the basics of configuring the X Window system during the installation process. See Chapter 7, "Configuring and Customizing the X Window System," for more detail.

A later section of this chapter discusses the Red Hat Installer's Bootdisk creation screen, explains why you want to create a boot disk as part of the installation process, and welcomes you to the world of Red Hat Linux. By the end of this chapter, you will have provided the Red Hat Installer with all the information required to install Red Hat Linux on your system, and you will be watching the installation process as it turns your computer system into a powerful Linux workstation.

Selecting Grouped Packages

The following sections discuss the requirements for adding grouped packages related to Red Hat's workstation, server, and custom installation classes. The amount of disk space required is rounded up slightly to guarantee that you have sufficient space available.

Selecting Packages for Red Hat's Workstation Installation Class

If you selected Red Hat's Workstation installation class, the Package Group Selection window displays, letting you specify whether you want to install the package that makes up the GNOME desktop environment, the KDE desktop environment, and/or a package of games for Linux. You can install all or none of these packages. Unless you have a definite preference for GNOME or KDE, or are installing Red Hat onto a system with a small amount of disk space, I generally recommend installing them all. This enables you to experiment with the two desktop environments to find out which one best suits your needs, and games are always a pleasant diversion. Rounding up, the requirements for these packages are the following:

- A basic workstation class install requires around 720MB.
- The GNOME package requires approximately another 120MB.
- The KDE package requires approximately 140MB.
- The games package requires approximately 40MB of disk space.

If you are using Red Hat's Workstation installation class, after making your selections using the mouse or the spacebar, you can skip to the section titled "Verifying Package Dependencies" later in this chapter.

Selecting Packages for Red Hat's Server Installation Class

If you selected Red Hat's Server installation class, the Red Hat Installer lets you select from a list of additional servers associated with this installation class. Rounding up, the requirements for these packages are the following:

- The basic amount of disk space required for a Red Hat Server installation is 450MB.
- To add a News Server requires an additional 10MB.
- Including an NFS Server adds 1MB to this total.
- A Web server adds 1MB to this total.
- A DNS Name Server adds 5MB to this total.

If you are installing a Server installation class, you can skip directly to the section "Configuring the X Window System."

Selecting Packages for Red Hat's Custom Installation Class

If you selected Custom as your installation class in the previous chapter, the next step in the process is to select the specific software that you want to install.

For installation and distribution purposes, Red Hat Linux groups software into packages, which are the core software required for a specific application. Packages usually include a specific application, configuration files that it uses, libraries specific to that application, and documentation associated with that application. Packages do not include any other applications or system libraries used by an application, but they identify any external packages that are required. For example, a package containing a security auditing application written in Perl would not include Perl, but would identify a Perl package as a requirement.

Red Hat uses the Red Hat Package Manager (RPM) to track and manage packages. A package manager enables a Linux system administrator to easily install new packages. By encapsulating the requirements of a specific application, packages make it easy to install or upgrade any application or set of libraries without reinstalling an entire Linux distribution, losing customized configuration files, or rebooting the system (depending on what you're installing, of course.)

If you are installing Red Hat Linux using its Custom installation class, the Red Hat Installer groups conceptually related sets of packages into the following sets. These sets are listed in the order that they appear in the Package Groups dialog box:

- **Printer Support**—The fonts, applications, system configuration files, and utilities required to print to the variety of printers supported by Red Hat Linux.
- **X Window System**—The fonts, client applications, X Window system server, and utilities related to the X Window system.
- **GNOME**—The window manager and utilities related to the GNU Object Model Environment (GNOME) X Window system desktop environment.
- **KDE**—The window manager and utilities related to the K Desktop Environment (KDE) X Window system desktop environment.
- **Mail/WWW/News Tools**—Utilities and required libraries related to reading and sending email, interacting with Web servers, and reading and posting messages to Usenet newsgroups. This set does not include the servers themselves—these are separately selected in other sets.
- **DOS/Windows Connectivity**—Applications for emulating DOS systems and interacting with DOS and Windows systems from your Linux system.
- **Graphics Manipulation**—Applications, libraries, and related utilities for creating, editing, and converting graphics files in different formats.
- **Games**—A variety of text-oriented and graphical games that use the X Window system, the command line, or the Linux console.
- **Multimedia Support**—Applications, libraries, and related utilities for creating, editing, and converting audio and video files in different formats.

- **Laptop Support**—Applications, libraries, and related utilities for exchanging data between laptops and desktop systems running Red Hat Linux.
- **Networked Workstation**—Applications, libraries, and related utilities for using your Red Hat system on a network and interacting with other networked systems.
- **Dialup Workstation**—Applications, libraries, and related utilities for connecting your Red Hat system to other systems over the telephone or through any serial connection to another system.
- **News Server**—A server application for obtaining and posting to Usenet newsgroups.
- **NFS Server**—The Network File System (NFS) server and related libraries and utilities.
- **SMB (Samba) Server**—A Server Message Block (SMB) server that enables you to mount and access shared Windows file systems over a network from your Linux system, or to access files in the Linux file system from Windows systems.
- **IPX/NetWare Connectivity**—Utilities and libraries necessary for interacting with networked systems that use the Internetwork Packet Exchange (IPX) network protocol, such as Novell NetWare systems.
- **Anonymous FTP Server**—A File Transfer Protocol (FTP) server and associated configuration files that enable users without accounts on your system to upload and download files over a network.
- **Web Server**—The Apache Web server and related configuration utilities.
- **DNS Name Server**—The Domain Name Service (DNS) server, used to automatically map hostnames to Internet Protocol (IP) addresses.
- **SQL Server**—A Structured Query Language (SQL) database server and related libraries and utilities.
- **Network Management Workstation**—Utilities and related libraries for workstations used for network analysis (tcpdump) and troubleshooting NIS, SNMP, and the Berkeley r-commands (`rdate`, `rsh`, `rcp`, and so on).
- **Authoring/Publishing**—Applications for editing, formatting, printing, and viewing troff, lout, and Tex/Latex documents.
- **Emacs**—Versions of the Editor Macros (Emacs) text editor for the X Window system and for standard terminal/console windows.
- **Development**—Compilers, preprocessors, libraries, include files, and related utilities for developing programs and managing application development on Linux systems, including X Window system applications.
- **Kernel Development**—The source for the Linux kernel distributed with the version of Red Hat Linux that you are installing.
- **Utilities**—System maintenance and monitoring utilities for Linux, as well as utilities for the X Window system and network management.

A final set of packages, labeled Everything, literally installs all the packages on the Red Hat CD. In general, if you have the disk space and are not intimidated by installing packages and applications that you might not use, installing everything on the CD is a good idea. If you happen to read about an interesting application in the Red Hat distribution, installing everything ensures that it is installed on your system. Installing all available packages when installing Red Hat Linux is simpler than subsequently locating individual packages on the Red Hat CD, identifying their requirements, and then installing them manually.

Selecting Individual Packages

Unless you select the package group labeled Everything, the package groups listed in the previous section select only certain packages for installation on your system. The Package Groups dialog box also provides a Select Individual Packages option to enable you to add individual packages to the package groups selected on the Package Group Selection screen. Selecting this option and then selecting Next or OK (depending on whether you're using the text-mode or the X Window system installer) displays a more detailed Package Group Selection dialog box, with an even more detailed list of packages to choose from. This list consists of sets of packages that you can expand by pressing Return when the cursor is over the names of the options. When a list of packages is expanded, you can select the names of specific packages to add that package to the list of those that will be installed on your system.

NOTE

Packages preceded by an asterisk or active selection box in the Select Individual Packages dialog box are already selected for installation either because they are part of the base Red Hat installation, because you already have selected them, or because you already have selected grouped packages of which they are a part.

Selecting packages for installation using the Individual Packages dialog box still takes advantage of the Red Hat Package Manager's knowledge of dependencies for these packages. After you select individual packages for installation and then select Next, RPM displays a Package Dependencies screen. This screen lists any unsatisfied requirements for the packages you've selected—in other words, any packages required by the packages you've selected that were not themselves selected.

The Package Dependencies screen displays a two-column list of selected packages and any unsatisfied requirements. You can select the Install Packages to Satisfy Dependencies check box and then select OK to automatically satisfy those dependencies.

The next sections discuss sets of packages that you might want to select to add specific capabilities to the Red Hat system you're installing. Red Hat's predefined installation classes make it easier than ever to automatically install the software needed for basic types of Linux systems. The only disadvantage of this approach is that it isn't easy to figure out what packages to add in order to add specific capabilities to your system. For example, the Server installation class doesn't include things such as the X Window system because Red Hat assumes that you're installing a server system that no one will be using as a desktop system. While this is usually the case, it's often convenient to be able to run the X Window system on a server console when installing new software or reconfiguring various server packages.

If you're using a Custom installation class, you can add the sets of packages described in the next few sections during the installation process. The package group in which each individual package is located is listed after the package. You also can use RPM to manually install these packages after you've installed a system using one of Red Hat's predefined installation classes. Instructions for locating and manually installing packages are given in the section "Locating Individual Packages," later in this chapter. Chapter 10, provides detailed information about using RPM.

Default Packages for Application Development

All Red Hat installation classes except the Custom installation class automatically install development tools including the following:

- `binutils`, a set of tools required for assembling and compiling applications on Red Hat systems.
- `bison`, a parser generator.
- `byacc`, a parser generator.
- `cpp`, the C preprocessor, used when compiling applications.
- `ElectricFence.a`, a debugging library that detects memory allocation violations.
- `flex`, a text (input) scanner.
- `gcc` and `g++`, the GNU compilers for C and C++.
- `gdb`, the standard GNU Debugger.
- libraries (both shared and static versions) such as glibc, fnlib, libtermcap, and glib (the GIMP toolkit). Static libraries end with the extension `.a` and are always linked into binaries. Shared libraries are only loaded into binaries when functions in those libraries are called. Programs linked with static libraries are therefore larger, but more portable since they have no external dependencies. Programs linked with shared libraries are smaller and can benefit from enhancements and corrections to the functions in those libraries because they will automatically link to newer versions of shared libraries as they are installed on your system.
- `make`, `pmake`, and `automake` for automating program builds and maintenance.
- `rcs` and `cvs` for software and documentation version control.
- `rpm-build` for creating RPM archives.

Adding Packages for the X Window System

As mentioned earlier, the GNOME and KDE workstation installation classes are mutually exclusive as far as the desktop environment goes. After using Linux for a while, you might find that you want to add applications that were built for the "other" desktop environment (that is, KDE if you're running GNOME and GNOME if you're running KDE) to your Linux system. Similarly, the Server installation class installs a few X Window system libraries and fonts, but no desktop environment or window managers. This makes it hard to do any real work on your server when you've been spoiled by the ease of use and ease of multitasking that the X Window system provides.

The next few sections list the packages necessary to add the GNOME desktop environment to a KDE or Server system, to add the KDE desktop environment to a GNOME Workstation or Server installation, and how to add the other window managers provided with your Red Hat distribution.

Packages for GNOME

The following is a list of the packages that you can install to add the GNOME desktop environment to a Custom installation, or to subsequently add GNOME to systems that you have installed as KDE Workstations or as Server installations:

- **control-center (User Interface/Desktops)**—Control center utilities for GNOME that enable users to configure the desktop background and theme, screensaver, window manager, system sounds, mouse behavior, and so on.
- **desktop-backgrounds (Applications/Multimedia)**—Desktop background images for use with desktop environments such as KDE and GNOME.
- **ee (Applications/Multimedia)**—The Electric Eyes image viewer and manipulation application for GNOME.
- **extace (Applications/Multimedia)**—An audio visualization plug-in for the Enlightened Sound Daemon (EsoundD) audio daemon, designed for use in GNOME.
- **gdm (User Interface/X)**—A highly configurable reimplementation of the X Display Manager (XDM), designed for use with GNOME.
- **gedit (Applications/Editors)**—A small but powerful text editor for the GNOME desktop environment.
- **gmc (User Interface/Desktops)**—The GNOME version of the Midnight Commander file manager.
- **gnome-audio (Applications/Multimedia)**—A package of sounds for GNOME events.
- **gnome-audio-extra (System Environment/Libraries)**—An optional set of sounds for GNOME events.
- **gnome-core (User Interface/Desktops)**—The basic programs and libraries that are needed to run GNOME. A GNOME-compliant window manager is also required.
- **gnome-games (Amusements/Games)**—Games for GNOME, including GnomeScott, ctali, freecell, gnibbles, gnobots, gnobots2, gnome-stones, gnomine, gnotravex, gtali, gturing, iagno, mahjongg, same-gnome, and sol.
- **gnome-libs (System Environment/Libraries)**—The shared libraries needed to run GNOME.
- **gnome-linuxconf (Applications/System)**—A GNOME front end for linuxconf, the Linux system configuration utility.

- **gnome-media (Applications/Multimedia)**—Media applications such as the GNOME CD player.
- **gnome-pim (Applications/Productivity)**—A Personal Information Manager (PIM) for GNOME that includes gnomecal, a personal calendar and to-do list, and gnomecard, a contact list of friends and business associates.
- **gnome-users-guide (Documentation)**—The GNOME Users' Guide.
- **gnome-utils (Applications/System)**—A set of GUI applications and desktop tools for GNOME, including Gcalc (a calculator), Gdialog (a dialog box creation tool), Gdiskfree (a disk space monitor), and many others.
- **gnorpm (Applications/System)**—A graphical front end to the RPM for GNOME.
- **gnotepad+ (Applications/Editors)**—A simple but versatile editor for GNOME.
- **gnumeric (Applications/Productivity)**—An impressive spreadsheet for GNOME. One of the best arguments for selecting GNOME over KDE.
- **gpgp (Applications/Cryptography)**—A GNOME front end for GNU Privacy Guard, a GNU implementation of pgp (Pretty Good Privacy).
- **gtop (Applications/System)**—A system monitor for GNOME that shows memory graphs and processes.
- **gxedit (Applications/Editors)**—A multifunction text editor built using the GNOME libraries and the GIMP Toolkit (GTK+).
- **libghttp (System Environment/Libraries)**—A library of functions used in the Web-based help for the GNOME desktop environment.
- **magicdev (Applications/System)**—A daemon to automatically mount and play CDs in the GNOME desktop environment.
- **rp3 (Applications/System)**—A Red Hat Linux utility for configuring PPP connections and activating and monitoring other network connections. The rp3 package includes a panel applet for use with the GNOME desktop environment.
- **switchdesk-gnome (User Interface/Desktops)**—A GNOME interface for the Desktop Switcher (switchdesk). If you install this, you'll also need to install switchdesk (User Interface/Desktops), a desktop environment switcher for GNOME, KDE, and AnotherLevel.
- **xmms-gnome (Applications/Multimedia)**—A panel applet that enables you to control the Xmms MP3 player.

Unlike KDE, GNOME doesn't come with a specific window manager. To use GNOME, you'll also have to install a GNOME-compliant window manager, such as any of the following:

- **Enlightenment (User Interface/Desktops)**—An X Window system window manager that is designed to be powerful, extensible, configurable, and attractive. If you install this window manager, you also will want to install the enlightenment-conf package (User Interface/Desktops), a configuration tool for the Enlightenment window manager.

- **Sawfish (User Interface/Desktops)**—A fast, light-weight, and powerful X Window system window manager. Sawfish is the default X Window system window manager installed in a Workstation installation using GNOME. Sawfish is extensible using the LISP programming language, which makes it a natural fit for emacs-lovers as well. If you install Sawfish, you'll probably also want to install the sawfish-themer package, which is an alternate set of themes that control the look and feel of the Sawfish window manager.
- **WindowMaker (User Interface/Desktops)**—An X Window system window manager that emulates the look and feel of the NeXTSTEP graphical user interface. If you install WindowMaker, you probably also will want to install the wmakerconf package (User Interface/Desktops), a configuration tool for WindowMaker.

Packages for KDE

The following is a list of the packages that you can install to add the KDE desktop environment during a Custom installation class, or to subsequently add KDE to systems that you have installed as GNOME workstations or as servers:

- **aktion (Applications/Multimedia)**—A movie player for KDE that supports many different file formats, including FLI, FLC, IFF, GIF87a, GIF89a, the GIF89a animation extensions, DL animations (formats 1, 2, and most of 3), Amiga MovieSetter animations, Utah Raster Toolkit RLE images and animations, AVI, and Quicktime.
- **desktop-backgrounds (Applications/Multimedia)**—Desktop background images for use with desktop environments such as KDE and GNOME.
- **kdeadmin (Applications/System)**—System administration tools for the K Desktop Environment, including kdat (tape backup), ksysv (sysV init editor), and kuser (user administration tool).
- **kdebase (User Interface/Desktops)**—Core applications for the K Desktop Environment, including kdm (replacement for xdm), kwm (window manager), kfm (file manager, Web browser, ftp client, and so on), konsole (xterm replacement), kpanel (application starter and desktop pager), kaudio (audio server), kdehelp (viewer for KDE help files, information, and man pages), kthememgr (system for managing alternate theme packages), plus other KDE components (kcheckpass, kikbd, kvt, kscreensaver, kcontrol, kfind, kfontmanager, kmenuedit, and kappfinder).
- **kdegames (Amusements/Games)**—Games for the K Desktop Environment. Included with this package are kabalone, kasteroids, kblackbox, kmahjongg, kmines, konquest, kpat, kpoker, kreversi, ksame, kshisen, ksokoban, ksmiletris, ksnake, and ksirtet.
- **kdegraphics (Applications/Multimedia)**—Graphics applications for the K Desktop Environment that include kdvi (displays TeX `.dvi` files), kfax (displays fax files), kfract (a fractal generator), kghostview (displays postscript files), kiconedit (icon editor), kpaint (a simple drawing program), ksnapshot (screen capture utility), and kview (an image viewer for GIF, JPEG, TIFF, and other graphics files).

- **kdelibs (Development/Libraries)**—Libraries for the K Desktop Environment, including kdecore (KDE core library), kdeui (user interface), kfm (file manager), khtmlw (HTML widget), kfile (file access), kspell (spelling checker), jscript (javascript), kab (address book), kimgio (image manipulation), and mediatool (sound, mixing, and animation).
- **kdemultimedia (Applications/Multimedia)**—Multimedia applications for the K Desktop Environment, including kmedia (media player), kmid (midi/karaoke player), kmidi (midi-to-wav player/converter), kmix (mixer), and kscd (CD audio player).
- **kdenetwork (Applications/Internet)**—Network applications for the K Desktop Environment, including karchie (ftp archive searcher), kbiff (mail delivery notification) kfinger ("finger" utility), kmail (mail client), knu (network utilities), korn (mailbox monitor tool), kppp (easy PPP connection configuration), krn (news reader), ktalkd (talk daemon), and ksirc (irc client).
- **kdesupport (Development/Libraries)**—Support libraries for the K Desktop Environment that are not explicitly part of it. These libraries include QwSpriteField, js (javascript), uulib, mimelib, and rdb. This package also provides extra KDE initialization files that are geared especially for Red Hat Linux systems.
- **kdetoys (Amusements/Graphics)**—Applications for the K Desktop Environment, including kmoon (displays various phases of the moon), kworldwatch (displays where in the world it is light and dark depending on the current time), and kodo (a mouse odometer that shows how far your mouse has traveled).
- **kdeutils (Applications/System)**—Utilities for the K Desktop Environment, including ark (tar/gzip archive manager), kab (address book), karm (personal time tracker), kcalc (scientific calculator), kedit (simple text editor), kfloppy (floppy formatting tool), khexedit (hex editor), kjots (note taker), klipper (Clipboard tool), kljettool(HP printer configuration tool), klpq (print queue manager), knotes (post-it notes for the desktop), kpm (process manager similar to top, but more advanced), and kwrite (improved text editor).
- **kdpms (Applications/System)**— Utilities that enable you to configure the power-saving functionality of your Display Power Management System (DPMS)-compatible monitor in KDE.
- **korganizer (Applications/Productivity)**—A complete calendar and scheduling program for KDE that supports exchanging data with other calendar applications through the industry-standard vCalendar file format.
- **kpackage (Applications/System)**—A graphical interface to the RPM package manager for the K Desktop Environment.
- **kpilot (Applications/Communications)**—Palm Pilot synchronization tools for KDE that enable you to back up and restore various Palm Pilot databases (Addressbook, ToDo List, Memos, and so on) and to install applications to the Palm Pilot.
- **kpppload (Applications/Internet)**—A PPP Link Monitor for the K Desktop Environment.

- **switchdesk-kde (User Interface/Desktops)**—A KDE interface for the Desktop Switcher (switchdesk). If you install this, you'll also have to install switchdesk (User Interface/Desktops), a desktop environment switcher for GNOME, KDE, and AnotherLevel.

Packages for Specific Window Managers

Unlike the GUIs used on personal computers, the X Window system provides a number of different window managers, each with its own look and feel. Using a window manager rather than a complete desktop environment such as GNOME or KDE places fewer demands on your system and provides a more lightweight environment in which to work. However, most window managers do not provide file managers and drag-and-drop utilities that many users find useful.

The following are some of the X Window system window managers that you can install on your system. For more information on using these window managers with the X Window system, see "Selecting and Using Different Window Managers" in Chapter 7.

- **AfterStep (User Interface/Desktops)**—An X window manager that emulates the look and feel of NeXTSTEP. If you install this package, you'll also want to install AfterStep-APPS (User Interface/Desktops); various applets, including power management, modem, sound, and load monitoring; and system status, for use with AfterStep and compatible window managers.
- **Enlightenment (User Interface/Desktops)**—An X Window System window manager that is designed to be powerful, extensible, configurable, and attractive. If you install this package, you'll probably also want to install enlightenment-conf (User Interface/Desktops), a configuration tool for the Enlightenment window manager.
- **fvwm (User Interface/Desktop)**—[The Fancy Virtual Window Manager, a highly-customizable X Window system window manager. If you install this package, you'll probably also want to install fvwm2-icons (User Interface/Desktops), graphics used by both the fvwm and fvwm2 window managers.
- **fvwm2 (User Interface/Desktops)**—An improved version of the fvwm window manager that is still actively under development. If you install this package, you'll probably also want to install AnotherLevel (User Interface/Desktops), a customized configuration for the fvwm2 window manager; and fvwm2-icons (User Interface/Desktops), graphics used by the fvwm and fvwm2 window managers.
- **Sawfish (User Interface/Desktops)**—A fast, light-weight, and powerful X Window System window manager. Sawfish is the default X Window system window manager installed in a workstation installation using GNOME. Sawfish is extensible using the LISP programming language, which makes it a natural fit for emacs-lovers as well. If you install Sawfish, you'll probably also want to install the sawfish-themer package, which is an alternate set of themes that control the look and feel of the Sawfish window manager.

- **WindowMaker (User Interface/Desktops)**—An X11 window manager that emulates the look and feel of the NeXTSTEP graphical user interface. If you install this package, you'll probably also want to install wmakerconf (User Interface/Desktops), a configuration tool for the WindowMaker window manager used for the X Window system.

Adding the X Window System to a Red Hat Server

Red Hat's Server installation class does not include support for the X Window system, which can make it hard to get any real work done on a sever console. To add the X Window system to a Red Hat server, you must install the packages for an X Window system desktop environment or X Window manager (as described in the previous three sections), plus the following packages:

- **qt (System Environment/Libraries)**—An object-oriented GUI toolkit that simplifies the task of writing and maintaining graphical user interface (GUI) applications for the X Window system.
- **Xaw3d (System Environment/Libraries)**—A library that provides three-dimensional versions of the original MIT Athena widget set for the X Window system.
- **Xconfigurator (User Interface/X Hardware Support)**—The Red Hat Linux configuration tool for the X Window system.
- **XFree86 (User Interface/X)**—The basic fonts, programs, and documents for a workstation running the X Window system.
- **XFree86-100dpi-fonts (User Interface/X)**—100dpi fonts for the X Window system.
- **XFree86-75dpi-fonts (User Interface/X)**—75dpi fonts for the X Window system.
- **XFree86-libs (System Environment/Libraries)**—The shared libraries needed by X Window system version 11, Release 6 applications on Linux.
- **XFree86-SVGA (User Interface/X Hardware Support)**—An XFree86 server for most simple framebuffer SVGA devices. This X Window system server will be sufficient to get X running on your server console; you subsequently might want to install an X Window system server that is tailored for your specific video hardware.
- **xinitrc (User Interface/X)**—The default startup script for the X Window system.
- **xpm (System Environment/Libraries)**— The XPM pixmap library for the X Window system, enabling applications to display color pixmapped images, and used by many popular X Window system applications.

Adding Packages for Database Development

Many commercial database vendors now have Linux versions of their products, but these can require a significant amount of disk space and execution overhead if all you're looking for is a small, SQL-compliant database. Several public-domain database packages and related utilities are available for Linux, the most powerful of which is the PostgreSQL SQL server. PostgreSQL is an advanced object-relational database management system (DBMS) that supports almost all SQL constructs (including transactions, subselections, and user-defined types and functions). This database and related utilities might provide all the features and power that you need. It is installed by default as part of Red Hat's Server installation class. You can easily add these packages to any Workstation or Custom installation class, space permitting. These packages are all located in the Applications/Databases section of the Individual Package List window:

- **db3utils**—The programs needed to use the Berkeley Database (Berkeley DB) embedded database for traditional and client/server applications.
- **mysql**—The programs needed to query and use a MySQL server. MySQL is a fast and powerful SQL server that is much less demanding of system resources than postgresl.
- **mysql-server**—The server component of the MySQL database package.
- **postgresl**—The programs needed to query and use a PostgreSQL server.
- **postgresl-jdbc**—Java-based client programs needed to access a PostgreSQL server.
- **postgresl-odbc**—The Open Database Connectivity (ODBC) driver needed to access a PostgreSQL server.
- **postgresl-perl**—The Perl-based client programs needed to access a PostgreSQL server.
- **postgresl-python**—The Python-based client programs needed to access a PostgreSQL server.
- **postgresl-server**—The libraries and programs needed for a PostgreSQL server.
- **postgresl-tcl**—The Tcl-based client programs and libraries needed for accessing a PostgreSQL server.
- **postgresl-test**—The source and binaries for the test suite distributed with PostgreSQL.

Adding External Office and Word Processing Packages

The Linux versions of the traditional UNIX TeX and troff word processors, known as TeTeX and groff, are automatically installed as part of both Red Hat Workstation install classes. These are text-based, markup-oriented word processors, in which you embed special commands in text files as you edit them and then process those files using other software that formats them and generates printable output. Many people have done a lot of work using these tools and still find them eminently useful today. However, most people's expectations of word processors today are very different from what these tools deliver—people want WYSIWYG (what you see is what you get) word processors that let you change fonts and styles on-the-fly and immediately see the effects of those changes.

The packages listed in this section are not located on any Red Hat CD, but these are common enough additions to Red Hat systems that it seemed reasonable to list them here to make it easier for you to find, download, and install them. Keep in mind that these are all large, time-consuming downloads.

- **AbiWord**—A powerful Open Source word processor, available from `http://www.abisource.com`.
- **ApplixWare**—A complete set of office applications, including a word processor, a spreadsheet, a presentation manager, and a graphics package. A demonstration version of this package is available from `http://www.applix.com/applixware/linux/main.cfm`.
- **Star Office**—A complete set of office applications, including a word processor, a spreadsheet, a presentation manager, and a graphics package. This entire suite is free, and can be found at `http://www.sun.com/products/staroffice`.
- **Word Perfect**—Corel provides a free Linux version of this classic and powerful word processor. The free version is fully functional and completely usable, and other versions with additional features are available very inexpensively. You can download this at `http://linux.corel.com/products/linuxproducts_wp8.htm`.

Adding Other Shells

By default, Red Hat installs the bash (Bourne-Again shell) and tcsh (enhanced csh) shells as part of all its installation classes. If you are already an experienced UNIX user and are used to ksh (Korn shell), you might want to add Linux shells that closely resemble it to your Linux system. These are located in the System Environment/Shells section of the Individual Package List window:

- **pdksh**—A public domain clone of ksh.
- **zsh**—An enhanced shell that is similar to ksh.

Adding Servers to KDE and GNOME Workstations

Red Hat's division of systems into Workstation and Server installation classes is appropriate in most cases. However, you might want to add certain servers to your GNOME or KDE workstation that are not part of the standard Workstation installation classes. These are located in the System Environment/Shells section of the Individual Package List window. The most common servers to add to a workstation are these:

- **apache**—The Apache Web server, the most popular and powerful Web server in use on the Internet today. If you are doing Web development on your GNOME or KDE workstation, you might find it convenient to have your own server to experiment with before releasing Web pages, graphics, or CGI and Perl scripts to your public Web server. If you are installing apache, you also might want to install mod_perl (also in System Environment/Daemons), a Perl interpreter for the Apache Web server that enables the Web server to directly execute Perl code.
- **inetd or xinetd**—The Internet daemon. xinetd is a more flexible and powerful version of the standard inetd used on Red Hat systems before Red Hat 6.2. Beginning with Red Hat 7.0, the Internet daemon is not installed as a part of a Workstation class install. If you want to support services such as inbound FTP, telnet, and so on on your system, you will want to install the inetd or xinetd package.

- **knfsd**—The kernel NFS server and related tools. These provide much better performance than the traditional Linux NFS server. Linux and UNIX tend to blur the differences between workstations and servers. For example, you might want to export certain directories from your workstation for the convenience of other members of any projects that you are working on. The NFS daemon and related tools are installed as part of Red Hat's Server installation class, but not as a default part of any other installation class.
- **samba**—Clients for interacting with Samba, the Windows networking software for Linux systems, are installed as a part of both Workstation installation classes, but the Samba server is not. The Samba server enables you to export file systems on your machine, making them available to Windows users over the network. You might want to export certain directories from your workstation for the convenience of other members of any projects that you are working on.

Locating Individual Packages

All the binary packages available for installation as part of Red Hat Linux are located in the `RedHat/RPMS` subdirectory of your Red Hat Linux CDs. Even if you do not install them as part of your initial Red Hat Linux installation, you can subsequently install packages using the `rpm` command, which is explained more detail in Chapter 11.

When your Linux system is up and running, you can locate any package that is part of the Red Hat distribution by doing the following:

1. Mount the first or second Red Hat CD using a command such as `mount /mnt/cdrom`.
2. Change your working directory of the Red Hat/RPMS directory of your first Red Hat installation CD using a command such as `cd /mnt/cdrom/RedHat/RPMS`.
3. Find the package you want. The names of the files containing the packages listed in the previous section consist of the package name, a version number, and the rpm extension. For example, to locate the package containing the gimp GNU image manipulation program, you would execute a command such as `ls *gimp*`.
4. Identify the package file(s) that you need to install, and install them using RPM, as explained in Chapter 10.

Verifying Package Dependencies

After selecting the packages that you want to install for any Red Hat Linux installation class, the Red Hat Installer analyzes the packages that you have selected and displays a screen that lists any "dependencies" that are present, but are unsatisfied, in the packages you have selected. These dependencies are other pieces of software that are required by the packages you have selected, but which are not actually present in them. If you do not somehow address these dependencies, the packages you install may not work correctly.

You are given three options:

- **Install Packages to Satisfy Dependencies**—This option tells the Red Hat Installer to locate and also install any other packages required by the packages you have selected.
- **Do Not Install Packages That Have Dependencies**—Do not install any of the previously selected packages that have dependencies on applications outside of those packages.
- **Ignore Package Dependencies**—This is almost always a poor choice, unless you recognize the specific piece of software on which the dependency exists, and know that it is an application that you will never use.

Text-Mode Installer: Package Installation Begins

If you are using the text-mode installer, the actual Red Hat installation begins at this point, after displaying a window identifying the name of the file in which a log of your installation will be saved

NOTE

If you are doing a Red Hat Custom installation and have select Everything as the list of packages to install, the Red Hat installer prompts you to insert the second CD during the installation process. Insert the second CD and select OK to proceed.

Configuring the X Window System

NOTE

Red Hat's text mode installer installs packages before configuring the X Window system on your computer. Red Hat's X Window system installer installs packages after configuring the X Window system on your computer. Some parts of configuring the X Window system are specific to the installer you are using—these are identified in the following sections.

The X Window system—commonly referred to as "X," which is anathema to true X Window system devotees—is a network-aware graphics windowing system that originally was developed at the Massachusetts Institute of Technology (MIT), but that is based on earlier windowing systems such as Stanford's W window system. (W comes right before X.) The X Window system provides a set of capabilities for creating and working with applications that is similar to what Microsoft Windows and the Macintosh operating system provide. The X Window system is the industry standard windowing system for computers running versions of UNIX, Linux, Compaq's VMS operating system, and many other operating systems. The X Window system was designed for use on multiprocessing networked computer systems and is far more powerful than the personal computer graphics systems mentioned earlier. On the other hand, user-friendliness is a relatively new concept to the X Window system.

The X Window system uses the terms client and server in slightly unique ways. An X Window system server is a process that runs on a single computer system and that manages the interaction between that system's graphics cards and monitors and any X Window system applications using those devices. X Window system applications are commonly known as clients. Because the X Window system is network-aware, clients running on one system can easily display their output as well as any windows that they create on any X Window system display that they are authorized to connect to. A third class of X Window system applications, known as window managers, manages the interaction between client windows and X servers. Window managers control how client windows are manipulated, managed, and displayed and also govern the decoration for client windows, such as buttons, menus, headers, resizing controls, and every other graphical bell and whistle that you can think of.

This section and Chapter 7, which gives a more detailed discussion of configuring and customizing the X Window system, both focus on getting the X Window system installed and running on your Red Hat Linux system. Discussing the details of using the X Window system is outside the scope of this book, but many excellent guides to using various X Window system window managers and clients are available commercially and on the Web.

NOTE

If the default settings selected by the Red Hat Installer don't work for your hardware, or if you don't want to deal with configuring the X Window system at this point, the second X Configuration screen gives you the option to skip configuring X at this time. When the rest of your Red Hat system is installed and configured, see Chapter 7 for information on configuring the X Window system on your computer.

Requirements for Running the X Window System

If you are using Red Hat's graphical installer, you can skip to the next section because this installer runs under the X Window system, and your system therefore is capable of running the X Window system. The Red Hat X Window system installer runs at a "safe" resolution for most monitors and graphics cards, not at the best resolution possible for your graphics card and monitor. This section and Chapter 7 help you configure the X Window system to take advantage of the capabilities of your graphics card, chip, and monitor. Don't panic if Red Hat's X Window system looks bad on your system—we'll fix that.

The basic requirements for running the X Window system on a Linux system are

- A graphics card or chip with 1MB or better of memory, capable of displaying graphics at a resolution of 600×480 or better.

- A monitor capable of displaying graphics at a resolution of 600×480 or better.
- A mouse or other point-and-click device.

If you press the Return key when you see the Welcome to Red Hat! screen after you boot your system from a Red Hat CD or disk, the installer program probes your system's hardware to see whether your computer's video circuitry and monitor have sufficient memory and power to run any version of the X Window system. The installer also checks to see whether a mouse or similar point-and-click device is found on your system. Just because Red Hat could not start the X Window system version of the installer does not mean that you cannot run the X Window system. The most common causes of not starting the X Window system version of the Red Hat Installer are the following:

- You typed `text` at the boot prompt on the first Welcome to Red Hat! screen. This runs Red Hat's text-mode installer regardless of the capabilities of your system.
- The installer could not detect a mouse or similar input device, such as a tablet or trackball, on your system. Regardless of the capabilities of your graphics card, chip, and monitor, you cannot run the X Window system without one of these devices because they are the primary way in which you interact with X Window system clients (such as the installer).
- Red Hat's X Window system installer could not uniquely identify your graphics card, chip, and monitor well enough to start the X Window system, or the installer might start it in an unusable mode. Hardware such as older, low-resolution monitors and motherboards with integrated video hardware could cause problems using Red Hat's X Window system installer, rendering it unreadable. If you encounter any problems using the X Window system installer, reboot your system and start the text-mode Red Hat installer by entering the word `text` and pressing Enter when you see the first Welcome to Red Hat! splash screen. Don't worry—there's still an excellent chance that you'll get the X Window system running in this chapter or Chapter 7.

Basic X Window System Configuration

Whether you are using Red Hat's graphical or text-mode installers, both provide the opportunity to configure the X Window system for the X Window system server that is most appropriate for your graphics card or chip and your monitor.

Selecting a Monitor

If you are using Red Hat's X Window system–based installer, the installer attempts to identify your monitor at this point. If you are using Red Hat's text mode installer, skip this section.

Detecting the capabilities of your monitor can be quite difficult. Millions of generic monitors are available today that vary slightly in capabilities, and laptop manufacturers usually don't have the courtesy to identify the type of LCD display used in your laptop. Red Hat's installer uses DDC, the Display Data Channel facility that enables monitors to provide information about the capabilities that they support.

The Red Hat Installer first attempts to probe your monitor to identify its capabilities. If this is successful, the X Window system installer displays a Monitors window, listing the results obtained from probing your system. You should always accept these values when configuring the X Window system for the first time. If they are incorrect, you can always run the XConfigurator utility separately to try to devise a more optimal X Window system configuration.

If the Red Hat Installer cannot identify your monitor by probing, the X Configuration screen displays a scrollable window from which you must select your monitor (if you're lucky), another monitor with capabilities that are exactly the same as yours, or a generic monitor (and then supply detailed information about its capabilities).

NOTE

If you must select a monitor manually, it is extremely important that you either select the correct monitor from this list or supply the correct information about your monitor when prompted to do so. The X Window system works your graphics circuitry and monitor very hard, and pushing these beyond their capabilities can damage them. Find the scraps of documentation that came with your monitor, contact the vendor, or search the Web for this information. You must have these details unless you are thoroughly versed in the hardware aspects of computer graphics cards and display devices or are willing to take a chance.

Following are some tips on selecting a monitor:

- If you are configuring the X Window system on a laptop, look for a monitor description that begins with the name of the vendor who made the laptop. For example, many of the LCD screens used in IBM ThinkPads are listed as various models of IBM TFT Panel (where TFT stands for Thin Film Transistor or some more amusing phrase).
- If in doubt and other monitors from the same vendor as yours are listed, it is usually safe to select an older, less-capable monitor from the same vendor. You can always fine-tune your X Window system configuration as described in Chapter 7, but getting the X Window system running in the first place will make your Linux system a friendlier and more usable system, especially if you are new to Linux.
- When in doubt, select Generic Monitor, use those settings for now, and read Chapter 7 for information on experimenting with other X Window system settings.
- You can always skip the X Window system configuration section for now by selecting Skip X Configuration. After the rest of your Red Hat system is installed and configured, see Chapter 7 for information on configuring your X Window system settings.

Selecting a Video Card or Chip Set

After you complete the package selection section of the Red Hat Installation process, the installer enters the initial X Configuration section. If you are running the X Window system–based installer, Red Hat already has identified your video card or chip set. If you are running the text-based installer, the installer now attempts to identify your video card or chip set. If it cannot uniquely identify your video hardware (which is rarely the case), the text installer displays "Which video card do you have?" onscreen. If this displays, consult the documentation that came with your system and select the most appropriate video card or chip set from the list.

Both the Red Hat X Window system and text-mode installers automatically probe your video hardware when they first display the X Configuration screen. If you are using Red Hat's text mode installer, the results of probing your hardware are displayed on the screen in a window labeled "X probe results."

Specifying Video Memory

NOTE

This section only displays if you are using Red Hat's text-mode installer.

Next, the Red Hat text-mode installer displays a screen that prompts you for the amount of physical memory found on your video card. Select the appropriate amount and select or click OK.

Specifying Your Clock Chip

NOTE

This section only displays if you are using Red Hat's text-mode installer.

Next, the Red Hat text-mode installer displays a screen that prompts you for the type of programmable clock chip found on your video card. This chip is responsible for synchronizing video output at various rates and frequencies. Unless you're sure that your video card contains a clock chip, select the default option No Clock Chip and select or click OK to proceed.

Probing for Clocks

NOTE

This section only displays if you are using Red Hat's text-mode installer.

Next, the Red Hat text-mode installer displays a screen that asks you whether you want the X Configurator to probe your video card for clock chips or RAMDAC (Random Access Memory Digital-to-Analog Converter) used to display graphics on your monitor screen. This is usually the right thing to do. Select or click the Probe button to proceed. If the probe of your video card is successful, a subsequent dialog will display the values detected and ask if you want to use them. If the probe fails, a dialog stating that the default values will be used is displayed. Select or click OK to proceed.

Selecting Video Modes

This section only displays if you are using Red Hat's text-mode installer.

Next, the Red Hat text-mode installer displays a screen that enables you to select the video resolutions and bit depths (the number of bits of color used for each pixel on your screen) to be used with the X Window system on your computer. You must select at least one value. I typically select the same range of video modes in each of the three bit depths (8-bit, 16-bit, and 24-bit). I personally prefer to use either 800×600 or 1024×768, but many people also select 1280×1024 and 1600×1200. The maximum value you should select depends on the capabilities of your video card and the size of your monitor. In Red Hat's text-mode installer, you can use the arrow keys to move up and down within a row, and the Tab key to move from row to row or to the OK button. Once you're finished selecting modes, select or click OK to proceed.

Testing Your X Window System Settings

This section only displays if you are using Red Hat's text-mode installer.

When you've selected your monitor, an appropriate alternative, or a generic type, select Test This Configuration to start the X Window system with your current settings. The installer will try to start the X Window system and will time out after 10 seconds. Even if your screen is totally unreadable, you can just wait 10 seconds (and then try other settings).

If you've found that only a generic monitor setting works but that the quality of that display is unsuitable, you can select the Customize X Configuration option on the X Configuration screen. After selecting this option, select Next to display a screen on which you can select better resolutions that might work with your current settings. You can start at the highest available resolution and color depth (bits per pixel), and work your way down to hopefully find better settings than the defaults for the monitor you've selected.

Other X Window System Configuration Options

The Use Graphical Login option on the X Configuration screen configures your Red Hat system to automatically start an X Window system application called the X Display Manager (xdm) and to use this when logging in on the console of your Red Hat system. This is a good idea if the system you are installing is intended for users who do not want to start a specific window manager (or users who do not know how to do so), or if you have a standard X Window system configuration that is shared by all the users in your computing environment.

As a long-time Linux/UNIX geek, I personally prefer not to select this option and to start my X Window manager du jour using the `startx` or `xinit` commands. Not using the X Display Manager and starting X with these commands makes it much easier to experiment with different window managers.

Different ways of starting the X Window system are discussed in more detail in Chapter 7.

X Window System Installer: Package Installation Begins

If you are using the X Window system installer, the actual Red Hat installation begins at this point, after displaying a window identifying the name of the file in which a log of your installation will be saved.

NOTE

If you are doing a Red Hat Custom installation and have selected Everything as the list of packages to install, the Red Hat installer prompts you to insert the second CD during the installation process. Insert the second CD and select OK to proceed.

Creating Boot Disks

After installing Red Hat Linux and beginning the X Window system installation and configuration process, the Red Hat Installer displays the Bootdisk screen, which enables you to create a boot disk for your system that doesn't require LILO. Creating such a boot disk is always a good idea. The boot disks you used to begin the installation process aren't suitable for use when trying to resolve a system problem because they are designed for use during a generic installation. Therefore, they don't have any special information about your system's configuration or any specific tools that you may need to use to try to recover from system problems.

If you ever need to use it, such a boot disk will be invaluable. If you ever have system problems serious enough to need to use this boot disk, you'll have to make sure that your system's boot sequence is configured to boot from a floppy disk before attempting to boot from the hard drive. To do this, you can follow the boot sequence configuration information in Chapter 3, "Beginning Your Red Hat Installation."

To create a boot floppy, select Yes on the Bootdisk screen. The boot disk is created at the end of the Red Hat installation process on your system.

Congratulations!

Congratulations! A summary screen displays, reminding you to remove any boot media and then reboot your system by selecting OK. The Red Hat installers automatically eject the CD from which you have installed Red Hat Linux—remove the CDs quickly, as the installers automatically close the CD drawer after rebooting.

After rebooting, you're running Red Hat Linux 7.0!

CHAPTER 6

Starting and Stopping Red Hat Linux

When you have a Red Hat Linux system installed and running, you'll probably want to take a bit of time to familiarize yourself with how the system boots and how it starts and stops various services and associated processes. Perhaps most importantly, you'll need to learn how to shut down the system or at least prevent other people from using it while you add and configure new hardware, reconfigure existing hardware or services, or enhance system security to protect yourself from ever-smarter hackers with more sophisticated tools.

If you've administered UNIX systems before, you're in luck. Linux systems follow the startup/shutdown models of SYSV UNIX systems. Linux systems also preserve enough of the startup/shutdown model of BSD UNIX systems so that no one will be totally lost, but everyone gets to learn something.

This chapter explains the sequence of events that take place when you boot a Red Hat Linux system, beginning with the actual motherboard boot process. Subsequent sections discuss using the Linux Loader (which is not mandatory, but is highly recommended), the kernel boot process, and the different run levels provided by Red Hat Linux.

The final sections of this chapter explain how to resolve hardware problems that might keep you from being able to use all the devices attached to your system, and how to manually start and stop Linux system services if you are experiencing problems. The final section explains how to shut down Red Hat Linux systems, either to the point at which you can power them off, or to the point at which you are the only user and can do hardware and software maintenance and reconfiguration.

The BIOS Boot Process

As explained in Chapter 3, "Beginning Your Red Hat Installation," the basic input/output system (BIOS) chip is located on your motherboard. The BIOS chip controls your system's initial interaction with all its peripherals, from keyboard and mouse ports to floppy, disk, and CD-ROM drives. Other boards in your system might have their own BIOS chips, specifically cards for more advanced I/O support such as SCSI and Firewire support.

When you power up your system, the motherboard loads the BIOS and probes the status of all its interfaces, including those to storage devices where your operating system is located. As explained in Chapter 3, different BIOS chips have different mechanisms for accessing and controlling the boot sequence, which determines the devices from which your system will attempt to boot and in what order.

NOTE

After you've installed and configured Red Hat Linux on your system, you probably will want to password-protect the BIOS on the motherboard so that no one but you can modify the sequence in which it attempts to boot from various devices. You probably also will want to remove floppy and removable media devices from the boot sequence so that no malicious individual can boot your system from his own media and either break in or delete information.

After your system has verified the health of the motherboard and the existence of various peripherals, it follows the boot sequence and tries to load the Master Boot Record (MBR) from devices in the order that they are listed. The MBR is located in the first sector of cylinder 0, track 0, head 0 on each storage device attached to your system. (Track 0 of most devices is usually reserved for boot information—most partitions actually begin with cylinder 0, sector 0, head 1.)

The MBR describes how the device it is associated with is partitioned. The MBR also contains the actual boot loader, which can identify any bootable partitions on the device. Boot loaders generally do one of three things:

1. Pass control directly to an operating system, such as Linux or DOS.
2. Serve as multiboot utilities. Boot loaders such as the Linux Loader (LILO), PowerQuest's Boot Magic, or the Windows NT boot loader all fall into this category.
3. Start a virus. Although this is meant to be somewhat amusing, it really isn't funny at all. There are no Linux viruses, although there are plenty of malicious utilities. However, if you have configured your system to boot either Linux or any DOS/Windows combination, it's quite possible that an MBR virus could infect your system from a DOS/Window session, which then would be run the next time you boot your system. You can protect yourself against this to some extent by activating the option on most motherboards to enable virus-checking. At the BIOS level, virus-checking generally just warns you when any application tries to write to the MBR of any of your drives.

At this point, most Linux systems run LILO, which is discussed in the next section.

Configuring the Linux Loader

The Linux Loader (LILO) is a powerful, flexible boot loader that uses a configuration file to describe any options you have when booting your system. This configuration file is located in the Linux file system, in the file `/etc/lilo.conf`, by default. LILO configuration files consist of a set of global options followed by a number of sections with unique names, one for each device that you want to boot from. Global options apply to all bootable partitions in the file unless they are overridden following that image/other statement.

NOTE

If your system boots only one operating system (Linux, of course) and you never plan to compile your own kernel, you can skip this section for now and move on to the section "Booting Red Hat Linux." Some of the information in this section on making your Linux system more secure might still be of interest later.

A sample `lilo.conf` file for a multiboot system looks like the following:

```
boot=/dev/hda
map=/boot/map
install=/boot/boot.b
vga=ask
prompt
timeout=100
default=linux

image=/boot/vmlinuz-2.2.12-20
        label=linux
        initrd=/boot/initrd-2.2.12-20.img
        read-only
        root=/dev/hda5

other=/dev/hda1
        label=dos
```

Each image statement defines one Linux kernel image and associated information. The Linux kernel is the core part of the Linux operating system, handing all of the input and output to and from different devices, managing running processes and memory allocation, and so on. An easy way to think of the Linux kernel is that it is the equivalent of the DOS/Windows `command.com` file or the Macintosh System file on serious steroids. A LILO configuration file can contain 16 different image statements, or up to 15 image statements and one other statement.

The full documentation for LILO is installed in `/usr/doc` when you install the LILO package from your Red Hat distribution. The majority of the commands that can appear in a `lilo.conf` file are described in the reference page for `lilo.conf`, found in the online manual by typing **man lilo.conf** on a Linux system. As a quick reference, the most commonly used global options are shown in the previous example, and have the following meanings:

- **boot**—Identifies the boot device.
- **default**—Identifies the label associated with the image or other partition that LILO should boot if you do not specify another label before the period specified by the timeout keyword expires.
- **install**—Identifies the location of a file that LILO should use as the actual boot block. Your system's BIOS must be capable of accessing the partition on which this file is located.
- **map**— Identifies a file that begins with a magic number (to verify its authenticity), contains a command line (optional) and options to run when booting, and contains pointers to the first block of each bootable image referred to in the `lilo.conf` file. Your system's BIOS must be capable of accessing the partition on which this file is located.
- **prompt**—Requires that you enter the label associated with the image or the name of any boot options that you want to supply to the boot process. This is overridden by the timeout option when that option expires.
- **timeout**—Specifies the amount of time, in tenths of a second, that Linux will wait before booting the default or first image in your `lilo.conf` file.

NOTE

When deploying Linux systems that do not boot multiple operating systems, setting the timeout value to 0 is a good security measure. Systems with this setting automatically boot the default or first image listed in the `/etc/lilo.conf` file without giving anyone the opportunity to specify alternate boot options.

- **vga**—Specifies the VGA video mode to be used when the console is in standard terminal mode (that is, during the boot process and when not running the X Window system). You can specify fixed video resolutions from 80×24 (the default) to 130×44. Using the `vga=ask` setting displays a list of possible options and lets you select one.

The most commonly used options associated with specific boot images or other files are

- **initrd**—Specifies a file to be loaded at boot-time as a RAM disk.
- **label**—A unique name associated with each image or other file.
- **read-only**—Specifies that the file system should initially be mounted read-only so that it can be checked for errors before being subsequently being mounted in read/write form.
- **root**—The physical partition that contains the Linux partition to be mounted as "/".

When LILO starts, it displays the LILO: prompt. At this point and before the timeout period elapses, you can press Tab to see a list of the boot options on your system, enter the label for any of the bootable partitions on your system, or press Return to tell LILO to boot the partition whose label is identified by the `default` keyword.

NOTE

If your Linux system is an SMP system, the default `lilo.conf` file created for your system contains at least two image entries, one for SMP mode (`label=linux`), and one for uniprocessor mode (`label=linux-up`) if you encounter problems running with both processors. They are automatically mapped to multiprocessor and uniprocessor versions of the Linux kernel if the Red Hat Installer can detect that your machine has more than one processor.

As mentioned in the discussion of partitions in Chapter 2, "Preparing Your System for Red Hat," the `/boot` partition is typically used to hold different Linux kernels that you are experimenting with. If you are hacking the kernel and want to test your changes, you would copy your new kernel to the `/boot` partition and add another entry to `/etc/lilo.conf`, perhaps like the following:

```
image=/boot/vmlinuz-caching-controller-1.0.9-test
        label=caching
        read-only
        root=/dev/hdc1
```

This section defines a special kernel image, also located on the `/boot` partition, that I was using when testing drivers for a caching disk controller. The label for this boot option is caching, and the root partition for my experiments was `/dev/hdc1`. (Hint: When experimenting with drivers that change how and when data is saved to disk, do not test this with any data that you depend upon.)

Whenever you make a change to the contents of your `lilo.conf` file, you must rerun the `/etc/lilo` command to create a new map file and verify the syntax of your `lilo.conf` file. If you are modifying your LILO options, you should always make sure that you have a bootable floppy available, in case you somehow damage your system's MBR.

If you damage your system's MBR on a multiboot system that also runs DOS, you can get the machine's DOS environment up and running quickly with the following procedure:

1. Boot from a bootable DOS disk that contains the FDISK utility.
2. Execute the `FDISK /MBR` command to restore the DOS MBR to the disk. This overwrites only the boot loader code in the MBR, not the partition table.
3. Make the DOS partition active using the `FDISK` command.

Booting Red Hat Linux

After LILO reads its configuration file, it begins the process of booting either the default Linux kernel or any other kernel that you specify. LILO does this by reading the specified map file to find the appropriate kernel, identifying any RAM disks to load to expedite the boot process, and then loading the kernel into memory and executing it.

As the kernel starts, it displays many messages on your screen as it probes your hardware, sets internal configuration options based on the video and memory detected, and then starts the `/sbin/init` process to start the system processes and servers that are required to actually make your system usable.

Overview of Red Hat Run Levels

The init program is the parent of all other processes on a Linux system. After it is started by the kernel, the init program reads the `/etc/inittab` file, which defines the commands used for system initialization and the system's default run level.

Linux and all other SYSV-based UNIX-likes use the term *run level* to refer to the collection of system processes and servers that should (or should not) be running to use your system in a specific way. For example, if you want people to log in on your Linux system and get some work done, you'll want all system services to be available. You will want a login prompt displayed on the console and any other terminals attached to your system so that you can log in, and you'll want to make the ftp and telnet daemons available so that people can access your machine over the network. On the other hand, if you are doing system maintenance tasks such as moving files and directories around, adding disks or file systems, and so on, you really don't want anyone to be able to remotely access your system until you're done changing things. Linux provides different run levels to simplify identifying different sets of processes and system services that should be available for different types of tasks.

Different UNIX-like systems use certain run levels for different purposes. Red Hat Linux uses the following run levels:

- **0: Halt**—Nothing is running. This is used to prepare your system for being turned off.
- **1: Single user mode**—This run level is used to perform system maintenance. No inbound network services are available, and the console is the only available terminal on your system.
- **2: Multiuser mode without NFS and other network services**—If your system isn't connected to a network, this run level is the same as run level 3.
- **3: Full multiuser mode**—All network services are running, and all terminals attached to your system are available. Any authorized user can log in on your system and do whatever is needed.
- **4: Unused**—You can use this run level to create your own custom set of services if you routinely want to make your system available in specific ways. For example, if you are using your system as a database server, you can use this run level for database testing. This would enable you to export databases in read-only mode to verify connectivity and privileges without letting anyone actually modify data.
- **5: X11 display manager**—This run level is used when an X Window system display manager is running on the console.

- **6: Reboot**—This run level is used to shut down and reboot your system. This run level is essentially the same as run level 0, except that it reboots your system rather than halting it.

Run levels actually work in two directions. Ordinarily, you want to bring your system up to a specific run level, such as multiuser mode. In this case, the init process runs the commands necessary to get to run level 3. On the other hand, you can imagine running your system in run level 3 (multiuser mode) and then discovering a problem that you can fix only when no other users are using your system (run level 1, single-user mode). For this reason, two flavors of the scripts are associated with each Red Hat run level: startup scripts that begin with a capital "S," and kill scripts that begin with a capital "K." These guarantee that only processes associated with a specific run level are active at that run level, providing a mechanism for terminating any processes that are inappropriate for that run level. Although you might not need this information at this point, it's important to realize that each run level provides a mechanism for both starting and stopping specific services. I'll discuss customizing run levels in more detail later in this chapter.

Overview of `/etc/inittab`

Each Red Hat Linux run level is defined by an entry in the `/etc/inittab` file, as is other important information used by the init process. The following is an excerpt from the `/etc/inittab` showing these types of entries:

```
id:3:initdefault:
si::sysinit:/etc/rc.d/rc.sysinit
l0:0:wait:/etc/rc.d/rc 0
l1:1:wait:/etc/rc.d/rc 1
l2:2:wait:/etc/rc.d/rc 2
l3:3:wait:/etc/rc.d/rc 3
l4:4:wait:/etc/rc.d/rc 4
l5:5:wait:/etc/rc.d/rc 5
l6:6:wait:/etc/rc.d/rc 6
```

The format of each line in this file is as follows:

```
label:run level(s):init action:command
```

The `label` is an arbitrary label, the `run level` is any run levels associated with this entry, and the `init` keyword tells the init process when to execute the specified command and how to respond if the command fails.

The first two lines in this example provide important information for the init process when you first start your Red Hat system. The line that begins with `id` uses the `initdefault` command in the third field of this entry to identify your system's default run level as run level 3. In Red Hat Linux, when you first power on your system or subsequently restart it, the init process automatically brings the system up in run level 3. If you answered yes to the question about automatically starting the X Window system in the Configuring X portion of the Red Hat Installer, the default run level for your system will be run level 5 instead of run level 3.

The line that begins with `si` defines a shell script that the system uses to initialize internal variables and services when you first start the system, before moving to any other run level. The keyword `sysinit` tells the `init` command to perform the specified command to do system initialization before entering any run level.

Each of the lines beginning with `l` followed by a number specify the command that the system should execute to enter a specific run level. The next section of this chapter discusses system initialization, and is followed by a section that provides more details about what actually takes place when a system enters a certain run level.

System Initialization Overview

Many stages of system initialization are performed before moving to a specific run level, all of which are subject to change. This section provides an overview of system initialization and describes specific stages in that initialization that you might need to know about to add hardware to your system or to resolve disk problems. The one true source for everything that your system does during system initialization is the script identified by the `si` entry in your `/etc/inittab` file, usually `/etc/rc.d/rc.sysinit`.

NOTE

If your Red Hat Linux system boots with no problems and correctly initializes all your hardware, you can safely skip this section for now. If you ever add hardware to your system that Red Hat cannot identify or use, you can come back to this section for help.

The `si` entry in `/etc/inittab` defines a shell script to run to initialize the system itself before moving to any run level. This performs tasks such as setting the system's name and clock, and initializing various system services. To initialize different parts of your Red Hat Linux system, the system initialization script reads various configuration files located in `/etc/sysconfig`. For example, configuration information for network services is located in the file `/etc/sysconfig/network`. Much of the system configuration work done for you by the linuxconf program (discussed in Chapter 10, "Configuring Network Services") actually involves modifying these files and then restarting any services associated with them for the current run level.

One of the most important stages in system initialization occurs when your system identifies and loads any modules that it requires. Loadable modules are compiled files containing drivers for any devices that were not compiled into your kernel, but which are required by your system. Loadable modules are a key aspect of the flexibility of Linux because they enable Linux users to run the same kernel on many different hardware configurations. The specific modules needed to interact with your hardware are loaded during system initialization rather than having to be compiled into the kernel. Older versions of Linux (and UNIX, for that matter) required support for different devices to be compiled into the kernel. This meant that users often had to rebuild the kernel to add new hardware to their systems. This isn't as scary as it sounds, but it certainly was a pain even in the best of circumstances.

The final step in system initialization before entering a specific run level is to check the consistency of all the file systems that are to be mounted. The `/etc/rc.d/rc.sysinit` script does this by first verifying the consistency of the root file system (the file system to be mounted as `/`). If this file system is okay, the system initialization script then mounts that file system, reads the file `/etc/fstab` (file system table), and checks file systems in the order specified in that file. Verifying a file system is generally known as fsck'ing your file systems. The version of fsck (File System Consistency checK) that runs on your system depends on the type of file systems used on your system. Most Linux systems use ext2 file systems for data storage, so the Linux system actually runs `fsck.ext2` to check file systems of this type. Most of the problems encountered by any version of fsck, such as bad date/time stamps on files, are automatically corrected.

NOTE

Identifying the meaning and proper response to all possible fsck problems is an art form and is outside the scope of this book. If you encounter file system problems at this point, the `rc.sysinit` script automatically gives you the option of rebooting to log in as the root user and run fsck manually to try to resolve the problem. See the section of Chapter 9, "Troubleshooting fsck Problems" for general information on resolving common problems reported when checking file system consistency—and good luck!

Assuming that all goes well and that no problems are detected on your file systems, the `rc.sysinit` script then mounts those file systems as specified in `/etc/fstab`, logging each successful mount in the file `/etc/mtab` (mount table).

Entering a Run Level

The excerpt of the `/etc/inittab` file shown previously is as follows:

```
id:3:initdefault:
si::sysinit:/etc/rc.d/rc.sysinit
l0:0:wait:/etc/rc.d/rc 0
l1:1:wait:/etc/rc.d/rc 1
l2:2:wait:/etc/rc.d/rc 2
l3:3:wait:/etc/rc.d/rc 3
l4:4:wait:/etc/rc.d/rc 4
l5:5:wait:/etc/rc.d/rc 5
l6:6:wait:/etc/rc.d/rc 6
```

The lines beginning with `l` followed by a number specify the command that the system should execute to enter a specific run level. For example, the entry for run level 3 is the following:

```
l3:3:wait:/etc/rc.d/rc 3
```

This entry tells the init process to run the command `/etc/rc.d/rc 3` to get to run level 3, and to wait until that script executes successfully before doing anything else. To make it easier to manage different run levels, the scripts for each Red Hat run level are located in a separate directory. For example, to get to run level 3, the /etc/rc.d/rc script actually runs scripts located in the directory /etc/rc.d/rc3.d.

When moving to a specific run level, the /etc/rc.d/rc script first runs all the kill scripts associated with that run level to make sure that nothing is running that isn't appropriate for that run level. For run level 3, these would be all the scripts that begin with K and are located in the directory /etc/rc.d/rc3.d. The rc script then runs the startup scripts for the target run level to guarantee that the processes associated with that run level are active. For run level 3, these would be all the scripts that begin with S and that are located in the directory /etc/rc.d/rc3.d.

If you do a long directory listing of the files in any of the rc.* directories, you'll see something interesting:

```
[/etc/rc.d] ls -al rc3.d | more
lrwxrwxrwx 1 root  root       14 Sep 16  1997 K05innd -> ../init.d/innd
lrwxrwxrwx 1 root  root       15 Sep 16  1997 K10pulse -> ../init.d/pulse
[additional entries deleted]
```

All the kill and startup scripts in the directory for each run level are actually symbolic links to master scripts located in the directory /etc/rc.d/init.d. These scripts either start or stop services depending on how they are called. Using symbolic links to master scripts ensures that you have to modify only the scripts in one location (if you ever have to modify them at all). Because multiple run levels may execute the same startup and kill scripts, those run levels automatically pick up your changes to the master scripts.

/etc/inittab Commands Executed After Entering a Run Level

After running the script associated with a specific run level, the init process reads the rest of the /etc/inittab file, looking for other entries associated with the current run level. The next ones it finds are typically the ones that start the process that enables users to log in on the various virtual consoles provided by Linux. These entries are the following:

```
1:2345:respawn:/sbin/mingetty tty1
2:2345:respawn:/sbin/mingetty tty2
3:2345:respawn:/sbin/mingetty tty3
4:2345:respawn:/sbin/mingetty tty4
5:2345:respawn:/sbin/mingetty tty5
6:2345:respawn:/sbin/mingetty tty6
```

The respawn keyword in the third field tells the init process that it should restart any of these processes whenever they exit. The /sbin/mingetty program is an enhanced version of the standard UNIX getty program that displays a login prompt on a terminal, enables you to log in and enter your password there, and then starts a specified shell so that you can interact with the computer.

The consoles listed in this section are the same virtual consoles that were used during the Red Hat installation process, as described in Chapter 3. After you've installed your system, the virtual consoles defined by `/etc/inittab` are accessed by pressing the keys Alt+F1 through Alt+F6. Each of these consoles provides a character-based login, exactly as you would see if you were using a dumb terminal. When you start the X Window system, you still can switch to the other virtual consoles, but you must do so using the key sequence Ctrl+Alt+*Fx*, where *Fx* is the number of the function key that corresponds to the virtual console that you want to switch to. You can switch back to the X Window system at any time by pressing Alt+F7 from a character-based virtual console.

After starting the mingetty process on each virtual terminal, The init process then runs the commands located in the file `/etc/rc.d/rc.local`. This is a holdover from BSD UNIX systems, in which this file contained startup commands that were specific to a given system, such as commands for setting the hostname and so on. This file still is used by Red Hat Linux as a location from which to start commands that are specific to your system, even though some of these tasks—such as setting the hostname and IP address—now are done much earlier. I tend to use this file as a location from which to start system services, such as AppleTalk emulation, network port monitoring, and performance tweaks, that I've compiled and added myself. Whenever I upgrade a system, I then can simply check this file to see what things I've added to ensure that I've preserved them before upgrading.

Resolving Module and Hardware Startup Problems

As discussed earlier in this chapter, loadable modules provide a way for Linux to support many different types of hardware without requiring support for that hardware to be compiled into the kernel. Loadable modules are your last ray of hope when you start your Red Hat Linux system and see error messages as it attempts to initialize some of your hardware. Before deciding that a missing or incorrect loadable module is the culprit, you should always use the linuxconf program or other configuration utilities to verify that your hardware is configured correctly. For example, there's no point in trying to build a loadable module for your network card if the actual problem is that your system mistakenly shares a network address with a machine at a nearby university.

NOTE

If your Red Hat Linux system boots with no problems and correctly initializes all your hardware, you can safely skip this section for now. If you ever add hardware to your system that Red Hat cannot automatically identify or use, you can come back to this section for help.

Red Hat Linux provides a large collection of loadable modules for the most common network cards, video cards, parallel and serial ports, and so on found in Linux systems today. Most Linux users never have to use loadable modules other than those that are automatically provided and loaded during system initialization. However, for people whose hardware isn't automatically detected or is detected incorrectly (most commonly network cards), loadable modules provide a relatively easy way to add support for new hardware to your system without waiting for the next version of Red Hat Linux or modifying, recompiling, and installing a new kernel.

You can use loadable modules to correct three general types of hardware initialization problems:

1. If the Red Hat installer misidentified your network cards, or you specified the wrong type of network card when installing Linux, you can use loadable modules to try the drivers for other similar network cards.
2. You can use loadable modules to specify options for configuring your hardware, as is the case when you are using ISA network cards that require specific IO addresses and interrupt request vectors (IRQs).
3. You can compile and install a loadable module for an uncommon network card if you can find the drivers for it on the Internet or obtain the source code for a Linux driver from the vendor who manufactured or sold you the card.

When booting, Linux systems use the depmode and modprobe utilities to analyze your hardware and automatically load any modules that your hardware requires. Linux systems also automatically load any modules specified in the module configuration file, `/etc/conf.modules`. Modules are usually specific to a certain kernel version. The modules for your Red Hat Linux system are located in subdirectories of the directory `/lib/modules/`*`kernel-version`*, where *`kernel-version`* is the value you get by executing the `uname -r` command. The subdirectories of this directory are organized based on the type of device that the modules are associated with.

The next sections provide an example of using loadable modules to correct each of the three classes of problems listed earlier in this section. These each use network cards as an example because this is the most common type of problem I've had to resolve using loadable modules.

NOTE

The information in the following sections owes a huge debt to Donald Becker (`becker@cesdis.gsfc.nasa.gov`), who wrote many of the Ethernet drivers used on Linux systems and whose Web site provided the information I needed to build and load my first loadable Ethernet. He also wrote the code for that driver, which was handy, too.

Associating Specific Modules with Specific Interfaces

In the `/etc/conf.modules` file, the `alias` command can be used to associate specific interfaces with specific modules. For example, assume that you specified that your system uses an Intel EtherExpress card during the installation process, but your network card is actually an Intel EtherExpress Pro 10/100. The EtherExpress drives typically will report a "module busy" error when you boot your system, and you will not be able to access your network. In this case, you could put the following entry in your `/etc/conf.modules` file to load the correct driver:

```
alias eth0 eepro100
```

You then could reboot your system to see if this corrects the problem.

You also might need to modify the `/etc/conf.modules` file if your system uses more than one network card. By default, the Red Hat Installer detects and configures only the first network card it finds. You can activate other network cards by adding lines specifying their drivers to the `/etc/conf.modules` file (or by using the linuxconf application, as explained in Chapter 10).

Specifying Driver Options in `/etc/conf.modules`

Cards that are not plug-and-play, such as many ISA cards, usually can be configured via DIP switches and jumpers or will work only at certain IRQs or IO addresses. If you need to pass options to the driver for your cards, you can do this in the `/etc/conf.modules` file. Most ISA modules accept parameters such as `io=0x340` and `irq=9`. You can supply these sorts of options by placing an `options` command in `/etc/conf.modules` of the following form:

```
options driver argument=values argument=values ...
```

For example, you might specify the I/O port and IRQ used by a 3c59x Ethernet card like this:

```
alias eth0 3c59x
options 3c59x io=0x340 irq=9
```

Compiling Your Own Loadable Modules

If you can't find a version of a loadable module for your card that was built for your kernel version, your last chance to get the card working is to compile one yourself. You often can find the source code for such loadable modules by using a search engine on the World Wide Web and searching for phrases such as "module," "Linux," and the common identifier for your card. You also can post a message to one of the Linux newsgroups, asking if anyone has a driver for your card and can send you the source code.

Some prerequisites for compiling a loadable driver for your cards are listed here:

1. You must have loaded the package containing the source code for the kernel that you're currently using.
2. You must have installed the gcc C compiler on your system.
3. You must be able to get the source code for the driver onto your system, which is often difficult without being able to access the network. In the worst case, you can copy the source code to a DOS/Windows disk and use the Linux mtools utility to copy the file from the disk to your Linux system.

Comments in the source code for many drivers identify the command that you should use to compile them. If such information isn't present, try the following command line (substituting the name of the driver that you are compiling for `3c59x.c`):

```
gcc -DMODULE -D__KERNEL__ -Wall -Wstrict-prototypes \
  -I/usr/src/linux/net -O6 -c 3c59x.c \
  `[ -f /usr/include/linux/modversions.h ] && echo -DMODVERSIONS`
```

If this command completes successfully, you'll have the object file for your driver (in my example, the file `3c59x.o`) in your working directory. To test this module, use the `su` command to become the root user, and load the module using the command `insmod 3c59x.o` (the name of your driver file might be different). If your other network configuration information (IP address, netmask, default gateway, name server, and so on) is correct and this is the only Ethernet interface in your machine, you should then be able to bring up your Ethernet interface using the command `ifconfig eth0 YOUR_IP_ADDRESS`, where `YOUR_IP_ADDRESS` is the IP address of your machine. You then can test your Ethernet interface using a network command, such as `ping XXX.XXX.XXX.XXX`, where `XXX.XXX.XXX.XXX` is the IP address of a machine that you know should be reachable from your machine. If you get a message such as "Network is unreachable," you will have to use the `route` command to define a route to your local network. This command would take this form:

```
route add -net XXX.XXX.XXX.0 netmask 255.255.255.0 eth0
```

If this command succeeds, you can verify your local name server configuration by using the `ping` command to ping a host on your local network by name. You then can verify your default gateway configuration by trying to ping a remote host (that is, one that is not on your local network) that you know to be available.

If all these actions work, you should copy your compiled driver file to the correct location to be automatically loaded the next time your system boots. This is a subdirectory of `/lib/modules/kernel-version`. (You can identify the kernel version of your system using the `uname -r` command.) The drivers for Ethernet cards (which are all I've ever had to build and load manually) are located in the net subdirectory of the directory for your kernel version.

You then should create an entry in the file `/etc/conf.modules` of the form `alias eth0 your-module` to cause the system to load the correct module the next time it boots. Give only the basename of your module—you do not need to specify the `.o` extension.

Manually Starting Specific Services

The previous section familiarized you with the different run levels provided by Red Hat Linux and the scripts used to start and stop the processes and services associated with those run levels. This makes it easy to see how to start and stop specific services using those scripts, by running them manually when logged in as (or using `su` to become) the root user.

The key to starting any service manually is to make sure that the configuration files it uses are set up correctly, and then running the appropriate script to start that service.

For example, suppose that you want to start the Network File System (NFS) to be able to temporarily share your Red Hat CD-ROM for use in doing installs over the network.

You probably wouldn't want to permanently share your system's CD-ROM drive, so this would be something that you would want to manually enable. The list of file systems exported by NFS is contained in the file `/etc/exports`. To share the Red Hat disk in your CD-ROM drive via NFS, you first would log in root as or use `su` to become root, and mount the CD-ROM on your system using the `mount /dev/cdrom` command. You then would add an entry for this drive to `/etc/exports`, something like this:

```
/mnt/cdrom          (ro,insecure,all_squash)
```

You then can manually start the NFS services by changing to the directory `/etc/rc.d/init.d` and manually running the NFS startup script with a command line like the following:

```
./nfs start
```

You will see some messages on the console or in the window from which you executed the command as each NFS service starts, and your system's CD-ROM will be available over the network via NFS.

If you manually start specific services, it's important that you manually shut them down and deconfigure them before rebooting your system. Most of the startup scripts for each run level automatically start all configured services. In the case of NFS, you would want to remove the contents of the file `/etc/exports` before shutting down your system, to prevent Linux from automatically restarting NFS each time your system boots.

Terminating Specific Services

Specific services can be manually terminated in the same way that you started them, but by giving the `stop` argument to the init script. For example, suppose that you want to shut down the NFS server that was started in the previous section. To do this, you would log in as root or use `su` to become root, change to the directory `/etc/rc.d/init.d`, and execute a command like the following:

```
./nfs stop
```

You will see some messages on the console or in the window from which you executed the command, and all NFS services on your system will be stopped. Your system's CD-ROM will no longer be available over the network. You then should remove the contents of the file `/etc/exports` to prevent the init process from attempting to restart NFS the next time you boot your system.

Disabling Specific Network Services

Most of the TCP/IP network services on your machine actually are started by a single parent daemon process called the inet daemon (`/usr/sbin/inetd`). A daemon is a process that always runs in the background, watches for specific events, and reacts appropriately when those events occur. The inet daemon watches for attempts by other systems to contact specific network services on your system, and starts the appropriate service-specific daemon when it detects such attempts. Older UNIX systems ran separate daemons for each network service (such as FTP and telnet), which wasted computing cycles when those services were not being used because the daemons were still running. The inet daemon is more efficient because it is a single process that starts other daemons only when they are needed.

The daemons that can be started by the inet daemon are listed in its configuration file, `/etc/inetd.conf`. To disable specific services on your machine, you need to log in as root or use `su` to become root, and edit this file, commenting out the entries for any services that you don't want to run. For example, suppose that you do not want to allow users to connect to your systems using any of the r-commands, such as `rsh`, `rcp`, and `rlogin`. (These commands enable authorized remote users to start shells, copy files, and log in on your system without using separate commands such as `telnet` or `FTP`). To disable the services on your system without disabling all network services, you simply can comment out the entries for these services by putting a hash-mark in front of them in `/etc/inetd.conf`, as in the following example:

```
# shell stream  tcp     nowait  root    /usr/sbin/tcpd  in.rshd
# login stream  tcp     nowait  root    /usr/sbin/tcpd  in.rlogind
# exec  stream  tcp     nowait  root    /usr/sbin/tcpd  in.rexecd
```

You then can force the inetd process to reread its configuration file by identifying its process ID and sending it the hang-up and restart signal (`SIGHUP`), as in the following example:

```
# ps -ef | grep inetd
root       475     1  0 Feb13 ?        00:00:00 inetd
# kill -s SIGHUP 475
```

All other network services will function normally on your system, but the inet daemon will never start any of the daemons associated with the r-commands.

You might want to look through the file `/etc/inetd.conf` if you are curious about the type and number of network services that your system exports. One important aspect of network security is to minimize the number of network services your system(s) provides. You might be surprised at the number of different network services that can (and often are) provided by the inet daemon.

Shutting Down Red Hat Linux Systems

Because Linux is a complex system that supports multiple users and provides many network services, the files in your Linux file systems change often and even automatically, as in the case of log files. If you want to shut down your Linux system, you will want to do so in a clean, orderly fashion so that any users of your system have sufficient advance warning and so that there is no chance of file system corruption. Linux provides the `shutdown` command to enable you to perform such orderly shutdowns.

The basic syntax of the `shutdown` command is as follows:

```
/sbin/shutdown [option] +time "Message..."
```

For example, to schedule shutting down and halting your system in 10 minutes to add new hardware, you would log in as root or use `su` to become root, and execute the following command:

```
/sbin/shutdown -h +10 "Going down to add new hardware..."
```

This command displays your message to each user that is logged in, and redisplays it each time half the interval of time that you specified has elapsed. In this example, the message would be redisplayed after 5 minutes, 2.5 minutes, 1.25 minutes, and so on.

The most common options to the `shutdown` command are `-h` (halt the system) and `-r` (reboot the system). Aside from specific time values, you also can specify the time as `now` (as in, `shutdown -h now "Goodbye"`) to shut down the system immediately, with no warning.

As you might suspect, the `shutdown` command primarily displays your message, counts down the remaining time, and disallows new logins when the shutdown time is five minutes away. When the `shutdown` command actually runs, it forces your system to the appropriate run level using the init process—either run level 0 for powering your system down, or run level 6 for rebooting your system.

Faster Shutdown Methods for Emergencies

You might want to shut down your system immediately under certain circumstances, such as a crippling network attack or severe hardware problem. In these cases, the following commands (executed as root) are even faster than the `shutdown` command but are not quite as neat because they do not cleanly shut down services and unmount disks. What they lack in elegance, however, they make up for in terms of speed:

```
sync; sync; sync; /sbin/halt
sync; sync; sync; kill -9 1
```

The `sync` command in each of these examples forces any pending writes to be flushed to the disks. Three `sync` commands are used for two reasons: to guarantee that these write operations have time to complete, and because this is popular UNIX/Linux folklore.

Using the Standard Three-Finger Salute

When running on Lintel (Linux on Intel) hardware, Red Hat Linux systems respond to the classic Ctrl+Alt+Del key sequence by scheduling a reboot in three seconds. This is controlled by an entry in the `/etc/inittab` file, such as the following:

```
ca::ctrlaltdel:/sbin/shutdown -t3 -r now
```

When you are deploying Red Hat Linux systems for use in common areas, you might want to comment out this entry in `/etc/inittab` (by preceding it with a hash-mark) to prevent malicious users from randomly rebooting your systems whenever they are frustrated or bored.

CHAPTER 7

Configuring and Customizing the X Window System

Chapter 5, "Red Hat Installation: Basic Software Installation," explained X Window system configuration in the context of installing Red Hat Linux. Red Hat's text-mode installation process uses Red Hat's own Xconfigurator application for all Red Hat Workstation class systems, and as part of Custom installations where you've installed XFree86. (Adding the X Window system to Server-class installations was also discussed in Chapter 5.)

This chapter provides additional background information about the X Window system and the XFree86 Project, and discusses how to get detailed information about the chipset used in your video hardware. It then discusses how and when to use the Xconfigurator application to optimally configure the X Window system for your video hardware and monitor.

If the X Window system was successfully installed as part of the Red Hat installation process and you're satisfied with the resolution at which the X Window system is running, you might want to skip these first few sections and proceed to the later, more general-purpose portions of this chapter, beginning with the section entitled "Starting the X Window System." These discuss different ways of starting the X Window system to run window managers and desktop environments; discuss GNOME, the desktop environment best loved by Red Hat; and cover KDE, an alternate desktop environment with its own equally fanatic adherents.

This chapter concludes by discussing some of the most interesting window managers and the reasons for using them. Look for a show on this on Jerry Springer or Oprah sometime soon, as few things are more likely to cause a fistfight at a Linux or other UNIX-like party than the question, "Which is the best window manager?"

What Are the X Window System, X11R6, and XFree86?

The X Window system is one of the most attractive aspects of Linux and of almost any operating system running on modern bitmapped graphics workstations. As discussed in the "Configuring the X Window System" section of Chapter 5, the X Window system is a network-aware graphics windowing system that provides a similar set of capabilities for creating and working with such applications as Microsoft Windows and the Macintosh operating system. The X Window system is the industry standard windowing system for computers running versions of UNIX, Linux, Compaq's VMS operating system, and many other operating systems. The X Window system was designed to provide a common windowing environment on multiprocessing, networked computer systems, and is far more powerful than the personal computer graphics systems mentioned earlier. Versions of the X Window system are also available for all releases of Windows greater than 3.1, and for most versions of the MacOS. These run X Window system applications in the context of the native windowing systems for those platforms.

The X Window system originally was developed at the Massachusetts Institute of Technology (MIT), based on an earlier windowing system from Stanford (called W—after W comes X, get it?), and is currently under the custodianship of the Open Group (`www.opengroup.com`), who also are the custodians of a surprising number of other standards, including UNIX itself. (The most surprising aspect of this is the fact that they call themselves the Open Group while often charging royalties for anyone writing code that follows their standards. The code base is therefore open, but so are the wallets of anyone who wants to use it, which, of course, is passed on to the consumer.) The current release of the X Window system is X11 Revision 6.5, usually known simply as X11R6. Luckily, the Open Group seems to have (eventually) released X11R6.5 under the terms of the original X Window system license, permitting free redistribution of code based on its X Window system APIs (except Motif—more about that later).

The XFree86 Project, Inc. is a nonprofit group that produces XFree86, which is essentially an X11R6 port with added support for the input devices (mouse devices, track balls, IBM ThinkPad nipples, touch pads, and so on), video cards, and monitors used on systems with Intel or compatible processors. The XFree86 version of X11R6 is currently based on X11R6.3, and a port of the X11R6.4 code base is underway. The fact that XFree86 isn't based on X11R6.4 doesn't really matter for 99% of the X Window system users out there. The only X Window system users that might actually care are those who are trying to compile new X Window system applications that depend on some feature not yet found in XFree86. If you find yourself in that category, three aphorisms could help: "Patience is a virtue," "You can't beat the price," and "They're looking for volunteers."

Because XFree86 is the version of the X Window system provided with Red Hat Linux, the terms *XFree86* and *X Window system* are used somewhat interchangeably throughout the rest of this chapter. Wherever possible, I've tried to use *XFree86* where configuration options are specific to XFree86 and *X Window system* where they are not.

Using XF86—configure

Beginning with Xfree86 version 4, you can use the Xfree86 server itself to generate a sample XF86 configuration file. To test this file, you'll need to run Xfree86 with a command line like the following:

```
Xfree86 -xf86config ~/XF86config.new
```

This usually generates an adequate XF86 configuration file, but one that doesn't take full advantage of the capabilities of your monitor and video card.

Identifying Graphics Cards and Chip Sets

As discussed in Chapter 5, the X Window system consists of an X Window system server associated with one or more video cards (display adapters, in X Window system parlance) on a computer system, and any number of X Window system client applications that display their output using the servers. For simplicity's sake, I'll refer to these simply as *servers* and *clients* throughout the rest of this chapter.

Because the server is the interface between your clients and your video hardware and monitor, choosing the right server to install on your system is critically important to get the most colors and the best possible resolution from your video hardware. You'll need a good amount of information to correctly select an optimal server:

- The chipset used in your video card.
- The name of your video card itself (if it has one).
- The amount of memory on your video card.
- Whether your video card contains a clock chip. Clock chips are programmable chips that enable you to set the frequency of various video card options. These are found in only a limited number of older video cards. If you can't answer this question, you'll be able to specify that you don't have one during XFree86 configuration.
- Your monitor's horizontal and vertical sync rates, if these aren't specified as part of your monitor selection. The vertical sync rate is a range of rates at which the image on your entire monitor can be redrawn. The horizontal sync rate is the range of rates at which horizontal scan lines (the individual lines that the image on your monitor is actually composed of) can be drawn.
- The resolutions and number of colors your monitor supports.

The good news about obtaining all this information is that you should be able to find it all in the documentation for your video card and monitor, or at least from the Web sites of their manufacturers. You can obtain some of this information from the splash screen that is usually provided by your video BIOS when it initializes—this often lists the card name, chipset, and amount of available memory, though this goes by fast—write quickly! As a last resort, you can try examining the card itself—the video chip is usually a larger square or rectangular chip on your video card, and usually has the chip type printed on its top surface. I'd suggest opening up your machine only as a last resort if you don't have the documentation for the card or if you're comfortable removing and handling hardware; the information on the chip isn't everything you need, but it can at least get you started.

As a last resort, Red Hat Linux provides a utility called SuperProbe (note the uppercase letters S and P), which will directly probe your hardware and display any information that it can obtain about your chipset. You must run the SuperProbe utility when logged in or after having used the `su` command to obtain root privileges because it needs direct access to your video hardware. When you first start SuperProbe, it displays a message (see Figure 7.1) saying that its automatic probing can hang your video card and gives you five seconds to press Control+C to abort the process. I've never actually seen this happen, but it is possible, especially on older video cards. SuperProbe then displays a message providing as much information as possible about the capabilities, chipset, and RAMDAC and timing information of each video interface found in your system.

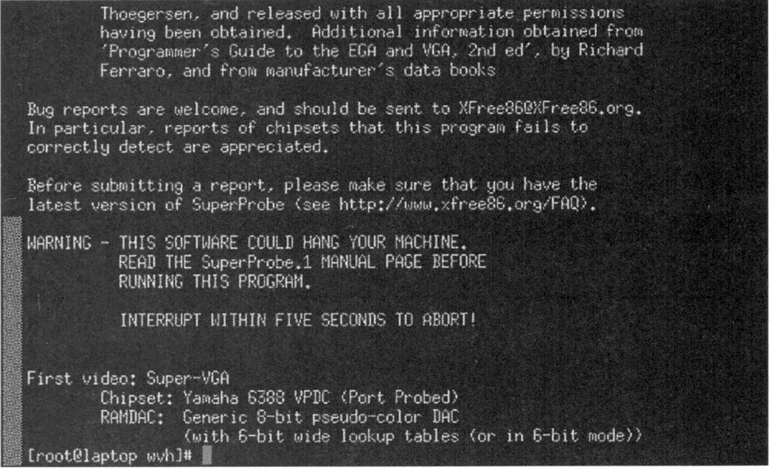

Figure 7.1

Sample SuperProbe output.

When you have the necessary information about your video card and monitor, you're ready to proceed with configuring or fine tuning the X Window system.

Using Xconfigurator

The Xconfigurator creates a configuration file for the XFree86 system that accurately describes your system's graphics and input hardware, and desired X Window system startup information. This configuration file is the file for versions 3.X and earlier of XF86Config, and XF86Config-4 for versions 4 and later of XFRee86, such as the one included with Red Hat 7.0. This file is a text file that is located in the directory /etc/X11. A symbolic link to this file is also located in the directory /usr/X11R6/lib/X11. When you start the X Window system on a system running XFree86, XFree86 reads this file and uses it to start the appropriate X Window system server with your specified resolution, a specified (or default) desktop environment or window manager, and any X Window system clients that you've specified in the appropriate fashion. That's a lot of "appropriates," but as you'll see later in the "Starting the X Window System" section, there are many different ways to use and start the X Window system, each of which has its own set of default actions. Like all good UNIX applications, the X Window system is highly configurable; when you've configured it to work the way that you want, "the right thing" will happen automatically in the future.

Red Hat runs its Xconfigurator application for you automatically as part of any text-mode Workstation-class installation, Custom installation in which you've installed XFree86, or Server-class installation to which you've added Xfree86. The Xconfigurator is a custom application from Red Hat that isn't found in other versions of Linux. Xconfigurator usually does a great job of correctly identifying your chipset, video card, and monitor whenever possible and creating a correct XFree86 configuration file for you. However, some video cards—especially older cards and the video circuitry on some newer, highly integrated motherboards—can't be easily identified. In these cases, you might want to skip configuring the X Window system as part of the installation process and manually configure it later. Red Hat's Xconfigurator application is designed to hide the potential complexity of configuring XFree86 by automatically setting most XFree86 bells and whistles for you.

The Xconfigurator utility can create an initial XF86 configuration file for you. You should always run this utility from a command prompt, not from within the X Window system, so that it can correctly restart and test your modified settings.

NOTE

If you already have a working XF86 configuration file (XF86Config or XF86Config-4) in the directory /etc/X11, you should always make a backup copy of the file /etc/X11/XF86Config before changing anything. This makes it easy to revert to your previous settings if you aren't happy with your changes by overwriting your new XF86Config file with your backup copy. Red Hat's Xconfigurator does not automatically save a copy of any previous XF86Config file for you, but it rewrites the same file each time you run it.

Because the Xconfigurator application modifies system configuration files, you'll have to either log in as or use the su command to become root before running it.

Using Red Hat's Xconfigurator

When you start the Xconfigurator from a command prompt, it first displays a Welcome screen. This screen provides some background about the XFree86 configuration file and identifies a text file on your Linux system that gives you more information about the XFree86 configuration process. This text file is the file /usr/X11R6/lib/X11/doc/README.Config. You shouldn't actually need to read this file unless you want more detailed information about the configuration process.

After displaying this screen, Xconfigurator probes your video hardware and attempts to identify the chipset or card that is present. If it can't uniquely identify your hardware, you'll see a Which Video Card Do You Have? screen. If this screen displays, consult the documentation that came with your system, and select the most appropriate video card or chipset from the list.

The next Xconfigurator screen contains a scrollable window from which you must select your monitor, another monitor with capabilities that are exactly the same as yours, or a generic monitor (listed under 'G' in the monitor selection window) and then supply detailed information about its capabilities.

If you're using the Xconfigurator to configure XFree86 for the first time, you can skip to any portion of this list to see whether your monitor is listed by typing the first letter that uniquely identifies your monitor. It's very important that you either select the correct monitor from this list or supply the correct information about your monitor when prompted to do so. XFree86 can be very demanding of your graphics chipset, video card, and monitor; pushing these beyond their capabilities can actually damage any and all of the three. Red Hat's Xconfigurator does a good job of probing hardware whenever possible, but it's always a good idea to have collected the information about your chipset, video card, and monitor as outlined earlier in this chapter before proceeding.

Some tips on selecting a monitor follow:

- If you are configuring the X Window system on a laptop, look for a monitor description that begins with the name of the vendor that made the laptop. For example, many of the LCD screens used in IBM ThinkPads are listed as various models of "IBM TFT Panel" (where TFT stands for Thin Film Transistor or some more amusing phrase).
- If you're in doubt and other monitors from the same vendor as yours are listed, it is usually safe to select an older, less-capable monitor from the same vendor. You can always fine-tune your X Window system configuration as described in the remainder of this section, but getting the X Window system running in the first place will make your Linux system a friendlier and more usable system, especially if you are new to Linux.
- If your monitor isn't listed but you know both its horizontal and vertical sync rates and its maximum resolution, select Custom Monitor. Then choose the appropriate values from the subsequent screens for custom monitor configuration. If the exact ranges for your monitor's vertical and horizontal sync rates

aren't available, select values that are inside the ranges supported by your monitor. Do not select any values that are greater than those supported by your monitor.

- When in doubt, select Generic Monitor for now. Subsequent screens will probe your hardware to attempt to obtain the correct settings. If probing your chipset, video card, or monitor causes your system to hang, then reboot your system, restart the Xconfigurator. Don't allow the Xconfigurator to probe your system. Just select more conservative settings for your chipset, video card, and monitor.

The Xconfigurator next tries to identify the default resolution of your chipset or video card by probing your video circuitry. If you've had problems when automatically probing the video circuitry on this machine in the past, select Don't Probe and enter the correct values for the amount of video memory you have, your ClockChip, and the maximum video modes you'd like to use on the next few screens. Many video cards don't require probing. If the video card you've selected is among them, "No clockchip—don't probe" is selected when you first display the ClockChip screen.

If you let the Xconfigurator probe your video card and this completes successfully, accept the default video mode for now. If you're using the Xconfigurator to reconfigure your system, you can select Let Me Choose and enter values that you know to be correct.

In general, it's safe to try for the highest video modes that you'd like to see. If your video circuitry or monitor doesn't support them, the X server won't start correctly, and the Xconfigurator will automatically return you to an earlier screen to give you the opportunity to select the correct values.

When you've selected your monitor, an appropriate alternative, or a custom or generic type, and have entered or probed for the correct values, the Xconfigurator displays a Starting X screen. This screen warns you that it will now try starting the X server to test your current settings. If the X server won't start, then your settings are incorrect and the Xconfigurator will automatically return you to the Which Video Card Do You Have? or Monitor Setup screens to give you the opportunity to select the correct values. If the X server starts and is usable, select Yes in the "Can you see this message?" dialog box. If the X server starts but the screen is totally unreadable, you can just wait 10 seconds; the X server will automatically exit, and you can then go back to previous screens and try other settings.

If the X server starts, it looks good, and you select Yes in the "Can you see this message?" dialog box, the next screen displays a dialog box asking whether you want the Xconfigurator to automatically start X (sic) when booting. This starts a system application called xdm (the X Display Manager) or its KDE or GNOME equivalents (kdm or gdm). This also sets your default runlevel to 5 (X Window system support) and uses the appropriate display manager as the means for logging in on the console of your Red Hat system.

Automatically starting the X Window system when your system boots can limit your options for subsequently experimenting with other window managers and desktop environments (or make it more complex to experiment). I generally recommend against this if your system will be used by any experienced X Window system user or anyone who wants to experiment. You can always subsequently modify the default run level, as explained in Chapter 6, "Starting and Stopping Red Hat Linux," if you want to run a display manager. On the other hand, using a display manager might be a good idea if the system you are installing is intended for users who do not want to start a specific window manager or who do not know how to, or if you have a standard X Window system configuration that is shared by all the users in your computing environment.

Next, save your X Window system configuration (updating the file /etc/X11/XF86config), and exit the Xconfigurator.

Troubleshooting XFree86 Configuration

If you're having problems correctly configuring XFree86 on your system, don't despair. The directory /usr/X11R6/lib/X11/doc contains a number of helpful text files, some general and one for each of the X Window system servers that XFree86 provides. If you have any problems configuring a specific XFree86 server, check the help file for that server in that directory. The names of these files are of the form README.*server-name*, where *server-name* is something approximating the name of a specific chipset or graphics card. Check for both uppercase and lowercase filenames for the help file for your XFree86 server. For example, the help file for the X server for the S3 chipset is named README.S3, while the help file for the X server for the NeoMagic chipset is called README.neo. These files were contributed by the authors of the various servers and, therefore, don't follow a single naming convention.

The first and most useful way of diagnosing problems starting the X Window system on your computer is any error messages displayed by XFree86 when you attempt to start the X Window system.

NOTE

Before editing the XF86Config file, make sure that you save the current file and any previous versions somewhere else on your system. This is especially important if you had a working XF86Config file, were trying to fine-tune your XFree86 configuration, and are now having problems starting the X Window system using the modified XF86Config file.

To save the messages displayed by XFree86 when it starts, use a command such as the following from the BASH, CSH, or TCSH shells:

```
startx >& ./startx.out
```

This saves all startup and error messages in the file in the working directory called `startx.out`.

Examples of an XFree86 configuration problem that you can easily resolve by manually editing the /etc/X11/XF86Config file are messages like the following:

```
(—) SVGA: There is no mode definition name "NNNNxMMMM"
Fatal server error:
No valid modes found
```

This means that the default video resolution of NNNN by MMMM is not supported by the currently selected X server. In many cases, you can simply edit the XF86Config file to use another default video mode, by modifying the appropriate portions of the file and entries.

For information about resolving XF86Setup and XF86Config problems, it always makes sense to "use the source, Luke!"—in this case, not necessarily reading the source code (although that's an option), but checking the Frequently Asked Questions (FAQ) file for XFree86, located on the World Wide Web at `http://www.xfree86.org/FAQ`.

Keyboard Controls for XFree86

XFree86 is a Linux- and UNIX-like application, and it wouldn't be a good one unless it had a few trap doors that are accessible via keyboard commands. Three of these are extremely useful:

- **Ctrl+Alt+Backspace**—Simultaneously pressing the Ctrl, Alt, and Backspace keys while running XFree86 (regardless of the window manager or desktop environment you're running) exits the X server immediately. This kills any clients that are running without saving any unsaved changes to your files. For example, if you are running emacs and have modified any files without saving them, your changes will be lost.
  Ctrl+Alt+Backspace is an incredibly useful command that anyone who likes to experiment with different window managers probably will have to use someday. Without the correct configuration files, many window managers start successfully but don't map mouse commands to mouse actions. Therefore, you can't start any applications or even exit the window manager. An alternative to this command is to switch to one of Linux's virtual consoles, locate the X server process, and shoot it down using the *`kill -9`* command, but Control+Alt+Backspace is much faster.
- **Control+Alt+Keypad+**—Pressing the Ctrl, Alt, and the Plus key on your keypad (Shift+= does *not* work) causes the X server to immediately switch to the next highest video resolution that it supports. This key combination can be very useful if you have configured your X server to start in a low-resolution video mode and want to experiment with using higher-resolution modes that are supported by your X server.

- **Control+Alt+Keypad-**—Pressing the Ctrl, Alt, and the Minus key on your keypad (Shift+= does *not* work) causes the X server to immediately switch to the next lowest video resolution that it supports. This key combination can be very useful if you have configured your X server to start in a high-resolution video mode and want to experiment with using lower-resolution modes that are supported by your X server.

Starting the X Window System

The fact that Linux has its roots in UNIX and that there are potentially a zillion developers working on any Open Source project means that Linux always provides more than one way to accomplish almost any task. Nowhere in Linux and UNIX is this more true than in the number of ways to start the X Window system and associated window managers and desktop environments. Of course, most people have a favorite way of starting the X Window system. This section explains the hierarchy of these methods, tells how to modify them, and covers the magic configuration files used by each of them.

Using a Display Manager

Using an X Window system display manager means that the default init state of your system is state 5. It also requires that your system automatically start either xdm, kdm, or gdm depending on the X Window system environment that you're running (standard XFree86 and the AnotherLevel window manager; the KDE desktop environment and the kwm window manager; or the GNOME desktop environment and GNOME-compatible window managers such as Sawfish and Enlightenment, respectively).

Using /etc/inittab, the init process runs the /etc/X11/prefdm script to figure out which display manager to run based on the contents of the file /etc/sysconfig/desktop. This file contains a single line of the form:

```
DESKTOP="desktop"
```

Here, `desktop` is one of KDE, GNOME, or AnotherLevel. (The AnotherLevel desktop is actually being phased out, so you should only use it if you absolutely love it.) If you've installed everything (KDE, GNOME, and all the standard XFree86 software) using Red Hat's Custom installation class, modifying the file /etc/sysconfig/desktop is the fastest way to switch between desktop environments. You can also use specialized commands such as switchdesk-gkde and switchdesk-gnome to do the same thing, but I prefer the personal touch. You can even insert commands to explicitly start KDE or GNOME in your personal ~/.xinitrc or systemwide xinitrc scripts, but this is much more time-consuming and error-prone than simply tweaking /etc/sysconfig/desktop.

Using the `startx` Command

The `startx` script provides a slightly more robust and capable front end to the xinit program (discussed in the next section). In general, the `startx` command is the preferred way of starting an X Window system window manager or desktop environment for anyone who doesn't use a display manager.

When executed, the `startx` command checks the standard initialization files used by the `xinit` command and also checks the file ~/.xserverrc, if present, to determine which X server to start. If no ~/.xserverrc file is present, the `startx` command checks for the presence of a default file, /etc/X11/xinit/xserverrc, to specify which X server to start. If this file does not exist, the `startx` script defaults to starting the server named X, which is typically a symbolic link to the specific X server for your video card and chipset. All these options for starting a specific X server are rarely used, but they are present as a bell and whistle if you want to run a different server for some reason.

The `startx` command is actually a shell script, located in /usr/X11R6/bin. This sample script is provided as a starting point for system administrators who want to standardize various aspects of the X Window system startup environment on their systems. The `startx` command uses copies of the default configuration files used by the `xinit` command (xinitrc, Xmodmap, and Xclients) to simplify setting up sitewide configurations. This prevents you from having to modify the default files used by the `xinit` command, which should not be modified because they are present as a final default. The copies of these files used by the `startx` command are located in the directory /etc/X11/xinit, while the default configuration files used by the `xinit` command are located in the directory /usr/X11R6/lib/X11/xinit. This is the most basic difference between the `startx` and `xinit` commands.

The `startx` script also simplifies passing additional arguments to the `xinit` command, the most significant of which is the `bpp` (bits per pixel) command used to start your X server with a different color depth than the default for that server. For example, to start your X server with a color depth of 16bpp, you would use the following command:

```
startx -- -bpp 16
```

The `startx` script next automates some aspects of X Window system security using the `xauth` command. See the online manual page for the `xauth` command for more information (`man xauth`).

When the `startx` script has processed its arguments and generated a security token (cookie) for your X Window system server session, it executes the `xinit` command, which is described in the next section.

Using the `xinit` Command

The `xinit` command uses a relatively large number of files located in a user's home directory to attempt to set personal defaults for using the X Window system. Like the `startx` commands, `xinit` falls back to systemwide configuration files located in the directory /usr/X11R6/lib/X11/xinit if per-user versions of these files aren't found. To make things even more flexible (and potentially confusing), if `xinit` is called from the `startx` script, it actually uses a set of default configuration files located in /etc/X11/xinit. The sequence in which these files are checked for and used is as follows:

1. The `xinit` command looks for the file ~/.xinitrc (the ~/ nomenclature refers to a user's home—that is, login—directory) to determine which window manager to run and which clients to start. The ~/.xinitrc file is a simple command file

that contains an optional entry to start a specific X Window system window manager and other optional entries to start some number of X Window system clients.

2. If no ~/.xinitrc file is present and `xinit` was not called from the `startx` script, the system file /usr/X11R6/lib/X11/xinit/xinitrc is used to determine what clients to start. If `xinit` was executed automatically by the `startx` script, it uses the system file /etc/X11/xinit/xinitrc as its default. Unless modified, on Red Hat systems these default xinitrc scripts do the following:
    1. The scripts load the X resources specified in ~/.Xresources. If no ~/.Xresources file exists, `xinit` uses the defaults in the file /etc/X11/xinit/Xresources if called from `startx`, or the defaults specified in /usr/X11R6/lib/X11/xinit/Xresources if simply executed as `xinit` from the command line.
    2. The scripts load the X keyboard rebindings specified in ~/.Xmodmap. If no ~/.Xmodmap file exists, `xinit` uses the defaults in the file /etc/X11/xinit/Xmodmap if called from `startx`, or the defaults specified in /usr/X11R6/lib/X11/xinit/Xmodmap if simply executed as `xinit` from the command line.
    3. The scripts load any X keyboard mappings specified in ~/.Xkbmap. If no ~/.Xkbmap file exists, `xinit` uses the defaults in the file /etc/X11/xinit/Xkbmap if called from `startx`, or the defaults specified in /usr/X11R6/lib/X11/xinit/Xkbmap if simply executed as `xinit` from the command line.
    4. The scripts start any X Window system clients specified in ~/.Xclients. If no ~/.Xclients file exists, `xinit` uses the defaults in the file /etc/X11/xinit/Xclients if called from `startx`, or the defaults specified in /usr/X11R6/lib/X11/xinit/Xclients if simply executed as `xinit` from the command line.
    5. The default Xclient files check for the existence of a file called ~/.wm_style, which, if present, contains the name of the Window manager to start.
    6. If no window manager is already running by this point, the /etc/X11/xinit/xinitrc script then tries to start the /usr/X11R6/bin/fvwm window manager, if it is installed on your system. If this window manager is not installed on your system, /etc/X11/xinit/xinitrc then defaults to starting the twm window manager, discussed later in this chapter.

Like the `startx` script discussed in the previous section, the system default X Window system initialization file /usr/X11R6/lib/X11/xinit/xinitrc is actually designed to be copied and used as the genesis of your own ~/.xinitrc or a sitewide X Window system initialization file.

The xinitrc file

The most important aspect of whichever xinitrc file you end up using is that it can start a window manager and multiple clients by specifying the full path name to the X Window system clients that you want to start (or just the name of the client, if you're sure that it's in your execution path). You should always start a window manager before starting any X window system clients.

Each client entry in this file except for the last one should be followed by an ampersand, which means to start the client in the background. The last client entry in this file should begin with the command `exec` and not end with an ampersand. The `exec` command tells Linux to replace the `xinit` command in memory with whatever command follows the `exec` command. This makes the client that you start using `exec` the controlling client for your X Window system session. When this client exits (that is, when you terminate it), your X Window system session ends and the command prompt is redisplayed.

The following is a sample ~/.xinitrc file that starts the Window Maker window manager, starts an xterm, and then starts the `xconsole` process as the controlling command for this X Window system session:

```
/usr/X11R6/bin/wmaker &
/usr/X11R6/bin/xterm&
exec /usr/X11R6/bin/xconsole
```

When you terminate the `xconsole` command, your other X Window system processes will exit and you will be returned to the console window from which you ran `xinit` or `startx`.

A Suggested Method for Starting Window Managers

The bewildering number of personal, systemwide, and default configuration files discussed in the previous sections can be overwhelming. Here's how I start the X Window system and window manager du jour on my system:

1. If I want to start a desktop environment, I modify the file `/etc/sysconfig/desktop` to identify that desktop environment, as described earlier in this chapter. Whenever I don't want to run a desktop environment, I delete this file. I then delete the file .xinitrc in my home directory.
2. If I want to run a window manager rather than a desktop environment (which I usually do because I'm a hard-core X Window system fanatic), I keep a number of files in my home directory with names such as .xinitrc.afterstep, .xinitrc.wmaker, .xinitrc.sawfish, and so on. Each of these files contains the single line, `exec <full-path-to-window-manager>`, where `<full-path-to-window-manager>` is the full path to where that X Window system server is installed on my system. Enabling each user to have their own .xinitrc file makes it possible for different users to each start their own window manager of choice, without modifying central system files that would therefore impose their tastes on others.

   To switch between window managers (which I like to do), I create a symbolic link to one of these files with the name .xinitrc. This makes the window manager the controlling process for the `startx/xinit` process, which seems reasonable to me. If I want to run a desktop environment, I delete the symbolic link called .xinitrc and thus get the default window manager used by each desktop environment. The window manager-specific files therefore are preserved but not used unless I recreate the symbolic link.

Using GNOME

Recently, X Window system window managers have graduated to true desktop managers like the ones you'd find on Macintosh, Windows, and old XEROX systems. Desktop managers, also commonly known as desktop environments, typically support drag-and-drop actions, provide a file manager of some sort, and have easy ways to tie applications to buttons, icons, and menu items. GNOME (GNU Network Object Model Environment—GNU stands for "GNU's Not UNIX") is an Open Source desktop environment on free steroids. GNOME is not a window manager, but it requires that one be present on your system. By default, the Sawfish window manager is used with GNOME, but any other GNOME-compliant window manager can easily be used, including Enlightenment, Sawfish, Window Maker, and IceWM (plus FVWM, SCWM, AfterStep, and QVWM in the near future). Figure 7.2 shows GNOME running a few applications on one of my home systems.

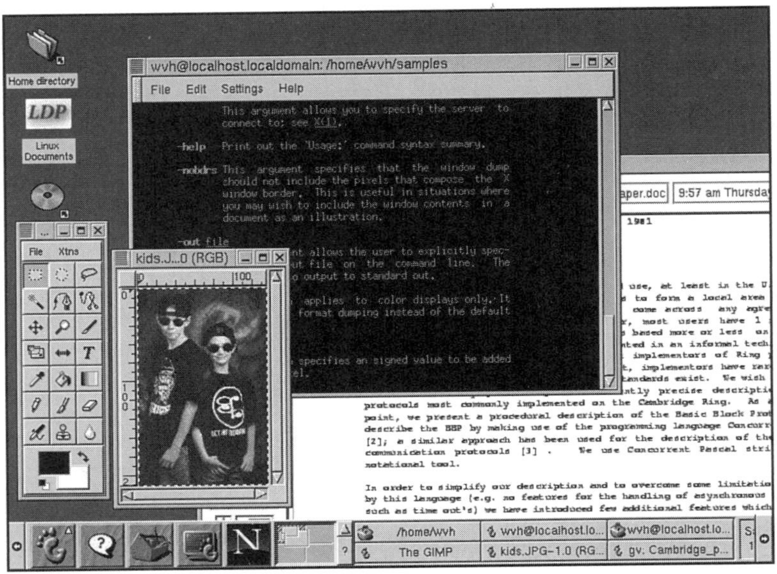

Figure 7.2

The GNOME desktop environment.

GNOME deserves a book all its own—discussing all the bells and whistles provided with GNOME would bloat this book faster than drinking a thousand gallons of water on a summer's day. For general information about GNOME on Red Hat, see the section "GNOME Workstations," in Chapter 2, "Preparing your System for Red Hat." For more information about GNOME, visit the GNOME Web site at `http://www.gnome.org`.

The most important aspect of GNOME is the pager at the bottom of the screen, which provides four virtual desktops by default and from which you can start any installed X Window system application. To configure GNOME's background, screen saver, and so on, click the toolbox icon in the pager to display the GNOME control center.

To exit from GNOME, click the GNOME footprint icon in the pager, and select the Log Out command at the bottom of the pop-up menu. This displays a dialog box that lets you save your current desktop setup and specify whether you want to log out, halt, or reboot the machine. For the latter two operations, you'll be prompted for your password.

Using KDE

Recently, X Window system window managers have graduated to true desktop managers like the ones you'd find on Macintosh, Windows, and old XEROX systems. Desktop managers, also commonly known as desktop environments, typically support drag-and-drop operations, provide a file manager of some sort, and have easy ways to tie applications to buttons, icons, and menu items. KDE (K Desktop Environment) is a desktop environment that is designed to provide normal computer users with a standard, easy-to-use graphical desktop environment. KDE was initially inspired by the Common Desktop Environment (CDE), which was cooperatively designed by major UNIX vendors such as IBM and Sun Microsystems. CDE was designed and built using the Open Group's Motif X Window system libraries, which meant that vendors wishing to deploy CDE had to license Motif. This was obviously was unsuitable in the free, Open Source environment of Linux, so KDE was written to provide a free, Open Source alternative. The KDE project originally was sponsored by a number of Linux vendors, including Caldera, Delix, O'Reilly Associates, and SuSE. Figure 7.3 shows the K Desktop Environment running on one of my home Linux systems.

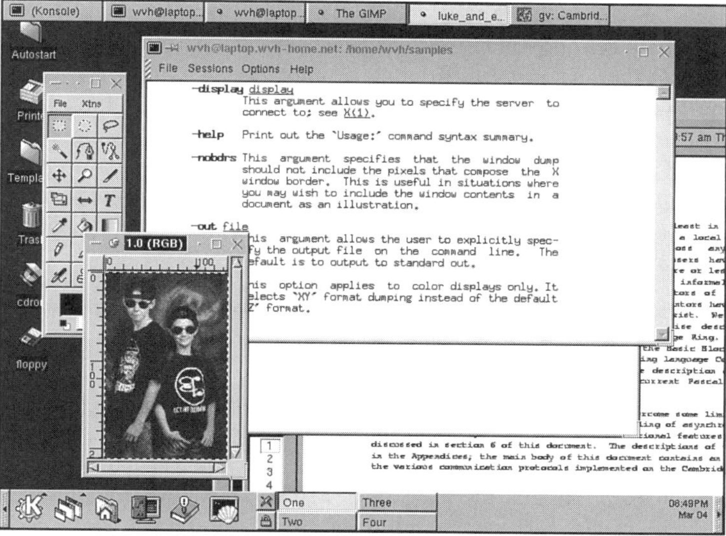

Figure 7.3

The K Desktop Environment.

KDE deserves a book all its own—discussing all the bells and whistles provided with KDE would bloat this book faster than a thousand cubic feet of helium. For general information about KDE on Red Hat, see the section "KDE Workstations," in Chapter 2. For more detailed information about KDE, see the K Desktop Environment Web site at `http://www.kde.org`.

Like GNOME, the most important aspect of KDE is the pager at the bottom of the screen, which provides four virtual desktops by default and from which you can start any installed X Window system application. To configure KDE's background, screen saver, and so on, click the icon of a circuit board in front of a monitor in the pager to display the KDE control center.

To exit from KDE, click the KDE logo icon in the pager, and select the Log Out command at the bottom of the pop-up menu. This displays a dialog box that lets you save your current desktop settings before exiting.

Selecting and Using Different Window Managers

Window managers are the applications that manage other applications on systems running the X Window system. Window managers control things such as what the decoration around client windows looks like, how windows are minimized, whether they can be iconified, and where they end up when minimized or iconified. I love X Window system window managers because they are someone's creative expression of how a desktop should work and can most easily be used. Whenever I hear about a new window manager, I immediately download and compile it, just to try it out. I've burned a good many hours over the years in this essentially pointless but extremely interesting task.

The window managers provided on your Red Hat CD include enlightenment, kwm, twm, Window Maker, AfterStep, sawmill, and multiple versions of fvwm. This section provides an overview of a few of these, primarily to show just how flexible the X Window system is and to illustrate how many great window managers there are to choose from. This section does not discuss kwm and enlightenment because these are used by default as part of KDE and GNOME, respectively. The window managers discussed in this section are my personal favorites—if you want to move beyond the confines of a desktop environment, feel free to experiment!

A great introduction to many of the X Window system window managers and desktop environments available for Linux can be found at `http://www.PLiG.org/xwinman/`.

TWM: The Classic Window Manager

Once known as Tom's Window Manager, after its original author, Tom LeStrange, TWM is the oldest and most stable window manager shipped with Red Hat. Located in the directory /usr/X11R6/bin, the executable version of TWM is called twm and is a great window manager with just enough frills to make it eminently usable. Figure 7.4 shows the twm window manager running a few applications on one of my Linux systems.

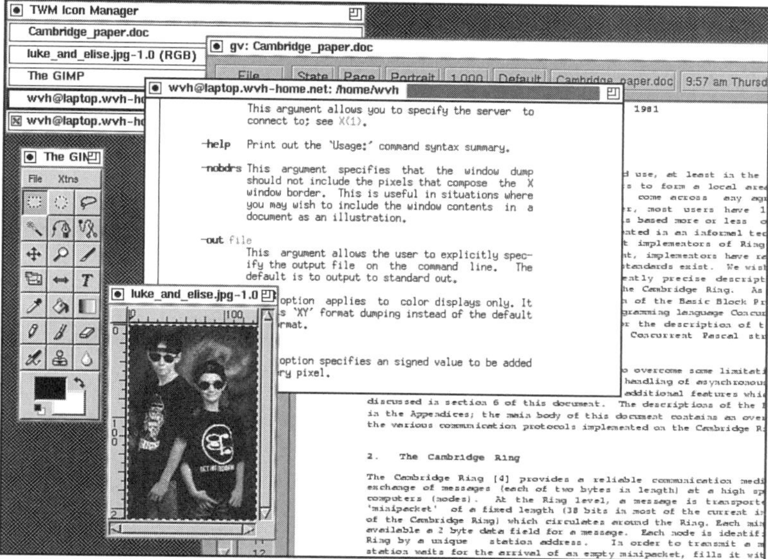

Figure 7.4

The TWM window manager.

TWM menus, commands, fonts, and just about anything else can be customized using the file .twmrc, located in your home directory. If you don't have a personal copy of this file, the systemwide configuration file /usr/X11R6/lib/X11/twm/system.twmrc is used to set basic twm menu commands and internal options.

Window Maker

Window Maker is a fast, lightweight window manager modeled after the NextStep window manager formerly used on workstations from NeXT computer, and it has outlived its inspiration. Located in the directory /usr/X11R6/bin, the Window Maker binary is called wmaker. Interesting features of Window Maker (and the similar window manager, AfterStep) are its capability to iconify applications and its use of a docking bar to provide shortcuts to commonly used applications. Figure 7.5 shows the Window Maker window manager running a few applications on one of my Linux systems.

Window Maker menus, commands, fonts, and just about anything else can be customized using the file ~/GNUstep/Defaults/WindowMaker, located in your home directory. This file and its associated directories are created automatically the first time you start Window Maker. System defaults for Window Maker are located in subdirectories of /usr/share/WindowMaker.

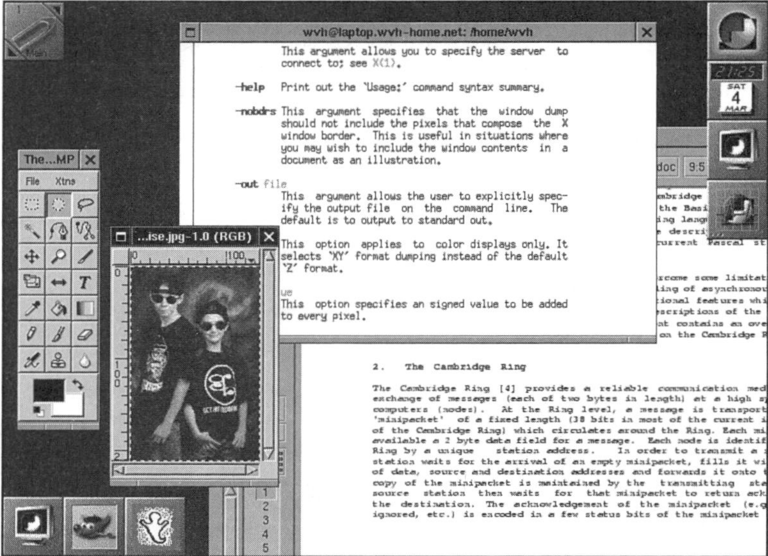

Figure 7.5

The Window Maker window manager.

fvwm95

This Windows 95/98-style variant on the Fancy Virtual Window Manager, Version 2, is actually just a special configuration for the fvwm2 window manager. The fvwm2 window manager running this graphical theme is often used to minimize culture shock when moving users from Windows systems to Linux systems. Located in the directory /usr/X11R6/bin, fvwm2 is started with the Windows 95 theme by running the command `RunWM.Fvwm95`. Fvwm95 features a Start menu, similar to that of Windows 95 and 98; provides a taskbar at the bottom of the screen, which is similar to that used by these versions of Windows; and displays the system time at the lower right of the taskbar. Figure 7.6 shows the fvwm95 window manager running on one of my Linux systems.

Why anyone would want to make a Linux system look like a Windows system is beyond me, unless to make new users comfortable. Seeing it running on a Linux system is good for a lot of double-takes, though.

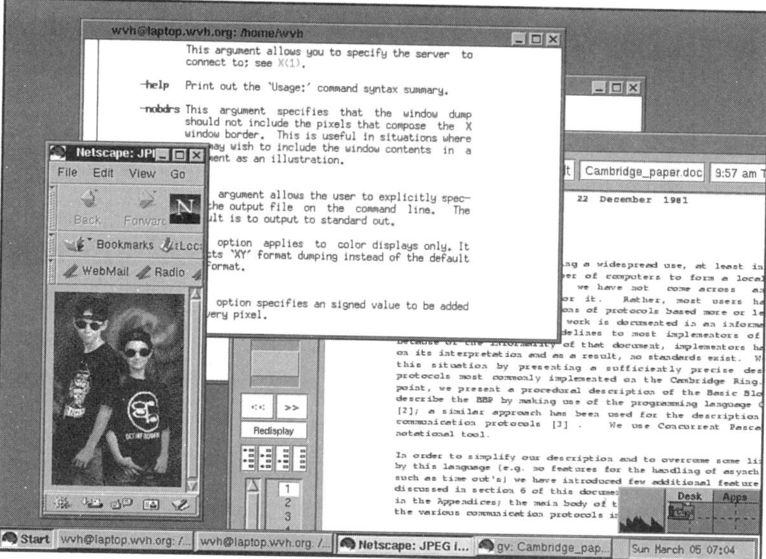

Figure 7.6

The fvwm95 window manager.

SawFish

SawFish, formerly known as SawMill, is a relatively young extensible window manager that uses a LISP-based scripting language. All window decorations are configurable, and all user-interface policy is controlled using the extension language. SawFish is designed as a fast, light-weight window manager, but it has a surprising number of graphical bells and whistles that are available by using different themes. The SawFish binary is located in the directory /usr/bin and is called sawmill. Your personal SawFish configuration is saved in a file in your home directory called .sawfishrc. SawFish themes can be installed by unpacking them in subdirectories of the directory ~/.sawfish/themes. You can configure SawFish either by writing Lisp code in a personal .sawmillrc file, or through an integrated customization system using GTK+. Figure 7.7 shows the SawFish window manager running on one of my Linux systems, using a GUI theme that makes it resemble the new Mac OS X “Aqua” GUI.

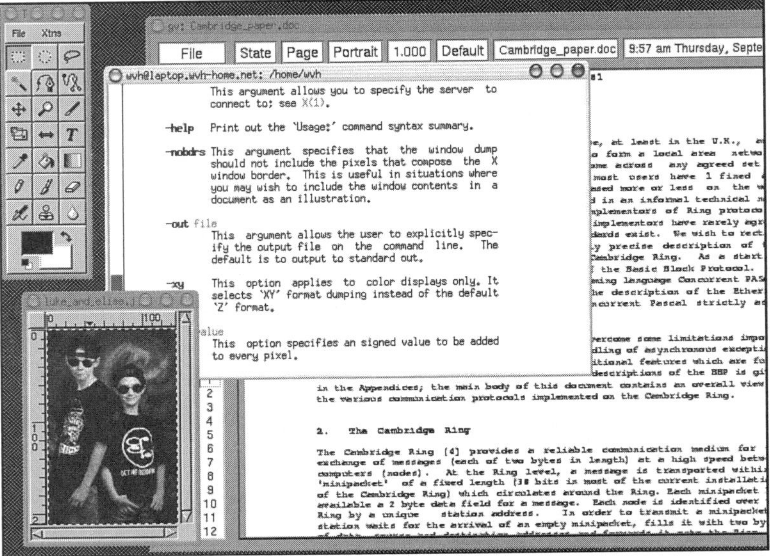

Figure 7.7

The SawFish window manager.

An impressive number of attractive SawFish themes are available from `http://sawmill.themes.org`. SawFIsh is actively under development. The latest SawFish sources and RPMs are always available on the Web from `ftp://sawmill.sourceforge.net/pub/sawmill`.

CHAPTER 8

Configuring Linux

This chapter begins discussing post-installation issues in configuring Linux. The first section discusses general issues in Linux system administration and introduces linuxconf, the central system administration application for Red Hat Linux systems. The linuxconf tool provides a single location for performing many system administration tasks, and either a starting or ending point for most others. As a central application for system administration, you must be logged in as root or have used the su command to assume the identity of the root user to run linuxconf.

Subsequent sections of this chapter discuss some of the most basic system administration tasks faced by everyone installing or configuring a Linux system for the first time. The first of these is adding printers to your Linux system and setting up the process of queuing print jobs to these printers. The next most popular system administration task is connecting your Linux systems to other systems or networks (such as the Internet) using a modem.

The remaining chapters of this book discuss more advanced system administration tasks for Linux. This chapter provides a starting point for understanding Linux system administration and the tools provided with Red Hat Linux to make your life easier.

System Administration on Linux Systems

One of the areas in which Linux still hasn't stabilized is in system administration, which is unfortunate because system administration is one of the most important aspects of any computer system. UNIX traditionally has provided a system administration environment that is best described as "poor" and "inconsistent." I've been a UNIX system administrator for

15 years or so, and have worked on UNIX systems from Apollo, DEC, HP, ISI, NBI, Sun, and other vendors during that time. All these had different system administration tools (usually text editors), used different configuration files, and required different types of arcane knowledge. The lack of a unified system administration environment, of a coherent desktop environment, and of user-quality commercial software has been the biggest stumbling blocks to the widespread adoption of UNIX over the years. Sound familiar? Linux is facing exactly the same problems, but its Open Source nature provides much hope that these problems can finally be fixed.

Different UNIX systems store the same types of configuration information in different files. Linux largely avoids this problem because the names and locations of most system configuration files are the same across Linux distributions—that's because the source code is the same. Regardless of the oneness of the underlying source code, different Linux distributions still provide different system administration tools. As a centralized tool for system administration, Red Hat provides linuxconf, a package with both X Window system and terminal-oriented interfaces, much like the Red Hat Installer. All linuxconf commands can also be executed from within command scripts, making linuxconf truly an administration tool for all seasons.

Figure 8.1 shows the linuxconf startup screen in the terminal-oriented version of Linuxconf. Figure 8.2 shows the linuxconf startup screen in the X Window system-based version of linuxconf. The X Window system interface is installed by default as part of both the KDE and the GNOME workstations, and is located in the GNOME-linuxconf-version-number package. This is a somewhat misleading name, however, because the X Window system interface for linuxconf works equally well under both GNOME and KDE.

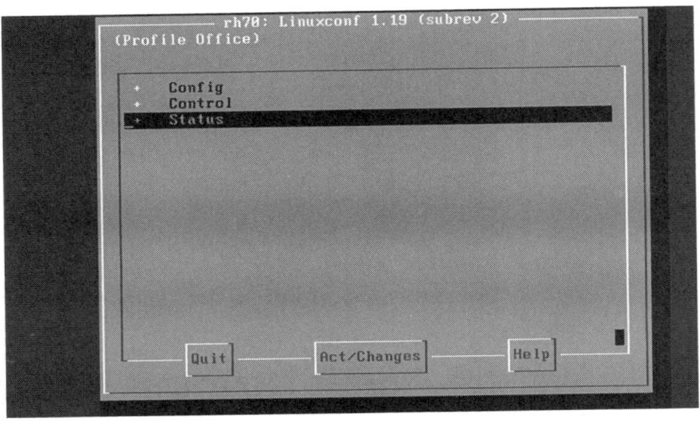

Figure 8.1

The terminal-oriented linuxconf interface.

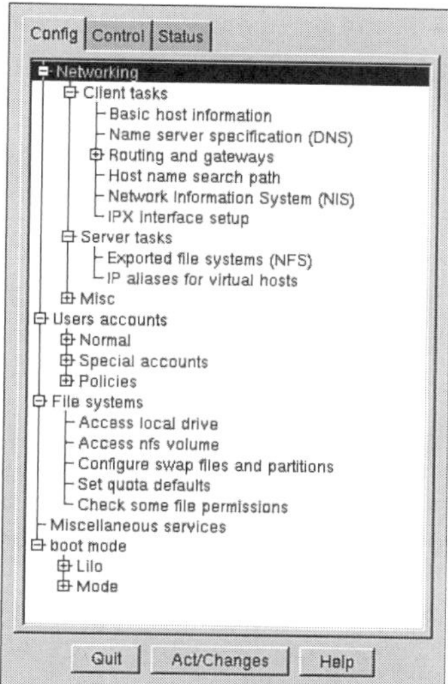

Figure 8.2

The Config.tab in the X Window system linuxconf interface.

All subsequent examples of linuxconf in this chapter show the X Window system interface for linuxconf. The organization of the commands, screens, and dialog boxes in linuxconf is exactly the same between the terminal-oriented and the X Window system interfaces—the latter simply looks better. To run the X Window system interface for linuxconf shown in this chapter, you must do the following:

- Be running an X Window system window manager or desktop environment
- Have the linuxconf-version package installed on your system
- Have the GNOME-linuxconf-version package installed on your system
- Be logged in as root or have used the `su` command to assume the identity of the root user
- Execute the command `/bin/linuxconf` from an xterm or console window in which the X Window system DISPLAY environment variable is set correctly

General Introduction to Red Hat's linuxconf Command

The linuxconf tool organizes Linux system administration tasks into three basic groups: those that configure different aspects of the system (Config), those that control the behavior of the system (Control), and those that provide status information about various aspects of Red Hat (Status). The difference between these can be subtle, and different aspects of some of the same services (such as accessing local and networked file systems) appear in both the Control and Config tabs. You view any of these sets of related commands by selecting the appropriate tab from the three tabs above the main linuxconf window.

The following two figures give you an overview of the commands available in each of the other linuxconf command groups. Figure 8.2 shows the X Window system version of linuxconf's Config tab. Figure 8.3 shows the X Window system version of Linuxconf's Control tab. Figure 8.4 shows the X Window system version of linuxconf's Status tab.

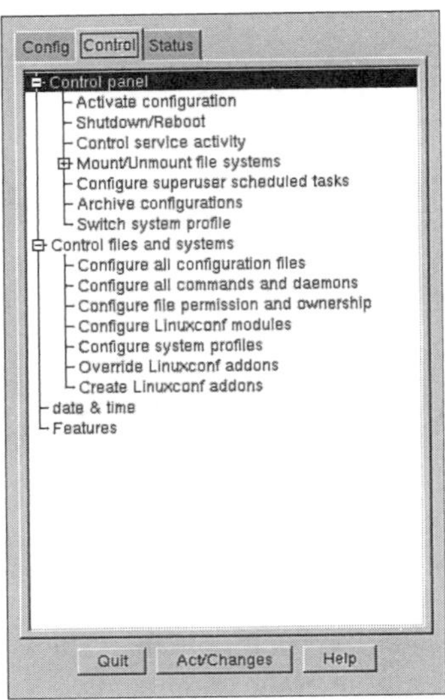

Figure 8.3

The Control section in linuxconf.

Figure 8.4

The Status section in linuxconf.

Sections of any linuxconf tab that are expandable are identified by a plus sign to the left of their names in the directory listing in the left panel of any linuxconf screen. To expand a section, click on the plus sign: The section expands, and the plus sign turns into a minus sign. To compress any section of the linuxconf directory, click on the minus sign to the left of its name: The section rolls up until only the name is visible, and the minus sign turns into a plus sign. You can scroll through the linuxconf directory by clicking and holding the left mouse button on the scrollbar in the center of the X Window system linuxconf dialog box, and dragging it up or down until you find the entry you want to modify.

When you display a panel or dialog box in the right portion of the X Window system linuxconf screen, a seperate or expanded window displays. You can move from one field to the next by pressing the Tab key. You also can move to any field by positioning the cursor in the field to which you want to move and then clicking the left mouse button—or, you can move to the previous field by holding down the `Shift` key and pressing `Tab`.

A good general rule when doing a system administration task on a Red Hat system is to try linuxconf first. If linuxconf supports the task that you want to do, it provides a well-designed interface for the task that is augmented by its online help. Even more impressive than its organization and centralization of various tasks is that linuxconf understands the implications of any changes you make to your system's configuration. You will find that linuxconf automatically keeps a list of any services that must be restarted (by running the appropriate scripts in `/etc/rc.d/init.d` or in the `/etc/rc.d/rc?.d` directory for the current run level) as a result of those changes. When you exit linuxconf after making any changes, linuxconf can preview a list of any init scripts that need to be restarted and can automatically shutdown and restart the associated services for you by running the appropriate init script. No reboots are necessary, unlike some other odious operating systems (Windows), although Windows 2000 fixes this problem in most respects.

Rather than providing a classic man page or other online reference information, linuxconf includes its own context-sensitive online help system. This online help is available from any linuxconf panel or tab by selecting the Help button, visible at the bottom of the preceding two screens and in the rest of the linuxconf examples in this chapter.

The best way to learn your way around linuxconf is to use it to perform some basic tasks. This tool provides a consistent set of tabbed dialog boxes that group related bits of information. The remainder of this section provides an example of using linuxconf to configure your network interface and set associated configuration information. This is something that you might need to do, for example, if your network card wasn't correctly recognized during installation or if you need to update your network configuration after upgrading Ethernet cards. Using linuxconf makes this task much easier than trying to locate all the configuration information stored in different locations on your Red Hat system. The next few sections explain which dialog boxes to use in linuxconf to configure or reconfigure an Ethernet adapter, and explain where the information you're entering is actually being used.

Configuring a Network Adapter Using linuxconf

The first step in configuring an Ethernet interface in linuxconf is to select the adapter that you want to configure. To do this, start linuxconf and select the Config, Networking, Client Tasks, Basic Host Information menu item.

Next, select the tab corresponding to the Ethernet adapter that you want to configure (in this case, the tab named Adapter 1). This displays the dialog box shown in Figure 8.5.

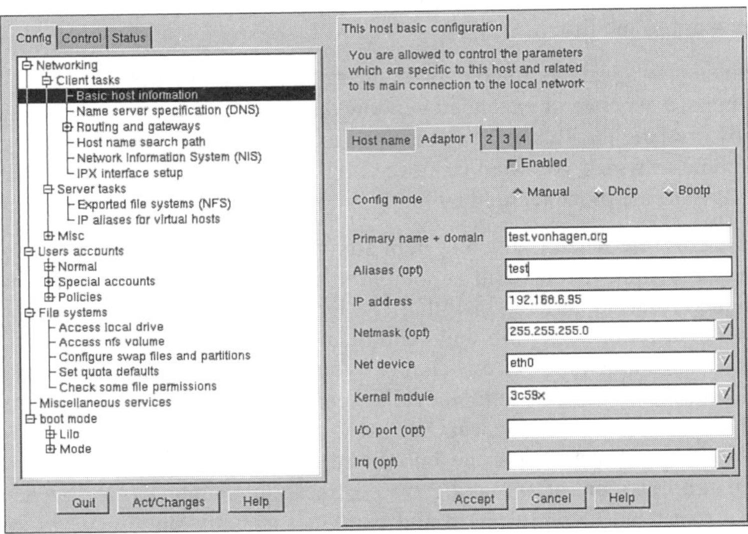

Figure 8.5

Configuring an Ethernet adapter in linuxconf.

First, make sure that the check box beside Enabled is selected to tell linuxconf to activate the selected Ethernet adapter. Next, select one of the Manual, DHCP, or Bootp Config modes, depending on how your system obtains its IP address. Select Manual if the machine has a specific IP address, and select DHCP (Dynamical Host Control Protocol) or Bootp (Boot Protocol) if your system obtains its IP address dynamically or its general configuration at boot time, depending on the protocol used.

Next, move the cursor to the Primary Name + Domain field, and enter the fully qualified name of your machine, including the domain. Figure 8.5 shows the fully qualified entry test for a machine named "test" in the Internet domain vonhagen.org. On the next line, you can enter any short aliases by which the machine you're configuring can also be found on the network. These aliases will be added to the end of the `/etc/hosts` file entry for your machine.

Next, if you selected Manual IP Config mode, enter the IP address of your machine in the IP Address field and the netmask for your machine in the Netmask field. Using a netmask expedites finding a host on the network by identifying the parts of the IP address that differ among hosts on your network. If you're using the DHCP or Bootp protocols to automatically obtain an Ethernet address and other configuration information, you don't need to fill in either of these fields unless you plan to reserve specific Bootp and DHCP addresses for the machine you're configuring.

Finally, you should select the network device that the Ethernet adapter you are defining is associated with, which is always `eth0` for machines with a single Ethernet card. Clicking on the arrow at the right of this field displays a drop-down list of your choices. Similarly, you must next select the kernel module to be loaded that contains the driver for the Ethernet card you are defining. Clicking the arrow at the right of the kernel module field displays a scrollable drop-down list of available kernel modules. You should first try to find one that is specifically designed for your Ethernet card or PCMCIA adapter. If no such module is listed, you can try a generic kernel module, such as `ne` or `ne2k-pci`, if your card advertises Novell-2000 compatibility. The net device and kernel module values are added to the file `/etc/conf.modules` to map the net device to its driver.

The final fields on this form are optional unless the I/O port and Interrupt Request Vector (IRQ) used by your Ethernet card are fixed and can't be automatically identified by the Linux kernel—that's a rare occurrence nowadays, but it still is necessary for some older cards.

After you've entered all the data on this dialog box, click Accept to save the new values you have entered. If you've made any changes to the settings on this dialog box, you will see the message "DNS has been updated." This is something of a misnomer if your system isn't running a nameserver, because the only generic hostname lookup file that has been updated in that case is the `/etc/hosts` file. Click OK to close this dialog box. If you are running a nameserver on this host, you still will need to update the name-to-IP and reverse IP-to-name mapping files, which you can do in the Config, Networking, Server Tasks, Domain Name Server (DNS) portion of linuxconf or even manually, using a text editor.

Changing Nameserver Specifications in linuxconf

To set the default domain, nameservers, and domains to search for unqualified names, select the Config, Networking, Client Tasks, Name Server Specification (DNS) command. The Resolver Configuration dialog box displays.

The entries in this dialog box are used to build or modify the `/etc/resolv.conf` configuration file, used by the system each time you connect to another network host by using a short or fully qualified host name. The Default Domain field specifies the domain to be searched first if you specify a short name, but it is actually ignored if you subsequently specify one or more search domains. Whichever of these entries (Default or Search) appears last in `/etc/resolv.conf` is the one that is actually used. Typically, the default domain is the first entry in the file, followed by an (optional) domain search list, followed by a list of nameservers to query, in that order. If you have only a single domain on your network, I suggest just using the default domain and leaving the search domains blank, as shown in Figure 8.6. However, if you have multiple domains on a single network for organizational purposes, you must be sure that the list of domains to search includes the default domain.

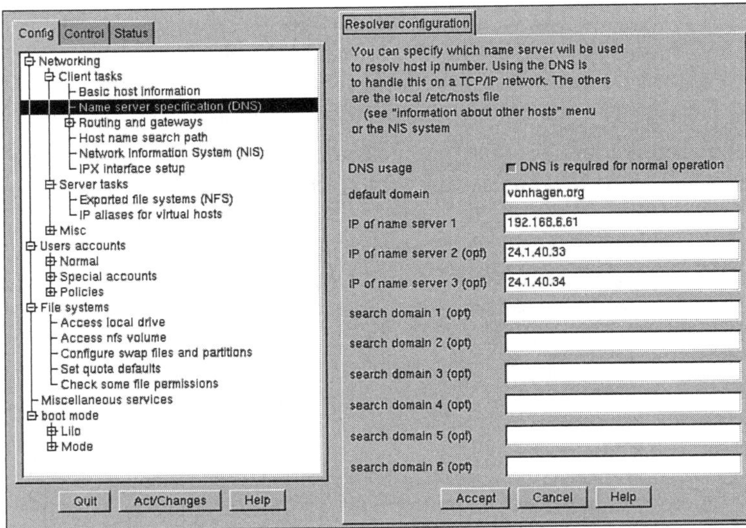

Figure 8.6

Configuring DNS information in linuxconf.

The list of nameserver IP addresses that you enter is interesting, especially if you are running a local nameserver for your personal domain but still need to find hosts outside your domain (such as hosts located elsewhere on the Internet). If you are running your own nameserver for your domain, you should always put that nameserver first—it is physically closest to you, is under your control, and therefore always should be updated with a complete list of your hosts and their current IP addresses. Figure 8.6 shows my personal nameserver first in the list (its address chosen from the list of nonrouted, private IP addresses), followed by two nameservers at my ISP for this location.

When you've entered all the data on this dialog box, click Accept to save the new values you have entered. The right dialog box in linuxconf closes.

Changing Gateway and Routing Information in linuxconf

The next step in configuring or reconfiguring an Ethernet interface is to identify the host through which all nonlocal IP address requests are routed. This is a host that typically has two Ethernet interfaces, one connected to the Internet or an ISP, and the other connected to your internal network.

To set the default gateway and enable routing between your local network and the Internet, select the Config, Networking, Client Tasks, Routing and Gateways, Set Defaults command. The Defaults dialog box displays.

Enter the IP address of the Ethernet interface on your gateway machine on your local network as the default gateway address; then select the Enable Routing button. The machine you specify must be configured to route Internet-bound packets between the two interfaces, but building and configuring a gateway is somewhat outside the scope of this book.

After you've entered all the data on this dialog box, click Accept to save the new values you have entered. The right dialog box in linuxconf closes.

The linuxconf tool provides several similar options to specify routing between different local domains, such as the Set Other Routes to Networks, Set Other Routes to Hosts, Set Routes to Alternate Local Nets, and Configure the Routed Daemon options, but these are more advanced features than can be easily explained in an introduction to linuxconf. See the context-sensitive, online help for these panels in linuxconf for more information.

Specifying the Hostname Search Path in linuxconf

A final critical aspect of correctly using the `/etc/hosts` file, your nameservers, and any other name services (such as Sun's Network Information System (NIS)) is to specify the order in which they are used on your system, known as the hostname search path, or whether they are used on your system at all.

To set the hostname search path, select the Config, Networking, Client Tasks, Routing and Gateways, Host Name Search Path command.

I typically use the `/etc/hosts` file first, followed by DNS, and I do not use NIS except for networks with hundreds of hosts where manually synchronizing the `/etc/passwd` and `/etc/group` files would otherwise be a nightmare. I use `/etc/hosts` first because the `/etc/hosts` file on all my machines maps most of the Internet banner ad companies back to my loopback interface (127.0.0.1), which causes loading banner ads to fail immediately, removes parasites, and generally improves bandwidth on my network immensely. (See `http://www.ecst.csuchico.edu/~atman/spam/adblock.shtml` for an excellent article on this topic.)

In the Host Name Search Path dialog box, first select the "Multiple IPs for One Host" check box if your `/etc/hosts` file or DNS contains entries for any dual boot systems that have the same IP address but different hostnames, depending on the operating system that they are running. Next, select the radio button that corresponds to the order in which you want to search the `/etc/hosts` file, DNS, and NIS. As mentioned, I usually use hosts, DNS search order.

After you've entered all the data in this dialog box, click Accept to save the new values you have entered. The right dialog box in linuxconf closes.

Previewing and Activating Changes in linuxconf

And now, the moment of truth. Click the Quit button in the bottom left corner of the linuxconf screen. If you've made any changes that require any Linux system service to restart, a dialog box such as the one shown in Figure 8.7 displays.

To see what init scripts Linuxconf believes must be re-executed to make your system's configuration match the information entered in linuxconf, click the Preview What Has to Be Done button. A Things to Do dialog box displays, as shown in Figure 8.8, listing the scripts that linuxconf will execute to synchronize your system. Unfortunately, though the window title is "Things to do," the preview screen displays entries like "Executing...<script-name>", which might lead you to believe that it was actually doing the work rather than just listing what will be done. The startup and shutdown scripts identified in this dialog will only actually be executed if you subsequently click the "Activate the changes" button. Click the window manager's close button to close the "Thing to do" dialog box.

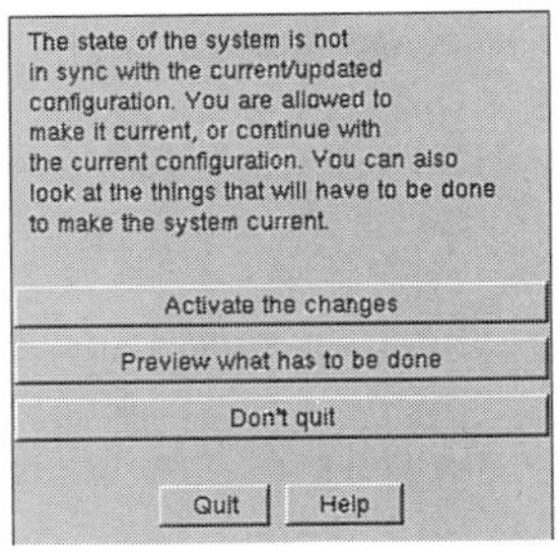

Figure 8.7

The dialog box for previewing or activating changes in linuxconf.

Figure 8.8

The Things to do preview dialog box in linuxconf.

At this point, you can either click the Activate the Changes button to synchronize your system's state with the changes you've made in linuxconf, click Don't Quit option to go back and make other changes in linuxconf, or click Quit to exit without actually making the changes you've specified in Linuxconf. They still will take place the next time you boot your system, so you almost always want to select Activate the Changes option at this point. If there are any problems, you can correct them now rather than forgetting what you changed and trying to run linuxconf on a system that may not even be capable of running the X Window system anymore. If all the changes were done successfully, the status of the system window closes. You may have to click Quit again to exit linuxconf. If any scripts fail to correctly restart services on your machine, the script that failed is identified, and you should re-examine the related linuxconf panels to determine whether you've made any typographical errors or incorrect selections that you should correct. This is often the case for typists like myself who manually enter Ethernet addresses!

This concludes the introduction to linuxconf. Whenever possible, subsequent sections of this book discuss Red Hat administrative tasks in the context of linuxconf both to show the amazing number of different administrative tasks that it encapsulates and to reinforce linuxconf as the best administrative application of its kind for Linux systems.

Installing and Configuring Printers

After the previous section's glowing recommendation of linuxconf as a central tool for most Red Hat system administration tasks, it's perfectly natural that the next section should discuss configuring printers, which must be done outside linuxconf, using Red Hat's dedicated printer configuration utility called printtool. Just one more growth opportunity for linuxconf at some point in the future, I suppose…

Red Hat's printtool is an X Window system application that immensely simplifies the task of defining local and networked printers on Linux systems. Information about available printers, their capabilities, and the applications used to pre- and post-process information sent to them is stored in the file `/etc/printcap` and can be a bear to edit manually. The printtool package makes defining printers, associated programs, and spool directories, and then testing these configurations extremely easy. (*Spooling* is just a historical term for setting up the mechanism by which different users can queue print jobs and the system will print them one at a time.) Because printtool modifies the file `/etc/printcap`, which is owned by the root user, you must be logged in as root or have used the `su` command to assume the identity of the root user before running the printtool command. You also must be running an X Window system window manager or desktop environment to use printtool. Figure 8.9 shows the printtool window as it looks before you've defined any printers.

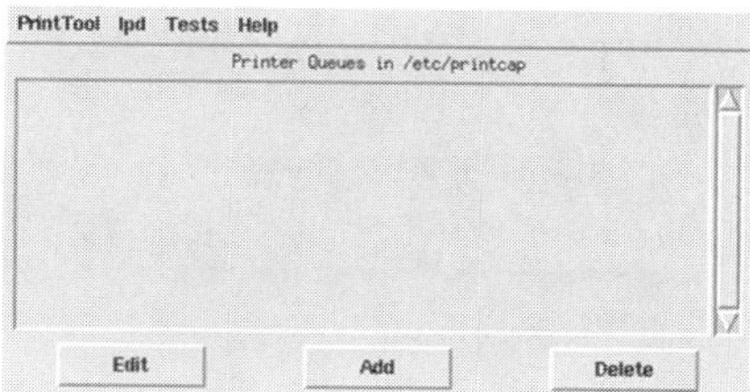

Figure 8.9

The main printtool window.

Click Add to define a printer. A dialog displays, prompting you to select the type of printer you are adding.

For local printers, click OK to proceed. The printtool utility then scans your system for ports to which printers could be selected, and displays a summary dialog box, as shown in Figure 8.10.

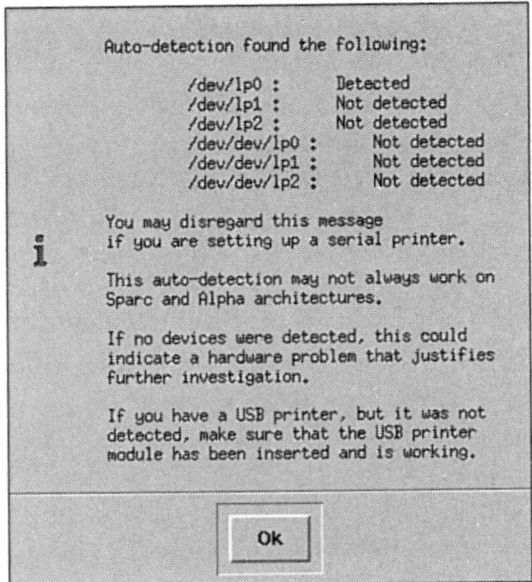

Figure 8.10

The Auto-Detect Results dialog box.

Click OK to close this window. The Edit Local Printer Entry dialog box displays, as shown in Figure 8.11.

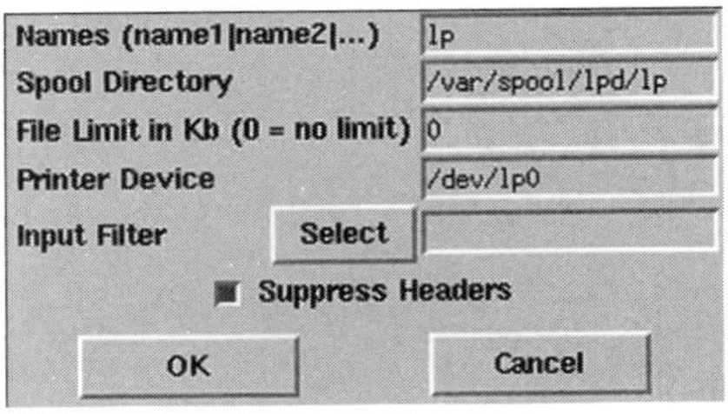

Figure 8.11

The Edit Local Printer Entry dialog box.

The critical piece of a printer definition is the printer filter, also referred to as the printer driver or input filter, which is a program that converts your input to the format that a printer can use, internally invoking programs called mpage and ghostscript to do the dirty work for you. To add a specific printer filter to the new printer definition that you're creating, click Select beside the Input Filter field in the Edit local Printer Entry dialog. The Configure Filter dialog box displays, as shown in Figure 8.12.

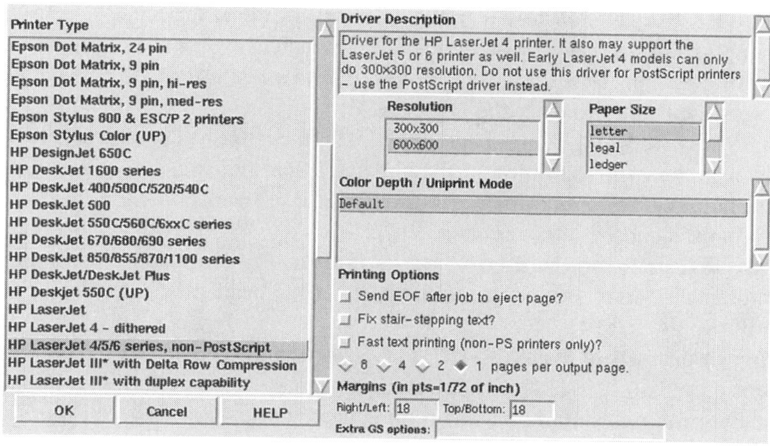

Figure 8.12

The Configure Filter dialog box.

The Configure Filter dialog box consists of two halves. The left half contains a scrollable list of available print filters, listed by printer type. Even if your specific printer isn't listed there, your printer probably supports one of the types of output used by the printers listed there. For example, the printer I currently use is a NEC SuperScript 660i. This printer isn't listed there, but the NEC SilentWriter 660i supports HP LaserJet 4 printer output, which is listed there, and which I've selected in Figure 8.12.

NOTE

When adding a printer to a Linux system, two invaluable sources of up-to-date printer information on the Web are the Linux Printer HOWTO (at `http://www.linuxdoc.org/HOWTO/Printing-HOWTO-4.html`) and Grant Taylor's CGI front end to a database of supported printers, the drivers used with them, and users' success and failure stories with different printers (at `http://www.picante.com/~gtaylor/pht/printer_list.cgi`).

The right half of the Configure Filter dialog box enables you to configure specific aspects of the print filter selected in the left half of the dialog box. Most printer filters enable you to specify the print resolution (typically 300 × 300 or 600 × 600) and the size of the paper in the printer's paper tray. Other standard printing options are described in the following list; using these options is explained in the "Fixing and Fine-Tuning Printing" section, later in this chapter. I strongly suggest that you accept the default options offered for your printer here, at least until you've successfully gotten some output from your printer.

- **Send EOF After Job to Eject Page**—Some printers, especially PostScript printers, require that an END-OF-FILE character be sent as the last character of a print job. This tells the printer driver that no more information is coming and forces the printer to eject the last page.
- **Fix Stair-Stepping Text**—Linux, UNIX, some print filters, and some printers differ in their interpretation of the character that indicates the end of a line of text output. This option toggles between the two most popular ways of interpreting the end-of-line character.
- **Fast Text printing (Non-PS Printers Only)**—Printers that accept only standard text input let you bypass some parts of the print filter if you're printing only simple text files.
- **Pages Per Output Page (8, 4, 2, 1)**—Selecting any value other than 1 shrinks your output so that 2, 4, or 8 pages appear on each page of output. Do *not* enable printing multiple pages on one output page when first configuring your printer because the printer test page (described later in this section) will not print correctly.

The final option on this dialog box enables you to control the size of the margins on your printed page, expressed in points, which are units that are each 1/72 of an inch.

After you've selected a print filter and selected the output resolution and appropriate paper on this dialog box, click OK to return to the Edit Local Printer Entry dialog box. Unless you really need to use other settings, you should accept the defaults offered on this dialog box, perhaps with the exception of Suppress Headers. In an environment where multiple people will be sharing the same printer, selecting this option generates a cover page for each print job. This cover page identifies the user who printed each print job, which may be handy when sorting lots of output. This option doesn't always work correctly for many Linux and UNIX printers, but it can be handy if it does. Experimenting with this option is explained in the next section, "Fixing and Fine-Tuning Printing."

Click OK to close the Edit Local Printer Entry dialog box; then select the appropriate item from the printtool Tests menu, and print a test page. This can be surprisingly unintuitive. For example, if you're using any laser printer that accepts input in a printer language (the most common of which are PCL, Hewlett-Packard's Printer Control Language, and PostScript), you will want to print a PostScript test page. This is because the ghostscript print filter application mentioned at the beginning of this section is working for you behind the scenes, converting the PostScript test page (if your printer isn't actually a PostScript printer) into the printer control language used by your printer.

Trust me—select Print Postscript Test Page option from the printtool Tests menu unless your printer prints only text output (in which case you should select the Print ASCII Test Page option), and watch your printer for your output. A confirming dialog box displays after the test page has been successfully sent to the printer.

If printing a Postscript test page, the page that prints should be framed by two boxes, inside which scaled Helvetica text beginning "This is the Red Hat Printtool PostScript Test Page" is displayed. If printing an ASCII test page, you should see fixed-width text that begins "If this is all you see, try enabling…"

Fixing and Fine-Tuning Printing

If your test output isn't correct or doesn't print, or if you want to enable printing multiple pages per single page of output, select the printer definition you modify, click Edit, and do the following:

- If you printed an ASCII test page, but your sample output page displays only the first line or shows lines that are not correctly left-aligned, click Select and enable the Fix Stair-Stepping Text Option.
- If you printed a PostScript test page, but your printer doesn't eject an output page, click Select and enable the Send EOF After Job to Eject Page option.
- If you specified printing a headers page, and the header page prints incorrectly but your test PostScript output page is correct, first click Select and then enable the Fix Stair-Stepping Text option. Try printing a test page again. If the headers work now, fine. If not, go back and disable the Fix Stair-Stepping Text Option and then enable the Suppress Headers option in the Edit Local Printer Entry dialog box. You won't be able to get print headers to separate your print jobs, but your printer will work correctly.
- If you printed a PostScript test page, but you want to print multiple pages per single page of output, click Select and then select the appropriate number of output pages per printed page. Selecting a value of 8 is handy if you want to print microfiche. Selecting a value of 4 or 2 can help you save paper if your eyes are excellent or just good.
- If you printed an ASCII test page that printed correctly, but you want to speed up printing text files in the future, click Select and enable the Fast text Printing (Non-PS Printers Only) option. Such printers let you expedite printing by shipping some parts of the print filter invisibly. However, you must not check this option if you have a PostScript printer because all you'll see are blinking lights followed by no output (or perhaps a page of PostScript error messages) as your printer attempts to interpret your text file as a set of PostScript instructions. This option is incompatible with setting the Pages Per Output Page option to any value other than 1.

CHAPTER 9

Using Local and Network Storage

This chapter explains how to expand your system by adding local or remote (networked) storage, and by enabling your system to interact with the file systems used on Windows computers. This chapter also discusses how to add additional swap space to your system if you find that you are running out of virtual memory. Where possible, this chapter discusses these tasks in terms of Red Hat's linuxconf graphical system administration utility.

The first section of this chapter explains how to add new disks and removable media to an existing Linux system; it also gives the names of different types of devices associated with different disk interfaces and types of removable storage media under Linux. In addition, this part discusses how to partition storage devices, explains how to create swap space to increase the amount of virtual memory available to your system, and covers how to integrate new partitions and swap space into your system using linuxconf.

NOTE

You may want to skip the next section if you're installing Linux on a laptop because adding new disks to a laptop can be tricky if you're limited by the physical space constraints of your system. PCMCIA disks and removable storage, such zip drives, are attractive alternatives for increasing the amount of storage space you have available on a laptop.

You may also want to skip the next section if you're installing Linux on a desktop system and currently have a reasonable amount of free space available. Although adding a disk drive to your system isn't a standard part of installing a Linux system, discovering that you need additional space is fairly common, especially after you've installed a number of Linux applications. When you need it, the next section may be invaluable. The information it provides on partitioning and creating file systems is difficult to find in the online documentation for Linux.

Adding New Disks and Storage Devices

During the life of every computer system, that system eventually will run out of usable disk space. Even after deleting extraneous files and archiving old, unused files and directories off onto archive media, the most common way of resolving disk space problems is to simply add another disk to the system, dividing it into manageably sized partitions and integrating them into your file system wherever they are most useful. As mentioned in Chapter 2, "Preparing Your System for Red Hat 7.0," separate partitions are associated with different directories for one or more of the following reasons:

- To isolate the contents of those directories from the system itself.
- To simplify increasing the amount of space associated with those directories.
- To reduce the overall sizes of the partitions and associated file systems on your system. The system fsck utility (file system consistency check) can verify and repair smaller file systems more quickly than large ones at boot time, especially nowadays, when fsck can check multiple partitions in parallel.
- To reduce the impact of the failure of any single disk or disk partition on your system as a whole. You can restore one or more smaller file systems from backup media much more quickly than you can restore a single huge partition. Smaller partitions also can be backed up more quickly during standard daily maintenance.

The Disk Druid process used when installing Linux provides an extremely friendly, largely intuitive interface for partitioning disks and defining associated partition data, such as partition type information. Unfortunately, you currently can use the Disk Druid only when installing Linux. You must use other Linux utilities, specifically the text-oriented /sbin/fdisk utility or the terminal-oriented /sbin/cfdisk utility, to partition disks and set partition type information when Linux is running.

This chapter describes using the /sbin/cfdisk utility (hereafter referred to as cfdisk) for these reasons:

- This utility is installed by default on Red Hat Workstation class installations.
- It provides a more usable interface than that provided by the fdisk utility.
- It is less widely documented than the old-style fdisk utility.

After the new disks are partitioned using the cfdisk utility and are formatted using /sbin/mkfs utility, the new partitions can be mounted and permanently added to your system using linuxconf.

Adding New Disks and Partitions: The Planning Phase

If you simply need more space on your system, you can quickly create a new file system and mount it on a new or unused directory on your current system.

However, if you need more space on an existing partition, you'll probably want to move an existing directory from a partition that is full onto its own partition. Good candidates for directories to move off existing partitions are directories such as the one that holds your Web server data files and logs (`/home/httpd`), or any project or system administration directories in which you actively archive and build new system software. As a general rule, move directories that you expect to continue to grow but that occupy enough disk space on a currently full partition that moving them to their own partitions will free sufficient space on the existing, full partition.

Poor choices for portions to split from the primary file systems are directories containing binaries or shared libraries that you require to boot or repair your system. Partitions occasionally develop corruption that prevents them from being successfully mounted. If you develop corruption in a partition that holds binaries, files, or shared libraries that your systems need to boot or operate correctly, you may need to reinstall Red Hat Linux to correct the problem.

The following is an overview of the process for adding new disks and partitions to an existing system:

1. Determine what portions of your existing file system you can move onto their own partitions. If you simply want to add additional disk space, decide where you want to mount the new partitions, and create any directories that you want to use as mount points.
2. Shut down your system and physically connect the new drives to your system, bringing the system back up in single user mode so that you can add new disks and move files and directories without interrupting the users of your system.
3. Partition the new disks using cfdisk. Create file systems on new partitions using mkfs or format them for use as swap space using mkswap, as appropriate.
4. Shut down any processes that are running in the directories that you will be moving, taking your system down to single user mode, if necessary.
5. Archive the current contents of the directories that you will be moving onto the new partitions.
6. Remove the contents of the existing directories.
7. Mount the new partitions appropriately, adding them to `/etc/fstab` so that they will be automatically mounted in the future.
8. Reload the archived data into the newly mounted partitions.
9. Restart any processes that should be running in the newly mounted partitions, and make the new partitions available to users.

The next sections of this chapter explain each step in this process in more detail.

Adding Disks to Your Linux System

The procedure for adding new hard disks to your Linux system depends on the type of disk interface to which you're adding the disks. The most common disk interfaces found in Linux systems are Integrated Drive Electronics (IDE) or Enhanced Integrated Drive Electronics (EIDE) interfaces. Most PC motherboards have two IDE or EIDE interfaces, each capable of supporting one master and one slave device. Other types of disk interfaces often found in Linux systems include Small Computer System Interface (SCSI) interfaces, which support at least seven devices, each uniquely identified by a numeric SCSI interface.

You must shut down your system to add new disks if they or the disk controller itself use any interface other than PCMCIA; this is because PCMCIA is designed to support the addition of new devices to a system while it is running. You do not need to shut down your system to mount and use any form of removable media. Red Hat does not currently support plug-and-play universal serial bus (USB) or Firewire interfaces that can be used with removable, plug-and-play hard drives.

NOTE

Using PCMCIA disk controllers and disks attached to them as boot media is possible using Linux's capability to load from a RAM disk and then switch control to a kernel or root file system located on the PCMCIA media. This topic, however, is far beyond the scope of this book. See the Web document `http://www.linux.org/help/ldp/howto/PCMCIA-HOWTO-5.html` for more information.

The devices on permanent hard disk interfaces are scanned and identified when your system boots. You should never add new disks to your system while it is running: Some more modern device interfaces such as USB and Firewire support hot-swappable devices, but these interfaces are not totally supported by the current releases of the Linux kernel. Many Redundant Array of Inexpensive/Independent Disks (RAID) controllers are software-controlled SCSI interfaces that support the removal and replacement of disks while the system is running, but these disks are usually mirrored portions of other file systems that are still in use on your system, even if one of the mirrors fails. You basically can't lose by shutting down your system to add new disks.

If you are adding IDE or EIDE disks to your system, first determine which IDE interface in your system can support an additional device. You usually can do this from the BIOS by examining the main BIOS screen that shows the devices currently attached to your system. If either of your IDE interfaces has an unused master or slave device, jumper your drive appropriately (configuring it as a master or a slave device) and attach it to that IDE interface in your system. Jumpers are small two-pin connectors on your disk that you connect to tell a disk whether it is a master or a slave device. Many drives list the jumper positions somewhere on the outside of the disk. If your drive does not, check the documentation that came with your disk, or search the manufacturer's Web site for jumper information.

If you are adding new SCSI disks to your system, set the address of the disk (using jumpers or a small numeric selector on the drive) to a numeric SCSI address that is not currently used on your system. Your SCSI card itself generally uses SCSI ID #0 or #7—the specific address used by the card should be identified by the SCSI BIOS when your system detects the card at boot time.

You should then reboot your system. Red Hat's Kudzu application should detect the new drives as part of the reboot process and should give you the option of configuring them into your system. This simply means that the new drives will automatically be recognized as a standard portion of your system, not that the new drives are ready for use in any sense. To add the new drives to your system, you must partition them and then format those partitions for use with Linux, as described in the next section.

To verify that the new drive is attached to your system and was found, and then to determine what its name is, you can use a command like the following. This sample command finds any messages related to disks named hda through hdd (IDE hard drives) in the `/var/log/messages` file where boot messages are stored:

```
grep hd[a-d] /var/log/messages
```

NOTE

For SCSI hard drives, you would substitute the disk name `sd[a-g]` for `hd[a-d]` in the previous example because most Linux SCSI disks use the generic SCSI driver.

The file `/var/log/messages` holds copies of any messages displayed on the screen when you boot your system. Subsequent reboots of your machine continue to append information to this file, so you'll want to focus on the last few lines of output displayed in response to the `grep` command, and tagged with the date of the last time you booted your system. Among the last few lines of output will be lines like the following:

```
Mar  5 16:49:06 twoproc kernel: hda: ST320430A, ATA DISK drive
Mar  5 16:49:06 twoproc kernel: hdb: WDC AC2850F, ATA DISK drive
Mar  5 16:49:06 twoproc kernel: hdc: CD-ROM 50X, ATAPI CDROM drive
```

You then can search this list for the name of the new disk you just added, making sure that you note the device that it is associated with. For demonstration purposes, I added a small Western Digital drive to my system, which is showing up as `hdb: WDC AC2850F, ATA DISK drive`.

To be totally sure that you are partitioning the right disk, you can use the `df` command to display the status of all disks that are currently mounted on your system:

```
[root]# df
Filesystem           1k-blocks      Used Available Use% Mounted on
/dev/hda5             19623156    689936  17936392   4% /
/dev/hda1                23302      5406     16693  24% /boot
```

Make absolutely sure that the basename of the disk you are planning to partition is not listed (this is hdb, in the case of the drive I added). You should also use the `swapon` command's summary option (`-s`) to make sure that the disk you are partitioning isn't already being used solely for swap space:

```
[root]# swapon -s Filename        Type           Size     Used     Priority
/dev/hda6                         partition      72252    0        -1
```

Because we know that the new drive is `/dev/hdb` and that it isn't being used for anything, it's now safe to partition it.

Partitioning New Disks

After you've attached the new disk and your system has recognized it at boot time, you use the `/sbin/cfdisk` command to repartition the disk. You'll need to be logged in as root on your system console or have used the `su` command to become the root user to be able to partition and format the new disks using the cfdisk utility.

NOTE

As discussed at the beginning of this chapter, the /sbin/fdisk program is an alternative to the /sbin/cfdisk program, but it uses a command-line interface and is generally less usable than /sbin/cfdisk.

To partition the new disk using the cfdisk program, follow these steps:

1. As root, start /sbin/cfdisk, supplying the name of the disk that you want to partition as an argument. The following example starts cfdisk, preparing to partitioning the new drive `/dev/hdb:/sbin/cfdisk /dev/hdb`.
2. The initial cfdisk screen, shown in Figure 9.1, displays a list of the current contents of the specified hard drive, either free space or existing partitions.

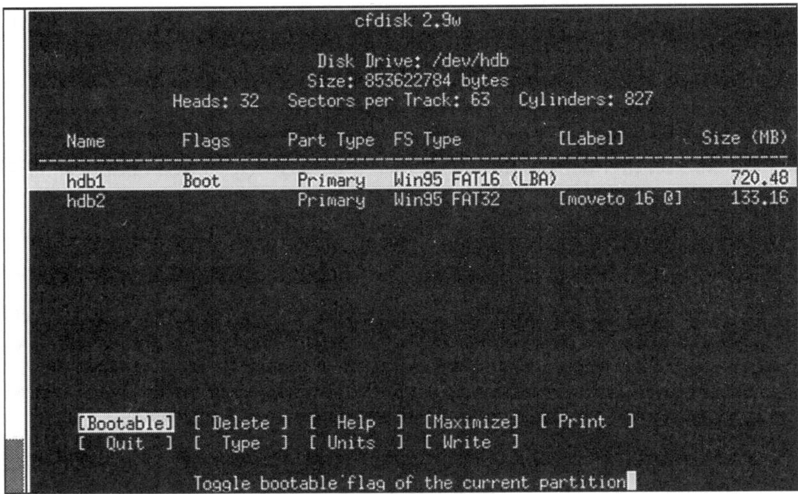

Figure 9.1

The cfdisk startup screen showing two existing partitions.

If any partitions are displayed and you are absolutely sure that they are not being used by your system, you must delete them before you can create new partitions. Deleting these partitions is irreversible, so be very careful. Figure 9.1 shows two existing DOS partitions that must be deleted before I can create Linux partitions on the drive. To delete existing partitions, use the Up or Down arrow key to highlight the name of each partition in turn, and press the D key to delete the highlighted partition. The entry for that partition is removed from the cfdisk display and is replaced with an entry for the amount of contiguous free space available on the disk. Figure 9.2 shows the cfdisk screen after deleting the two partitions shown in Figure 9.1.

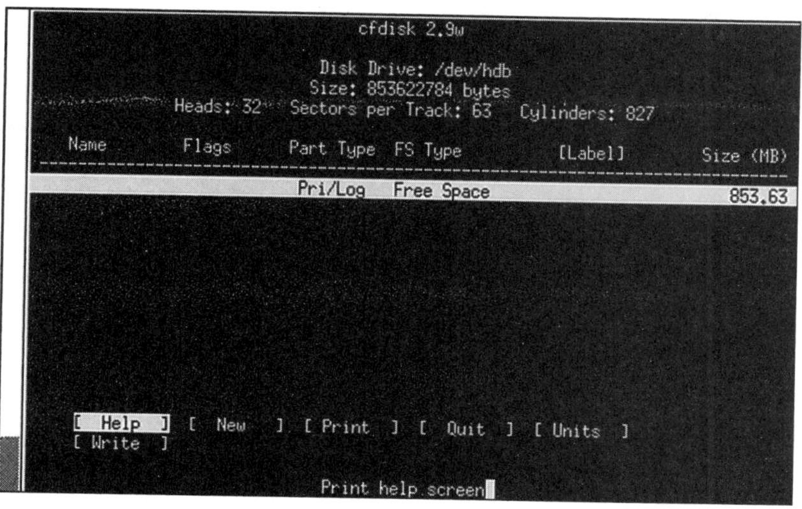

Figure 9.2

The cfdisk screen after deleting existing partitions.

3. Next, create the partition(s) that you want to have on the new disk. As a simple example, let's create two partitions, one for a Linux file system and one for an additional swap space partition.

   To create a new partition, press N (for New). The cfdisk program prompts you for the size of the partition, displaying the remaining free space on the disk as a default value. My test disk is small, so I'll create a 500MB data partition. Enter the size of the partition that you want to create in megabytes. The cfdisk program prompts you for whether to put the new partition at the beginning or the end of the available free space. Press E to select the beginning of the free space.

   Figure 9.3 shows the cfdisk screen after creating the initial partition.

   To create the second new partition, press N (for New). The cfdisk program prompts you for the size of the partition, displaying the remaining free space on the disk as a default value. My test disk is small, so I'll create a 500MB data partition. Enter the size of the partition that you want to create in megabytes. The cfdisk program prompts you for whether to put the new partition at the beginning or the end of the available free space. Press B to select the beginning of the free space.

   Figure 9.4 shows the cfdisk screen after creating the second partition.

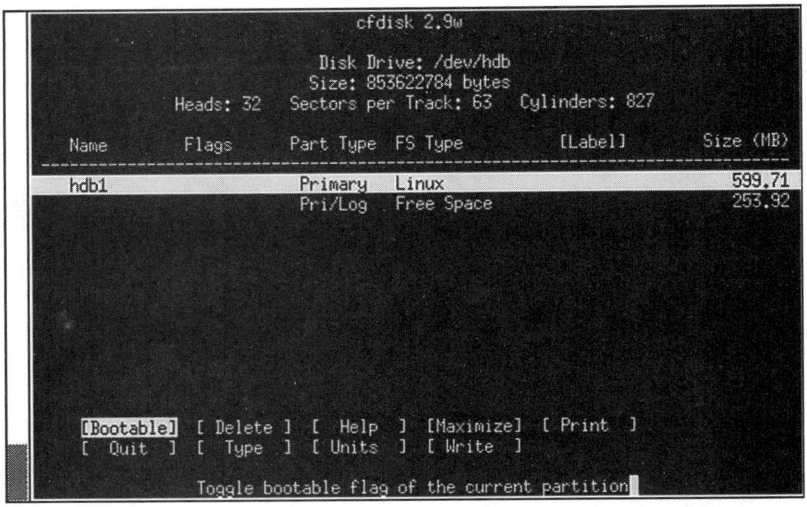

```
                              cfdisk 2.9w

                          Disk Drive: /dev/hdb
                         Size: 853622784 bytes
            Heads: 32   Sectors per Track: 63   Cylinders: 827

  Name         Flags      Part Type  FS Type          [Label]        Size (MB)
 ------------------------------------------------------------------------------
  hdb1                     Primary   Linux                              599.71
                           Pri/Log   Free Space                         253.92

    [Bootable]  [ Delete ]  [  Help  ]  [Maximize]  [ Print  ]
    [  Quit  ]  [  Type  ]  [ Units  ]  [ Write  ]

                Toggle bootable flag of the current partition
```

Figure 9.3

The cfdisk screen after creating a partition.

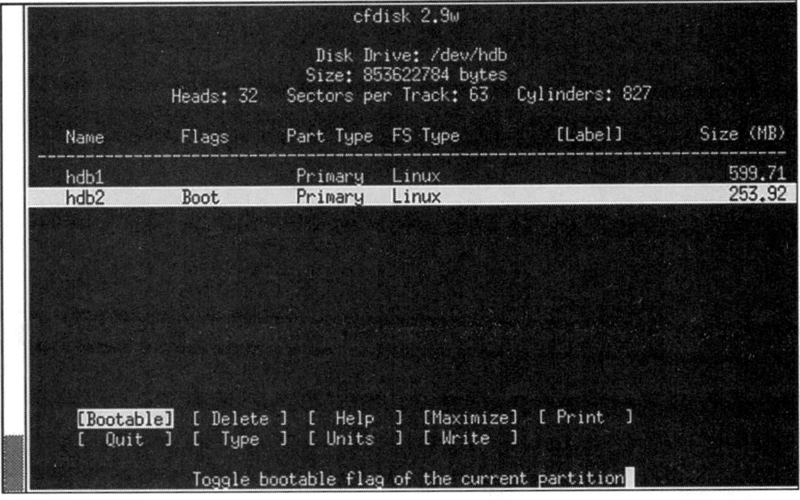

Figure 9.4

The cfdisk screen after creating a second partition.

4. Next, change the type of the second partition to type 82 (Linux swap). By default, both fdisk and cfdisk create partitions of the most common type of partition used on Linux systems, EXT2.

   To change the partition type, use the arrow keys to select the partition for which you want to change the type, and press T. A screen displays showing the most common Linux partition types. Press the spacebar to see the rest of the partition types, and enter **82** (the default value) for the new type of the selected partition.

Figure 9.5 shows the cfdisk screen after changing the type of the second partition.

```
                              cfdisk 2.9w

                         Disk Drive: /dev/hdb
                         Size: 853622784 bytes
          Heads: 32   Sectors per Track: 63   Cylinders: 827

 Name        Flags      Part Type  FS Type          [Label]        Size (MB)
------------------------------------------------------------------------------
 hdb1                   Primary    Linux                              599.71
 hdb2        Boot       Primary    Linux swap                         253.92




 [Bootable]  [ Delete ]  [  Help  ]  [Maximize]  [ Print  ]
 [  Quit  ]  [  Type  ]  [ Units  ]  [ Write  ]

           Toggle bootable flag of the current partition
```

Figure 9.5

The cfdisk screen after changing the type of the second partition.

5. Finally, you must write the new partition table out to the disk. To do this, press the Tab key until "Write" is selected, and press Return. The cfisk program prompts you to confirm that you want to write the new partition table to the disk. Enter **yes** and press Return to confirm.
6. Press Q to exit from the cfdisk program.

You are now ready to create a file system and a swap file system on the new partitions. Your partitions will be different than those in the example I'm using, but the principles and commands are the same.

Creating File Systems or Swap Space

As with most computer systems, partitions used by Linux systems must be preformatted to create structures that the operating system can use to successfully store and retrieve data on those partitions. On Linux and UNIX systems, formatted partitions used for storing files and directories are known as file systems. Such partitions are prepared for use by the system using the `/sbin/mkfs` command.

Aside from storing files and directories, Linux and UNIX systems also use partitions to support virtual memory. Partitions used for virtual memory are known as swap space because the system can swap data between working memory and these partitions. This gives the system the illusion that it has more working memory than is physically available. Processes that are inactive or that are waiting for resources that are temporarily unavailable can be temporarily swapped out of memory and written to the swap space, proving more room in physical memory for active processes. When the resources required by swapped processes become available, or simply when the system decides that it is their turn to run again, swapped processes are brought back into working memory, and their execution continues. The use of swap space in Linux and UNIX systems is actually far more granular than a per-process basis—Linux and UNIX systems can also write portions of active processes out to the swap space, providing more memory for the portion of a process that is actually running.

This section explains how to create Linux file systems on new partitions, how to create swap partitions, and how to add swap partitions to the list of swap space available to your system.

Creating a File System on a Disk Partition

After a Linux partition that is a standard Linux file system is created using the cfdisk or fdisk utilities, it is converted into a Linux file system using the `/sbin/mkfs` command. This program is actually a transparent front end for the file system formatting tools specific to different types of file systems (such as mkfs.ext2 for ext2 file systems, the default type of file system used on Linux systems).

NOTE

It is necessary to execute mkfs only when adding or repartitioning disks on your systems. The appropriate mkfs commands are automatically executed for you when installing Red Hat Linux and partitioning a disk as part of the installation process.

To create a Linux file system that you can subsequently mount and use to store file and directories, you must be logged in as the root user or have used the `su` command to assume the identity of the root user. You then execute the `/sbin/mkfs` command, supplying the same partition on which you want to create a file system as an argument.

Because you identified this as a "Linux Native" partition when you created it, an ext2 file system will be created on that partition.

CAUTION

Be very careful when executing this command. Supplying the name of an existing, mounted file system will totally destroy any data currently located on that partition. This also may crash your system if you erase files required by your current system. Always double-check the arguments that you supply to the `/sbin/mkfs` command before executing the command.

Continuing with the example in the “Partitioning New Disks” section of this chapter, you execute the following command to format the data partition that we created in that section:

```
[root@twoproc wvh]# mkfs /dev/hdb1
mke2fs 1.15, 18-Jul-1999 for EXT2 FS 0.5b, 95/08/09
Filesystem label=
```

```
OS type: Linux
Block size=4096 (log=2)
Fragment size=4096 (log=2)
73280 inodes, 146404 blocks
7320 blocks (5.00%) reserved for the super user
First data block=0
5 block groups
32768 blocks per group, 32768 fragments per group
14656 inodes per group
Superblock backups stored on blocks:
    32768, 98304,
Writing inode tables: done
Writing superblocks and filesystem accounting information: done
[root@twoproc wvh]#
```

At this point, you can update the system's list of available file systems, mount the new partition, and use it to store files and directories after setting the Linux permissions appropriately.

If you are adding a new partition to move existing files off an existing partition, you also can mount it and copy data into it, as described later in this chapter in the section "Moving Directory Hierarchies onto New Partitions."

Preparing Partitions for Use as Swap Space

Like partitions slated for use to store files and directories, partitions slated for use as swap space require some preparation before the system can use them. You can format partitions for use as swap space by using the `/sbin/mkswap` command, supplying the name of the partition that you want to prepare for use as swap space as an argument.

Continuing with the example in the "Partitioning New Disks" section of this chapter, you execute the following command to format the swap partition that we created in that section:

```
[root@twoproc wvh]# mkswap /dev/hdb2
Setting up swapspace version 1, size = 253915136 bytes
```

After creating the swap space, you can use either the command-line application /sbin/swapon to add and verify the addition of the new swap space, or linuxconf to add the new swap space, as discussed in the next section.

Using the `/sbin/swapon -s` command to display a summary of your current swap space usage, add the new swap space using the `swapon` command itself; then use the `swapon -s` command to display a summary of your new swap space usage. This is shown in the following examples:

```
[root@twoproc wvh]# swapon -s
Filename                        Type            Size    Used    Priority
/dev/hda6                       partition       72252   1912    -1
[root@twoproc wvh]# swapon /dev/hdb2
```

```
[root@twoproc wvh]# swapon -s
Filename                    Type          Size    Used    Priority
/dev/hda6                   partition     72252   1912    -1
/dev/hdb2                   partition     247960  0       -2
```

Using linuxconf to Permanently Add Swap Space

As discussed in the previous chapter, Red Hat Linux provides a centralized graphical environment for most system administration tasks through its linuxconf program. The linuxconf File System control panel provides access to tabbed dialog boxes that enable you to add, edit, or delete file system mount points and entries for swap space. These dialog boxes do not enable you to add, partition, or format disks, but they make it easy for you to quickly add new partitions and swap space, performing many otherwise complex options for you "automagically." This section and the next explain how linuxconf, like any good graphical tool for system administration, simplifies your administrative procedures while still guaranteeing that the right things happen.

Swap space is always created when you install your Red Hat Linux system, usually one to one and a half times the amount of memory in your system algorithm. However, if you subsequently add memory to your system or you end up running extremely large, demanding processes, you'll eventually want to add more swap space to increase the efficiency of your system. In cases where the processes that you are swapping are smaller than any of your swap partitions, having several smaller swap partitions (known as noncontiguous swap space) may even be more efficient than having one huge swap partition. This enables your system to write to one disk's swap partition while simultaneously swapping in a process from another disk. Another alternative to creating swap partitions is to create swap files (files in a standard Linux file system that Linux can use as though they were actual swap partitions), but this can degrade swap performance so substantially that it should really be done only in an emergency (or on systems used in batch mode when you don't really care how quickly a process finishes but when more swap space is necessary to enable those processes to run to completion).

Just as with file systems used for data storage, formatting and activating new swap partitions using the `/sbin/swapon` command doesn't update the list of available swap partitions that your system stores in `/etc/fstab`. When you activate swap partitions, you must guarantee that they will be automatically reactivated each time you reboot your system.

This is typically done in one of two ways:

- By using the linuxconf utility to add the new swap space or file system.
- By adding entries for the new swap partitions to `/etc/fstab` and then adding an explicit `/sbin/swapon -a` command to one of your system initialization files to activate all of them during system initialization. For more information about using the `swapon` command, use the `man 8 swapon` command.

The following example shows how to use linuxconf to add the new swap partition created in the previous section of this chapter:

1. Start linuxconf and select the Configure Swap File and Partitions entry from the File Systems portion of linuxconf's Config section. The screen shown in Figure 9.6 displays.

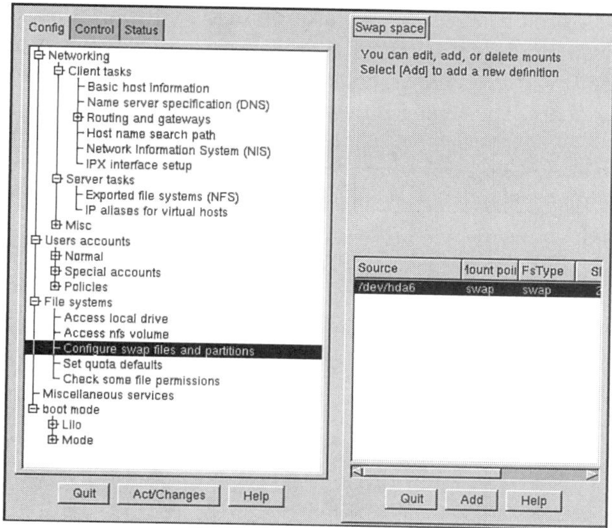

Figure 9.6

Linuxconf's Swap Space dialog box.

2. Click Add. The Volume Specification screen shown in Figure 9.7 displays.

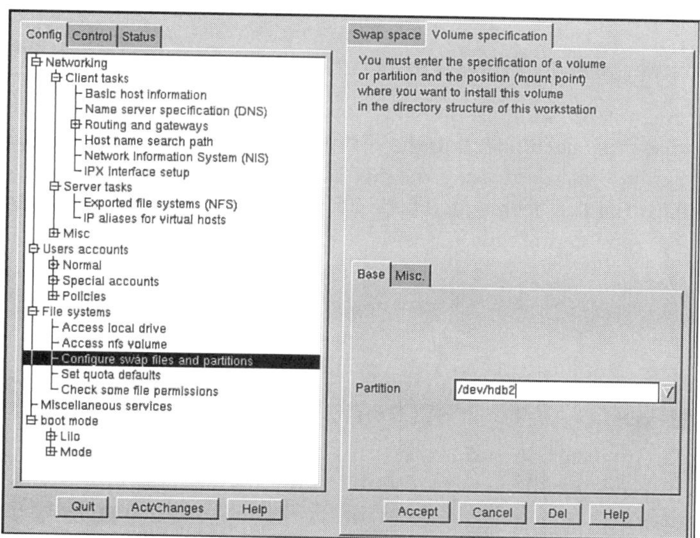

Figure 9.7

Linuxconf's Volume Specification dialog box.

3. Click the Down arrow beside the Partition field to display a list of all partitions of type Swap on disks that are local to your system. Select a swap partition that isn't currently mounted (`/dev/hdb2`, continuing with my previous example), and click Accept. The screen shown in Figure 9.8 displays.

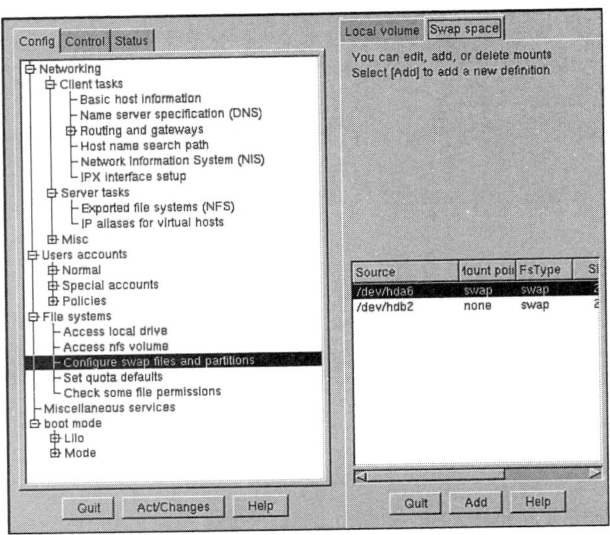

Figure 9.8

Linuxconf's Swap Space dialog box after adding new swap space.

This screen is the same as the one shown in Figure 9.6, except that the new swap space has been added to the list of swap partitions currently in use.

4. After exiting linuxconf using the Activate Changes option, verify that the new swap partition has been added and activated correctly using the command-line `/sbin/swapon` command:

```
[root]# /sbin/swapon -s
Filename                        Type        Size     Used      Priority
/dev/hda6                       partition   72252    0         -1
/dev/hdb2                       partition   128012   0         -3
```

Using linuxconf to Permanently Mount Partitions

Creating and mounting file systems doesn't automatically update your system's permanent list of available file systems, stored in the file `/etc/fstab`. Manually mounting a file system updates only the `/etc/mtab` file, which lists currently mounted file systems and is automatically updated each time your system boots.

To permanently add a new file system to the list of those that are mounted or used as swap space each time your system boots, you must add an entry for that file system to the Linux/UNIX file system table, stored in the text file `/etc/fstab`.

You can make newly mounted file systems a permanent part of your system in two general ways:

- By using the linuxconf utility to add the new swap space or file system.
- By adding entries for any new file systems to `/etc/fstab` and then putting an explicit `mount -a` command in one of your system to activate swap partitions each time you restart your system.

Using linuxconf is preferable because it provides a graphical environment for listing, adding, and removing file systems. For more information about the structure of the `fstab` file, use the `man 5 fstab` command to view the online manual page for this file. For more information about using the `mount` command, use the `man 8 mount` command.

Moving Directory Hierarchies onto New Partitions

As discussed earlier in this chapter, the most common reason for adding new disks to your system is running out of space on an existing partition. An easy way to expand the amount of space available in existing partitions on your system is to identify project- or process-specific directories (such as the directory for your Web server) that you can move onto partitions on new disks that you have added to your system. The commands used to move directory hierarchives (tar or recursive cp) are the same on all versions of Linux, and thus are not discussed in detail here.

After you've copied your existing data to the new partition, have mounted the new partition, and have ensured that everything is working correctly, you'll want to add an entry for the new partition to the file system table, `/etc/fstab`. This guarantees, for example, that the new partition is always mounted as `/home/httpd` (in this example) before your Web server is started. Updating the file system table is explained in the next section.

Mounting New Partitions Using linuxconf

To permanently mount one or more file systems in your Linux system, do the following:

1. Start linuxconf and select the Config tab, File Systems, Access Local Drive. The dialog box shown in Figure 9.9 displays.
2. Click Add. The dialog box shown in Figure 9.10 displays. Select the name of the new partition that you want to mount by clicking the Down arrow to the right of the Partition field. Select the type of that partition by clicking the Down arrow to the right of the Type field. Enter the name of the directory on which you want to permanently mount the new partition in the Mount Point field. This must be a directory that already exists. (If the new mount point doesn't already exist, switch to an xterm or console window, and create that directory.)

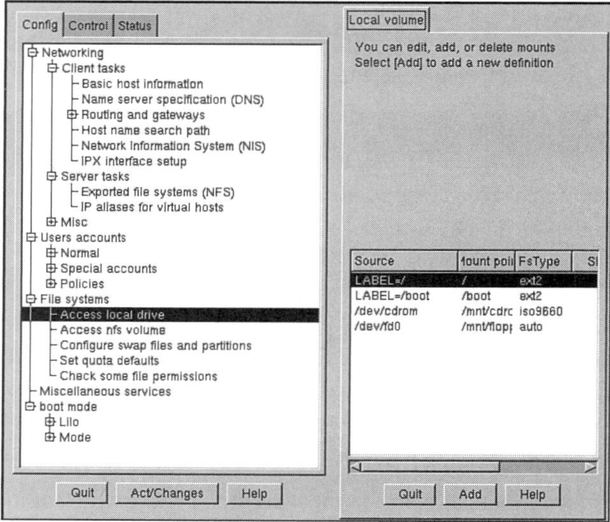

Figure 9.9

Linuxconf's Access Local Drive.

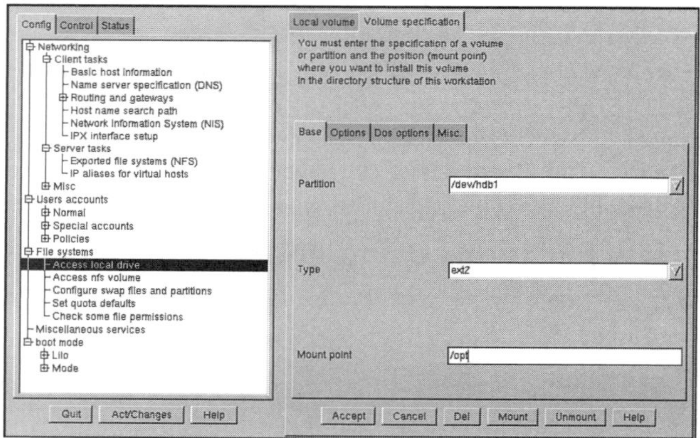

Figure 9.10

Linuxconf's Volume Specification dialog box.

3. Click the Mount button to test mounting the new partition on the specified directory. You will see linuxconf display a confirmation dialog box, as shown in Figure 9.11. Click Yes to mount the new partition and redisplay the previous screen.

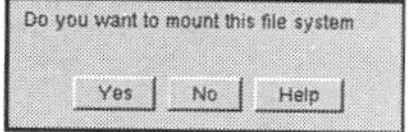

Figure 9.11

Linuxconf's Mount File System confirmation dialog box.

4. Click Accept to complete adding the new partition. The screen shown in Figure 9.12 displays. The only difference between this screen and the screen shown in Figure 9.9 is that the new partition is shown as being mounted on `/var`.

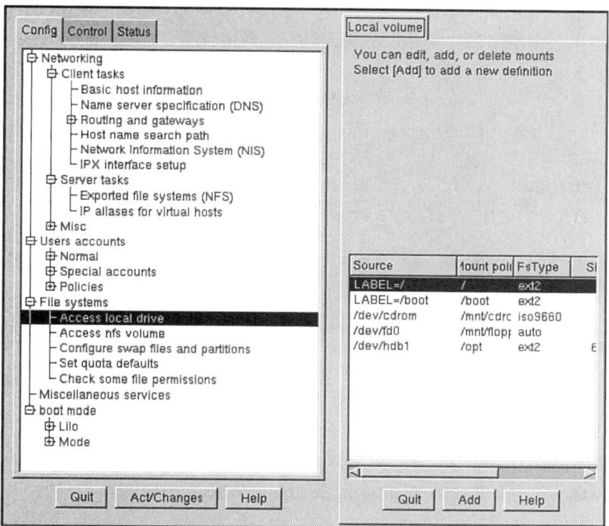

Figure 9.12

Linuxconf's Local Volume dialog box.

Using linuxconf to Add Removable Media to Your Linux System

Iomega zip drives, LS120 SuperDrives, and even floppy disks provide easy-to-use removable media for copying and archiving backup files or simply for exchanging data with other systems.

The easiest way to use these types of media is to create entries in your `/etc/fstab` file for these drives. In general, it's easiest to mount zip or LS120 disks, floppies, and so on in DOS format, just to maximize portability. (Think of DOS/Windows as the lowest common denominator of data storage across most computer systems today.) You can read and write DOS/Windows disks from Linux, but you also can access your backup files in a pinch from any DOS or Windows system.

Sample entries in an `/etc/fstab` file for zip and floppy drives in DOS/Windows format are the following:

```
/dev/fd0      /mnt/floppy    msdos   noauto,owner    0 0
/dev/hdd4     /mnt/zip       msdos   noauto,user     0 0
```

The first field identifies the partition to be mounted. In the case of removable media drives, this is usually a single partition that corresponds to the entire removable disk. The second field gives the mount point for that partition, which is the UNIX directory through which the partition can be accessed after it is successfully mounted.

The third field of any `/etc/fstab` entry identifies the format of the file system on that partition. These sample entries specify the msdos file system type because this is simplest for portability among multiple computer systems.

The entries in the fourth field of the `/etc/fstab` file are the most critical ones for removable media disks. Normally, only the superuser account (root) can mount and unmount partitions. However, if the fourth field contains the `user` keyword, any user can mount that partition. When a partition is mounted, only the user who mounted that partition (or the superuser, of course) can unmount it.

Another important keyword in the fourth field of `/etc/fstab` is the `noauto` keyword. Many systems mount partitions from `/etc/fstab` by issuing the command `/bin/mount -a`. The `-a` argument to the `mount` command tells the system to automatically mount all partitions listed in `/etc/fstab`. The `noauto` keyword excludes a device from being automatically mounted. Because removable media disks are, well, removable, you don't want the system to require their presence or forcibly attempt to mount them.

The last two columns identify the order in which the file system should be dumped when using Linux/UNIX backup and restore utilities, and the order in which that file system should be checked for consistency immediately after each reboot. As mentioned previously, when these fields are 0, the specified file system will never be dumped and is not checked for consistency when you reboot your system. As before, because removable media disks are removable, you don't want the system to try to dump them or check them for consistency if they are not present in your system.

You also can create `/etc/fstab` entries for removable drives using linuxconf. This is done using the same panels discussed in the previous section. Figure 9.13 shows the linuxconf file system description for an IDE zip drive.

When using linuxconf to mount removable media, you set the options discussed earlier in this section using the Options tab of the dialog box shown in Figure 9.13. Figure 9.14 shows appropriate Options settings for an IDE zip drive.

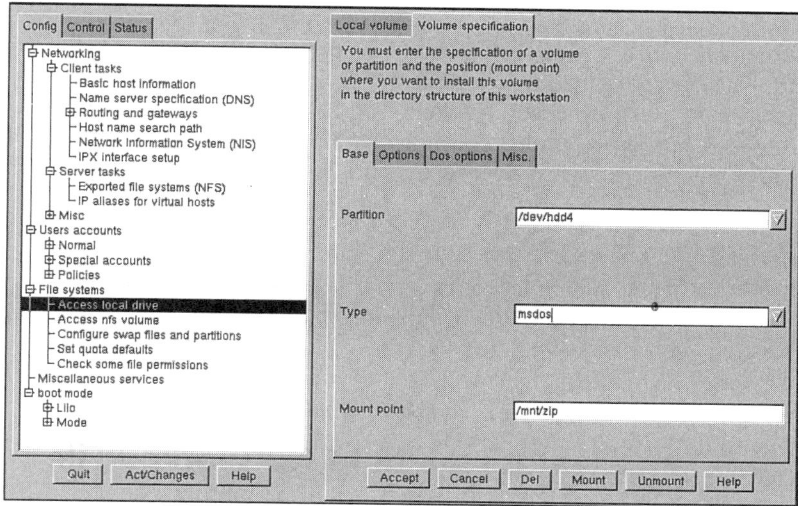

Figure 9.13

An IDE zip disk definition in linuxconf.

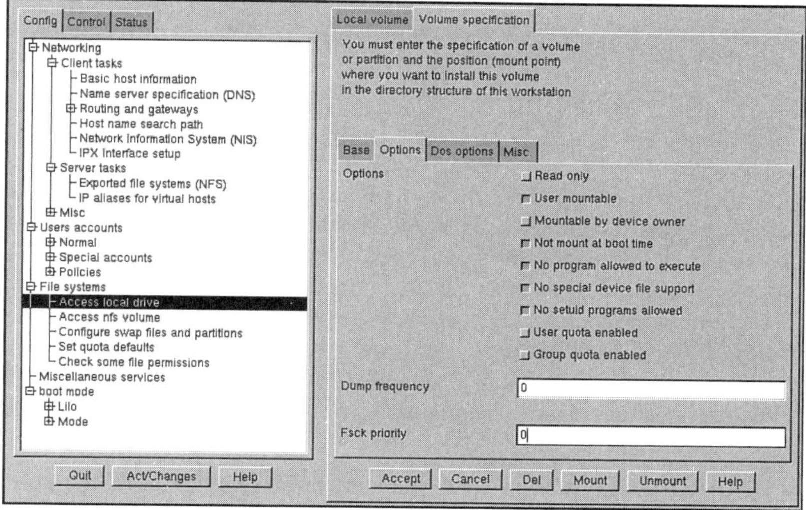

Figure 9.14

Options for an IDE zip disk definition in linuxconf.

Using Networked File Systems

The previous sections discussed issues in adding local storage to your computer system. An alternative to this approach is to share existing file systems over a network.

This enables you to create a single corporate computing environment in which all of your computers, whether Windows, Mac, or Linux/UNIX systems, are clients. In this scenario, your files are stored on centralized file server machines to which every client has equal access over the network, as long as it has the correct user privileges. These file servers can run any supported operating system and are simply computers that are dedicated to storing files and delivering them to clients over the network.

When correctly implemented in a business or academic environment, this unified client/server model can provide some significant advantages:

- It provides great opportunities for centralized system administration.
- It offloads the processing time required to share files and directories from desktop computers onto centralized servers.
- It relieves individual users and client computers of the responsibility of correctly maintaining, exporting, and backing up files and directories.

Popular Platform-Independent Networked File Systems

Specific platforms, such as the Apple Macintosh and various flavors of Windows, have their own mechanisms for sharing files over a network. Accessing each of these platform-specific networked file systems from Linux systems is discussed later in this chapter, as is interoperating with Novell NetWare file servers. However, in addition to these platform-specific networked file systems, several extremely powerful platform-independent networked file systems are also available. Originally developed for various UNIX systems, these all provide substantial advantages in networked environments.

AFS (`http://www.ibm.com/software/ts/integrate/filesharing`), Coda (`http://www.coda.cs.cmu.edu`), DFS (`http://www.ibm.com/software/ts/integrate/filesharing`), and NFS (`http://www.sun.com/software/white-papers/wp-nfs.sw/`) are all networked file systems that were designed as client/server software whose file servers could be accessed from many different types of computer systems. These networked file systems all include enhanced security mechanisms that augment the login, file, and directory security provided by any single operating system. These centralized client/server packages are well worth considering, especially in larger business or academic environments. These packages provide a single, enterprisewide solution to interoperability by providing a common foundation for networked data storage.

AFS and DFS are commercial products that are currently in use at thousands of sites, serving terabytes of data. IBM recently released the AFS source code under the IPL (IBM Public License), so free versions of AFS will soon be available. However, for better or for worse (but definitely for free), NFS is the most common platform-independent networked file system in use today.

Using NFS File Systems

NFS is the most common networked file system in use today, largely because it comes preinstalled and for free with almost every UNIX and UNIX-like system. NFS clients and servers are also available for systems such as DOS, Windows, and Macintosh. Like AFS, Coda, and DFS, NFS is a natural location in which to store centralized sets of files and directories that you want to export to multiple client systems, such as users' home directories and sitewide but system-dependant sets of software development tools.

For example, suppose that the home directories for all of your users are stored in the directory `/export` on your NFS file server. The password file for each of your systems (or a network-oriented password file, such as that provided by NIS) would list your users' home directories `/export/<user-name>`. Regardless of which system your users logged in on, they would get the same home directory. Similarly, suppose that you want to export all of the GNU tools for the different platforms in your environment, accessing them as `/usr/gnu` regardless of the type of system you're using. You could simply build binaries for each type of system that you support, storing them in `/export/gnu/solaris28`, `/export/gnu/hpux10.20`, `/export/gnu/redhat61`, and so on. You then could mount the appropriate exported directory as `/usr/gnu` on the appropriate type of system (`/export/gnu/solaris28` is mounted as `/usr/gnu` on Solaris 2.8 systems, and so on). Voila! All of the systems in your environment require only that `/usr/gnu/bin` be in your path, and the legendary "right thing" happens!

Configuring Directories Exported by an NFS Server

NFS is as easy to set up and use as it is to obtain. NFS uses the user ID (UID) and group ID (GID) of each user to determine who has access to exported files and directories. This means that all of your users should have the same user ID and group ID (found in their entries in the password file) on all systems to which NFS directories such as home directories are exported. This happens automagically if you are using networkwide authentication mechanisms such as the Network Information System (NIS). If you are simply replicating password files on different machines or are maintaining them in parallel, you must make sure that all of your users have the same UID and GID on all of your systems.

As discussed in this chapter and the previous chapter, Red Hat Linux provides a centralized graphical environment for many system administration tasks through its linuxconf program. Linuxconf's File System control provides access to a set of dialog boxes that enable you to add, edit, or delete NFS mount points. Figure 9.15 shows the linuxconf panel (Config, Networking, Server Tasks, Exported File Systems (NFS)) where you can define the directories exported by and NFS server.

Figure 9.16 shows the panel that displays if you click on any currently exported NFS directory listed on the panel shown in Figure 9.15. The panel shown in Figure 9.16 provides access to security options that are a subset of those discussed in the remainder of this section. These are sufficient for most purposes, but directly editing the `/etc/exports` file still provides the greatest control over NFS security.

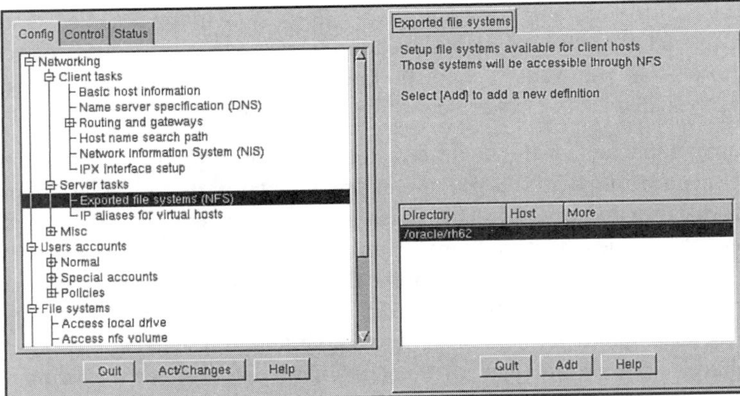

Figure 9.15

Defining exported NFS directories in linuxconf.

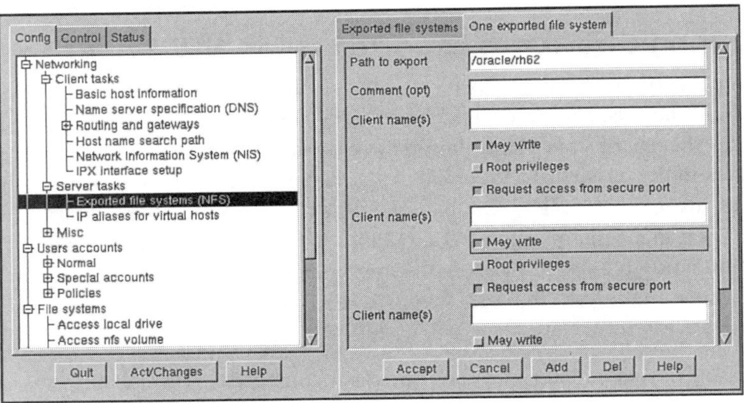

Figure 9.16

Setting security options on exported NFS directories in linuxconf.

Using linuxconf to configure your system for NFS liberates you from having to locate and understand the format of the configuration file actually used by the NFS subsystem, `/etc/exports`. The `/etc/exports` file is a text file with a large number of potential entries and options. Using linuxconf, you can graphically select the options you want. Then linuxconf generates the correct cryptic `/etc/exports` file for you when you exit from linuxconf and synchronizes your system with the changes you've made in linuxconf. If you're interested, see the man page for `/etc/exports` (`man 5 exports`) for complete information on these options. The remainder of this section discusses security options that are not covered by those provided through linuxconf but that you may find useful and significant, depending on the computing environment to which you are adding one or more Red Hat Linux systems.

To use NFS, your machine must be on a network and should have enough processor and memory resources to support remote users of the NFS file systems; 128MB of memory and a 500Mz processor or better should be fine. Dedicated NFS servers, systems that service only NFS requests, can get by with substantially fewer resources.

After you've created your `/etc/exports` file, you can start the NFS daemon and associated process by executing the following command (when logged in as or using the `su` command to become root):

```
/etc/rc.d/rc3.d/S70nfs start
```

When first started, NFS keeps a list of any exported file systems in the export table file `/var/lib/nfs/xtab`. This file has the same relationship to `/etc/exports` that `/etc/mtab` has to `/etc/fstab`. If you want to export other file systems via NFS when NFS is already running, you can execute the following command on your NFS file server (when logged in as or using the `su` command to become root):

```
/usr/sbin/exportfs -r
```

This command rereads the `/etc/exports` file and synchronizes `/var/lib/nfs/xtab` with it.

NOTE

On Red Hat systems, NFS starts eight copies of the NFS daemon to service NFS requests. To improve performance when large numbers of clients are accessing NFS volumes over the network, you can increase the number of copies of the NFS daemon that are started by changing the value of the `RPCNFSDCOUNT` variable in the startup script `/etc/rc.d/init.d/nfs`.

Accessing NFS Drives from Other Systems Using linuxconf

As discussed earlier in this chapter, NFS uses the user ID (UID) and group ID (GID) of each user to determine who has access to exported files and directories. Assuming that you have the same UID and GID on all of the system you want to share data with using NFS, you can mount an NFS volume by logging in as or using the `su` command to assume the identity of a user who has access, and then executing a command such as the following:

```
mount hostname:/remote-filesystem /local-directory
```

For example, to mount the remote file system `/archive` that is exported via NFS from the NFS server foobar, you would execute this command:

```
mount foobar:/archive /archive
```

When you're sure of the exported NFS directories that you want to permanently mount on your system, you could add entries to your system's `/etc/fstab` file for those file systems. Entries in `/etc/fstab` for NFS file systems have the following form:

```
foobar:/var/mail     /var/mail      nfs     rw,hard  0 0
foobar:/export/home  /export/home   nfs     rw,hard  0 0
```

These entries mount the directories `/var/mail` and `/export/home` that are exported by the host `foobar` as the local directories `/var/mail` and `/export/home`. The file system type is NFS, and the mount options indicate that the NFS file system is readable and writable (rw); the hard option indicates that the system will continue trying failed file operations indefinitely.

Red Hat's linuxconf administrative application also provides dialog boxes that you can use to graphically mount remote NFS file systems and automatically update the `/etc/fstab` file. Figure 9.17 shows the main linuxconf dialog box for mounting directories exported by another system in the Config, File Systems, Access NFS volume.

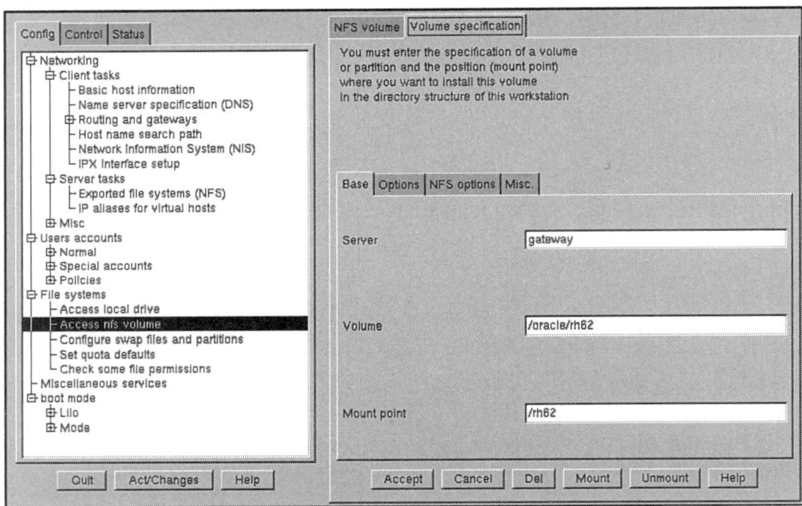

Figure 9.17

Using linuxconf to mount remote NFS directories.

Figure 9.18 shows the Options tab of the dialog box shown in Figure 9.17. The Options tab enables you to specify the way in which a remote NFS directory is mounted on your system.

Sharing Windows and Linux File Systems Using Samba

Samba is a free and impressive interface for Linux/UNIX systems to Windows Server Message Block (SMB) file systems. Samba enables Windows users to access UNIX file systems and resources transparently, just like any other Windows shared file system or networked resource. For example, with Samba running on a Linux/UNIX system on your network, Windows users can mount their UNIX home directories as networked Windows drives and can automatically print to UNIX printers just like any Windows printer. Samba is one of the truly great innovations of computing within recent memory, and its original author, Andrew Tridgell, deserves a hearty round of applause from every Linux/UNIX system administrator who has ever struggled to integrate Windows users into a real computing environment.

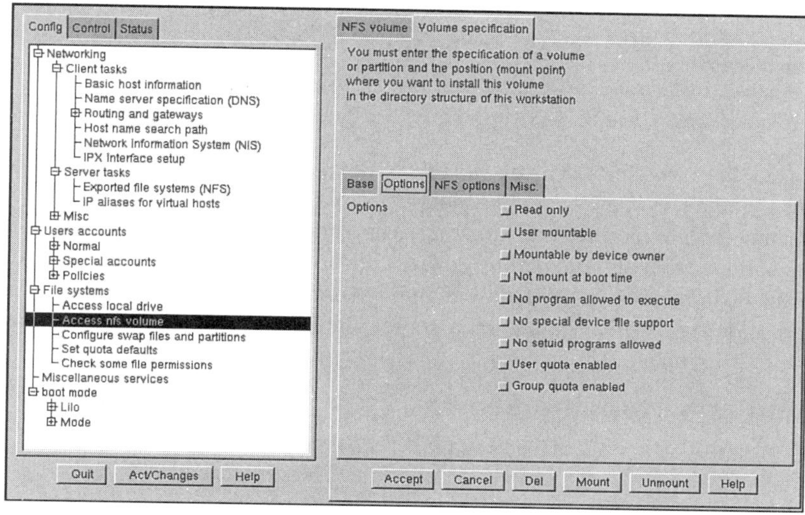

Figure 9.18

Options for mounting remote NFS directories in linuxconf.

Samba is also sometimes known as a Common Internet File Services (CIFS) server, a term coined by Microsoft to suggest the ubiquity of NetBIOS file systems on the Internet. That's a somewhat scary proposition, but knowing this alternate acronym may eliminate confusion if you see Samba referred to in this way.

Sharing Samba Directories Between PCs

Samba makes it easy to mount directories stored on Linux and UNIX-like systems as mapped network drives on PCs. Samba also enables you to capitalize on the Linux/UNIX group mechanism to allow multiple users to share and simultaneously work on mapped drives. Samba does this by providing an internal implementation of the file sharing and locking mechanisms found on actual Windows SMB drives.

The following example shows how to set up such a shared drive:

```
#
# The marketing directory, shared by Marketing Group
#
[mktg]
   comment = Marketing Data
   valid users = @mktg wvh
   write list = @mktg wvh
   force group = mktg
   path = /export/home/marketing
   public = no
```

```
   writable = yes
   write ok = yes
   printable = yes
   force create mode = 0770
   force directory mode = 0770
   share modes = yes
   locking = yes
   strict locking = yes
```

In this sample entry, the `valid users` and `write list` entries state that anyone who is a member of the Linux group mktg can mount or write to the shared drive mktg, found at the Linux path /export/home/marketing. The `force create` and `force directory` modes guarantee that any files or directories created in the shared drive will be created so that they can be read or written by members of the mktg group. The `share modes`, `locking`, and `strict locking` entries force Samba to implement Windows locking modes when anyone is editing files in the shared directory.

Starting and Stopping Samba

When you install Samba, only process kill files are created in the directories specific to various run levels where Samba is appropriate. These files, called K35smb, are symbolic links to the file `/etc/rc.d/init.d/smb`. To automatically activate Samba whenever your system boots, you must create associated start files, named S35smb by default, in your `/etc/rc.d/rc3.d` and `/etc/rc.d/rc5.d` directories. You can create these symbolic links (which are just pointers to another file) using commands such as the following:

```
cd /etc/rc.d/rc3.d
ln -s ../init.d/smb S35smb
cd /etc/rc.d/rc5.d
ln -s ../init.d/smb S35smb
```

These links guarantee that Samba will be started at boot time when the system processes either of the multiuser run levels, 3 or 5.

NOTE

> If you are running a Samba server on a Linux laptop that uses a PCMCIA Ethernet card, you will want to create the start and kill file links to `/etc/rc.d/init.d` with numbers higher than 45 where the PCMCIA drivers are initialized. This is when your Ethernet services will actually be activated. I typically create symbolic links to `/etc/rc.d/init.d/smb` with the names S55smb and K55smb to guarantee that the network is available before starting Samba.

After modifying its configuration file for the first time, you can execute this command to start Samba manually:

```
/etc/rc.d/init.d/smb start
```

To shut down Samba manually, you can execute this command:

```
/etc/rc.d/init.d/smb stop
```

Accessing Samba from a Windows Machine

When you've started Samba and it has reported success for both the SMB and NMB processes, go to a Windows machine and double-click the Network Neighborhood icon. An icon with the name of the Linux system that is running Samba should be displayed. You can traverse this icon by double-clicking until you get to the icon for the volume you want to access. To map that icon to a drive letter in windows, right-click that icon and select the Map Network Drive option. This brings up the standard drive mapping dialog box and associates the selected volume with a drive letter. You can even specify Reconnect at Login if you want to automatically remount this drive each time you boot your system and it connects to the appropriate network or IP address.

Linux Tools for Samba Administration

Linux provides several graphically oriented tools for Samba administration. The most commonly used of these is the Samba Web Administrative Tool (SWAT):

The Samba Web Administration Tool (SWAT) tool provides a highly usable interface for Samba administration using your favorite Web browser. To obtain the latest version of SWAT, see Red Hat's `http://www.redhat.com/apps/download/` site. After you install SWAT, modify the `/etc/services` and `/etc/inetd.conf` files on your Samba server, and restart the inetd, you can access SWAT through your favorite Web browser at the URL `http://hostname:901`, where `hostname` is the name of your Samba server. SWAT is a handy utility that makes it easy for you to check the status of your Samba server, but it doesn't provide a complete interface for most Samba administration tasks. Figure 9.19 shows SWAT running inside Netscape, displaying the Server Status page.

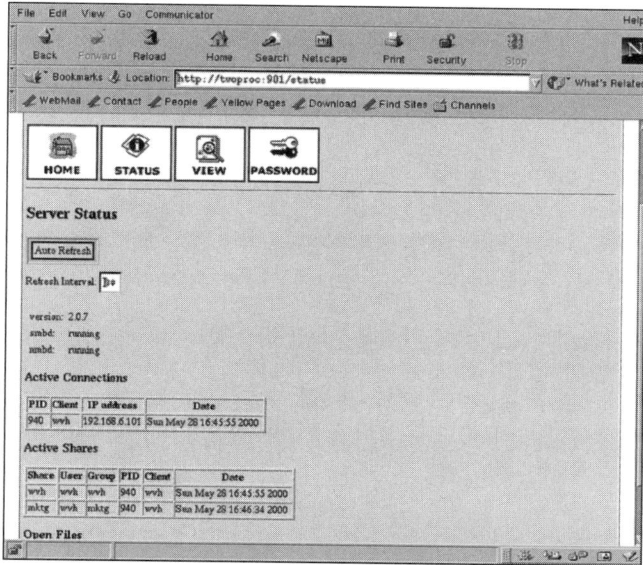

Figure 9.19

The SWAT tool for Samba administration.

You also can configure Samba using linuxconf, although linuxconf tends to rewrite your `smb.conf` file, sometimes making it harder to follow if you are accustomed to looking at it in text mode. Figure 9.20 shows the main screen for the Samba administration section of linuxconf.

Two other Samba-related utilities are worth mentioning. The `/usr/bin/smbclient` utility enables you to mount a shared Windows directory on your Linux system, using an interface much like the FTP program. The `/usr/bin/smbmount` program, although not a part of the Samba suite itself, is a very useful application for mounting shared Windows drives on PC systems so that you can back them up as part of your standard Linux/UNIX backups. This can be useful for taking snapshots of machines or for archiving critical files that were accidentally left on the PC rather than being saved to a Linux system via Samba.

NOTE

If you are using the smbmount utility to mount drives from Windows systems on your Linux system, the Windows systems either must be on all the time or must be configured to reawaken on a LAN request for Samba to access their data.

CHAPTER 10

Installing Other Software

After installing Red Hat on your system, you'll inevitably run across additional software that you want to install, either from the Red Hat CD distribution (if you're lucky), or from a download off the Internet. This chapter explains how to install additional software that wasn't installed automatically as part of your Red Hat installation. Luckily, and not surprisingly, Red Hat makes this easy (and bulletproof) to do.

One of the big differences between personal computers and UNIX systems has always been the ease with which personal computer applications can be installed. Most Windows software is installed using InstallShield, while most Mac software is installed using the VISE Installer. In both cases, the effect of using a standard package to install many different applications is that users know what to expect when they install a new software package.

UNIX and UNIX-like systems have never taken a coordinated approach toward installing software packages, partly because UNIX systems aren't exactly knee-deep in off-the-shelf software packages in the first place. UNIX systems don't even have a consistent vocabulary for describing the installation and upgrade process. Systems from Sun Microsystems install software from packages using `pkgadd`, systems from Hewlett-Packard install software from `depots` using `swinstall`, and so on.

Luckily, all previous UNIX and UNIX-like software for centralized software installation, maintenance, and dependency analysis has one thing in common: None does as good a job as the Red Hat Package Manager (RPM). As a testimonial to its capabilities, RPM originally was developed by Red Hat, but because of its capabilities and Open Source roots, it has since been adopted by most of the other major Linux players, including Caldera, SuSE, and Debian. Debian's version of RPM has some incompatible internal modifications and a change to the file extension from `.rpm` to `.deb`, so there is occasionally a downside to Open Source software.

This chapter explains what packages contain and how they are named, as well as how use to use RPM to install and update software, identify and resolve dependencies and conflicts, figure out what packages are associated with various files on your system, and list the contents of the packages that you install.

For those who want to know more, you're scaring me, but an excellent book solely about RPM is available from Red Hat and other fine Linux vendors. This book, entitled *Maximum RPM: Taking the Red Hat Package Manager to the Limit*, by Edward C. Bailey, is excellent. It contains detailed information about every RPM command, as well as a substantial amount of information that is useful primarily to those who are building rather than simply using RPM packages.

RPM Packages and Their Contents

RPM is aRPM is a command-line utility that is automatically installed early in the Red Hat installation process. All subsequent software installed on your Red Hat Linux system is then installed from RPM packages, which are specially prepared archive files that contain the following:

- The files associated with that specific package. For example, the X Window system version of the emacs text editor distributed with Red Hat 7.0 is contained in the package `emacs-X11-20.7-14.rpm`.
- A short description of the package.
- A package label, which is a unique identifier for the package that is contained in the package itself and that traditionally is also used as the name of the package. When you've installed a package on your system, the package label is stored in the RPM database rather than the name of the file from which you installed the package.

  A package label has three components, separated by dashes. The first portion of a package label is the name of the software contained in the package (in this case, emacs-X11). The second portion is the version of the software contained in the package (in this case, 20.5). The final portion of a package label is the package's release number (in this case, 7). This is a number chosen by the person who built the package, and it reflects the number of times that a package has been built and released for this version of the software.

  The name of the file containing a specific package is usually created by appending the extension `.rpm` to the package label. Storing the package label inside a package keeps the package independent of the name of the file from which it was installed. I can send you the emacs package in a file named `install-me.rpm`, and RPM won't get confused.

- A list of any other packages required by the package.
- A list of the files in the package itself.
- Linux command files (aka *scripts*) to run before installing or uninstalling the package.
- Linux command files (aka *scripts*) to run after installing or uninstalling the package.

Understanding Software and Package Dependencies

The key idea behind packages is to create relatively small sets of files that must be installed together for a specific piece of software to work on your system. Packages can contain many files, but generally they contain as few files as possible to install a specific library, utility, or application on your system.

To keep packages as small as possible, packages usually depend on other packages being installed on your system. The only alternative to this would be to package all the binaries, libraries, and support files required by each piece of software together. This all-in-one approach would quickly become unmanageable because many different pieces of software share a dependency on certain libraries and other utilities. If the same libraries were contained in multiple packages, installing these packages would quickly generate conflicts.

RPM's approach is to keep packages as small and focused as possible by maximizing the use of dependencies on other packages. Continuing with the example of the emacs text editor used in the previous section, actually two different versions of emacs can be installed on your system. The first of these (in the Red Hat 7.0 distribution) is `emacs-nox-20.7-14`, a non-X Window system version of emacs that must run within a console or a terminal emulation window. The other is `emacs-X11-20.7-14`, an X Window system version of emacs. Both of these packages contain only the binaries for their respective versions of emacs, and they share a dependency on the package `emacs-20.7-14`, which contains the support files required by any version of emacs.

Using the Red Hat Package Manager

To execute the `rpm` command, enter **`rpm`** from any shell, xterm, or console command prompt, followed by the RPM options that you want to use. (The rest of this chapter explains how to choose the right options to accomplish what you want to do.) Because the database of installed software maintained by RPM is located in `/var/lib/rpm` and is owned by the root user, you must be logged in as root or use the `su` command to assume the identity of the root users to execute any RPM commands that modify the RPM database in any way.

Besides the command-line version of RPM, different Red Hat desktop environments provide GUI front ends for RPM. Figure 10.1 shows gnorpm, the GUI interface to RPM for GNOME users. Figure 10.2 shows kpackage, the GUI interface to RPM for KDE users.

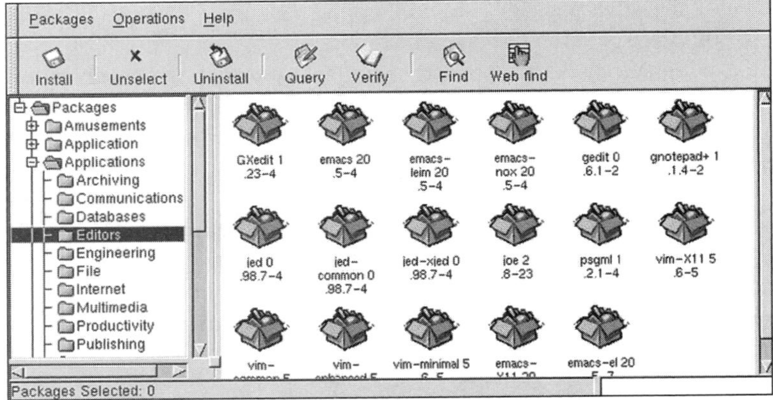

Figure 10.1

The gnorpm RPM GUI for KDE users.

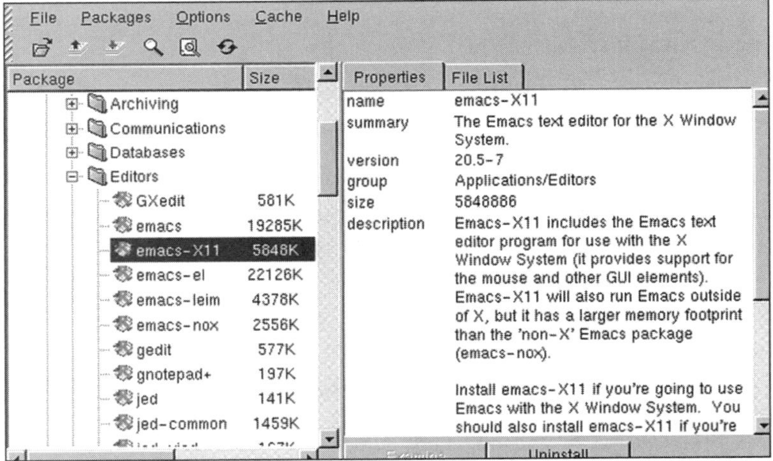

Figure 10.2

The kpackage RPM GUI for GNOME users.

Rather than exploring a specific GUI approach to RPM, this chapter focuses on using the RPM command line, which works in exactly the same way whether you are running the GNOME or KDE desktop environments, or a standard X Window system window manager.

What Actually Happens When Using RPM

RPM provides many features to simplify the lives of developers who are creating RPM packages. This translates into ease of use and power for those of us who simply use RPM to manage installing (and occasionally removing) software packages.

When installing or upgrading an RPM package, RPM does the following for you (invisibly, unless you are running RPM with the very verbose output option enabled, as explained in the section "Getting Verbose Output," later in this chapter):

- Analyzes your system to ensure that all package dependencies identified in the package you're installing have been satisfied. If any unsatisfied dependencies are found, RPM notifies you of them and exits without going any further. You can override this by running RPM again with the `--nodeps` option, but this isn't recommended unless you know exactly what you're doing and have a good reason for overriding RPM's dependency analysis.
- Runs any preinstall scripts identified in the RPM package you're installing or upgrading.
- Installs the package itself, saving any modified configuration files if you already have a previous version of the package installed.
- Runs any postinstall scripts identified in the RPM package you're installing or upgrading.

See the section "Installing and Updating Packages" later in this chapter for more information about installing and upgrading packages using RPM.

As you might hope, the steps for removing or erasing an installed RPM package are very parallel to those for installing a new package. When removing or erasing a package that is already installed, RPM does the following for you (invisibly, unless you are running RPM with the very verbose output option enabled, as explained later in the section "Getting Verbose Output"):

- Analyzes your system to ensure that it doesn't have other packages that depend on the package you're removing or erasing. If any such dependencies are found, RPM notifies you of them and exits without going any further. You can override this by running RPM with the `--nodeps` option, but this isn't recommended unless you know exactly what you're doing and have a good reason for overriding RPM's dependency analysis.
- Runs any pre-uninstall scripts identified in the RPM package you're erasing.
- Removes the specified package from your system, saving any modified configuration files.
- Runs any post-uninstall scripts identified in the RPM package you're erasing.

See the section "Removing Installed Packages" later in this chapter for more information about removing, uninstalling, and erasing packages using RPM.

Querying Files and Packages

Although they are not the sexiest aspects of RPM, two of its more useful aspects are the capability to quickly find out what packages are installed on your system and also to determine what package contains a specific file. Both of these types of information are easily available using options associated with RPM's `query` command (`-q`).

Continuing with the example emacs package used in previous sections, let's say that you hear through friends that a new version of emacs is available that provides some features that you need to run a friend's custom emacs macros. The first question you'll probably want to answer is, "What emacs packages are currently installed on my system?" However, to answer that question, you'll need to know what package the version of emacs on your system is associated with.

Red Hat's `query file` command (`-qf`) lets you identify the package that a specific file is associated with. The following is an example of using RPM's `query file` command to identify the package that emacs is associated with:

```
# which emacs
/usr/bin/emacs
# rpm -qf /usr/bin/emacs
emacs-X11-20.5-4
```

Of course, wizardly bash, csh, and tcsh users will see that I could have answered my question with a single command, namely this one:

```
# rpm -qf `which emacs`
emacs-X11-20.5-4
```

The capability to identify the package with which a specific file is associated is an incredibly useful feature of RPM. Try figuring out what software package installed a specific file on a Windows or Macintosh system, and get back to me in the 5 or 10 minutes that it takes for you to find that this is impossible!

After finding out which package the actual binary executable of emacs is associated with, another useful thing to know is what versions of all emacs-related packages are installed on your system. RPM lets you quickly answer this question through its `query all` (`-qa`) command, as in the following example:

```
# rpm -qa | more
setup-2.1.4-1
filesystem-1.3.5-1
basesystem-6.0-4
ldconfig-1.9.5-16
AfterStep-1.7.164-2
AfterStep-APPS-20000124-4
AnotherLevel-1.0-1
[ many other lines of output deleted ]
```

Unfortunately, this command produces 745 lines of output, from which identifying the emacs-specific entries can be a tad tricky. As in the query file example, you can use some UNIX/Linux features to obtain the specific output that you want to see, as in the following example:

```
# rpm -qa | grep -i emacs
emacs-20.5-4
emacs-X11-20.5-4
emacs-nox-20.5-4
emacs-el-20.5-4
```

This command filters the output of the RPM query all command through the UNIX/Linux grep command, looking for any package name that matches the string emacs, regardless of case. The more manageable output of this command tells you what you need to know: You have several emacs-related packages installed on your system, all of which are slightly older than the new emacs package that you'd heard about on the Web.

It's often useful or at least interesting to know what files are contained in a specific package. Not being able to look inside installable packages for Windows or the Macintosh is one of the more irritating aspects of the InstallShield or VISE installers for these platforms. Not surprisingly, RPM's query long command makes this easy, as in the following example:

```
# rpm -ql emacs-20.5-4
/etc/skel/.emacs
/usr/bin/b2m
/usr/bin/emacsclient
/usr/bin/etags
/usr/bin/gctagsiouspreviouspreviousous
/usr/bin/rcs-checkin
/usr/doc/emacs-20.5
/usr/doc/emacs-20.5/BUGS
/usr/doc/emacs-20.5/FAQ
[ additional output deleted ]
```

To query packages rather than the current state of your system, simply add the -p option to the RPM query command, and supply the name of the package that you want to examine rather than the name of the package label. For example, the following command examines a local package file for its contents, in long format:

```
# rpm -qlp emacs-20.5-7.i386.rpm
```

Installing and Updating Packages

RPM provides several commands to install (-i) and upgrade (-U) packages. The easiest to use and remember is the upgrade command. Upgrading a package installs the new package even if no previous version of that package is already installed. The advantage of upgrading a package rather than simply installing it is that if an earlier version of that package is already installed on your system, the upgrade command automatically removes the older version(s) of the package after installing the new one.

The following is an example of using the upgrade command to install a new version of the emacs support files on an older system:

```
# rpm -U emacs-20.5-7.i386.rpm
```

You can install or upgrade any package by executing this command, replacing the emacs-20.5-7.i386.rpm command with the name of the package you want to install on the command line.

Unless you run the RPM `upgrade` command with the very verbose option enabled (as explained in the next section), seeing no messages means that the package was successfully installed or upgraded. If you see messages about missing dependencies, you'll need to satisfy these, as explained in the "Understanding Software and Package Dependencies" section earlier in this chapter. Then retry installing or upgrading the package. I'd like to say more, but it just isn't necessary—RPM does the right thing for you.

If you want to install a package rather than upgrading one, you can accomplish the same thing as the upgrade option by executing the RPM `install` command, as in the following example:

```
# rpm -i emacs-20.5-7.i386.rpm
```

Getting Verbose Output

As discussed earlier in this chapter, one of the best features of RPM is its capability to tell you exactly what's in a package and what RPM is actually doing at any given point.

RPM provides three options that you can use to get additional information about the installation or upgrade process. These are the verbose (`-v`) option, the very verbose (`-vv`) option, and the hash (`-h`) option. By itself, the `-v` option displays slightly more information about the packages you're installing or upgrading, such as their names. The `-vv` option displays more information than you would probably want to know about each step in the installation process. The `-h` option displays hash marks during the actual installation process so that you actually know that something is happening. This can be surprisingly useful when installing large packages. It's sort of RPM's equivalent to a blinking light on a computer console that you can watch to see that something is actually occurring.

Here's some sample output from a generic RPM `install` command:

```
# rpm -i icewm-1.0.3-1.i386.rpm
```

Here's the same command after adding the `-h` switch:

```
# rpm -ih icewm-1.0.3-1.i386.rpm
##################################################
```

Here's the same command after adding the `-vv` switch:

```
# rpm -ivv icewm-1.0.3-1.i386.rpm
D: counting packages to install
D: found 1 packages
D: looking for packages to download
D: retrieved 0 packages
D: New Header signature
D: Signature size: 68
D: Signature pad : 4
D: sigsize       : 72
```

```
D: Header + Archive: 295386
D: expected size   : 295386
D: opening database mode 0x42 in /var/lib/rpm
D: found 0 source and 1 binary packages
D:  requires: ld-linux.so.2  satisfied by db provides.
[ many lines of output deleted ]
D:     file: /usr/doc/icewm-1.0.3/icewm.sgml action: create
D: running preinstall script (if any)
icewm-1.0.3-1
D: running postinstall scripts (if any)
```

Removing Installed Packages

RPM makes it easy to remove software from your system using its erase (`-e`) option. The following is an example of using this command to remove the emacs support files on an older system:

```
# rpm -e emacs-20.5-7
```

Note that this command specifies the label of the package that you want to erase, not the name of the file from which it was installed. You can use the RPM query commands, as explained earlier in this chapter in the "Querying Files and Packages" section, to find out the label for the package you want to erase if you don't have the package around or don't believe that the name of the package file corresponds to the actual package that it contains. You can erase any package by executing this command with the label of the package you want to erase on the command line.

Unless you run the RPM `erase` command with the `-vv` option enabled (as explained in the "Getting Verbose Output" section earlier in this chapter), seeing no messages means that the package was successfully erased. If you see messages about dependencies on the package you're trying to erase, you'll need to erase the other packages that depend on the one you're trying to erase. Or, you simply can ignore these, as explained in the "Understanding Software and Package Dependencies" section earlier in this chapter. Then retry erasing the package.

Finding New Packages

If the package you want to install isn't located on your Red Hat CD, you'll need to know either where to find it on the Web or just where to find it.

CAUTION

Many browsers automatically associate files with the RPM extension with Real Audio's Real Player software. If you're trying to download RPMs using a browser, and your browser insists on trying to play them using Real Player, you can work around this by going back to the page where the RPM was located. Hold down the Shift key while left-clicking (or simply clicking and holding, if you're using a Mac) on the link to the RPM package.

If you're looking for a specific package to install on your Red Hat system and don't actually have a link to a page that you can download the package from, don't despair. If you're looking for updates to Red Hat 7.0 packages that you know can resolve security problems, check Red Hat's site at `http://www.redhat.com/support/updates.html`. If you're looking for a random package (one that is not part of the official Red Hat distribution), you can browse or otherwise search several Internet sites for specific packages. My favorites of these are the RPM finder site (`http://rpmfind.net/linux/RPM/ByName.html`) and the RPM search site (`http://www.whichrpm.com/`). Both of these feature straightforward and usable mechanisms for finding specific packages based on different criteria, such as their name, the specific Linux distribution they're intended for, and so on.

Installing and Using Packages from Other Linux Distributions

As discussed in the "Mixing and Matching Software from Linux Distributions" section of Chapter 1, "Introduction to Red Hat Linux," one of the big advantages of Linux is that it's often possible to install and use software packages that were actually designed for or created using other Linux distributions, as long as a few basic points have been satisfied. The first of these is that the package must have been compiled and created for use on systems using the family of processors used in your system. For example, several Linux distributions are available for systems using Motorola/Apple/IBM PPC and 68000 processors. You'll never be able to execute binary packages compiled for these Linux distributions on a Linux system running on an x86, Pentium, or clone processor.

Aside from that basic issue, see the tips in the "Mixing and Matching Software from Linux Distributions" section of Chapter 1 for a discussion of other general issues. If the only package format you can find for the application you desperately want to install isn't totally compatible with Red Hat's RPM format, download and experiment with the alien package converter (on the Web at `http://kitenet.net/programs/alien/`). You'll be amazed at just how well this software works.

INDEX

Symbols

A

B

C

E

M

P

S